THE GLOBAL AGE OF REVOLUTIONS

The Revolutionary Age

Francis D. Cogliano, Christa Breault Dierksheide,
Eliga H. Gould, and Patrick Griffin, Editors

THE GLOBAL AGE OF REVOLUTIONS

A History from 1650 to Today

Edited by
Bryan A. Banks and Cindy Ermus

University of Virginia Press • *Charlottesville and London*

The University of Virginia Press is situated on the traditional lands of the Monacan Nation, and the Commonwealth of Virginia was and is home to many other Indigenous people. We pay our respect to all of them, past and present. We also honor the enslaved African and African American people who built the University of Virginia, and we recognize their descendants. We commit to fostering voices from these communities through our publications and to deepening our collective understanding of their histories and contributions.

University of Virginia Press
© 2026 by the Rector and Visitors of the University of Virginia
All rights reserved
Printed in the United States of America on acid-free paper

First published 2026

9 8 7 6 5 4 3 2 1

ISBN 978-0-8139-5455-4 (hardback)
ISBN 978-0-8139-5456-1 (paperback)
ISBN 978-0-8139-5457-8 (ebook)

Library of Congress Cataloging-in-Publication Data is available for this title.

Cover art: Sketch for "The Revolt of Cairo," Anne-Louis Girodet de Roussy-Trioson, ca. 1810. (The Art Institute of Chicago)
Cover design: Cecilia Sorochin

You place confidence in the actual state of society without reflecting that this state is subject to inevitable revolutions, and that it is impossible to foresee or to prevent that which may confront your children. The great become small, the rich become poor, the monarch becomes a subject. Are the blows of Fortune so rare that you can count on being exempt from them? We are approaching a state of crisis and a century of revolutions.
—Jean-Jacques Rousseau, *Émile; ou, De l'éducation*, 1762

CONTENTS

Preface ix

Introduction 1

Part 1. What Was the Age of Revolutions?

Religious Republican Revolutions in an Age of Confessionalization 11
BRYAN A. BANKS

The Ages of Revolution 19
DAN EDELSTEIN

The Invention of Representative Democracy 32
KATLYN MARIE CARTER

Gender and the Age of Revolutions in Private Lives 41
DENISE Z. DAVIDSON

The Global Age of Revolutions: An Anticolonial Approach 52
CHRISTY PICHICHERO

Part 2. Where Was the Age of Revolutions?

The Sète Affair of 1721: Crisis and Resistance in the
Early Eighteenth-Century French Colonies 69
CINDY ERMUS

Cherokees in the Age of Revolutions 80
KATE FULLAGAR

French Imperial Failures in Siam and Persia:
Asian Revolutions in the Age of Revolutions 91
JUNKO THÉRÈSE TAKEDA

Why Haiti Should Be at the Center of the Age of Revolutions 101
LAURENT DUBOIS

Locating West Africa in the Age of Revolutions   111
BRONWEN EVERILL

(In)forming Meiji: Two Revolutions in Nineteenth-Century Japan   121
GIDEON FUJIWARA

Part 3. Are We Still Living in the Age of Revolutions?

The Intimate Life of Books in Iran's 1979 Revolution   137
NAGHMEH SOHRABI

Two, Three . . . Many Túpacs: The Enduring Afterlife of an
Andean Rebel   146
MIGUEL LA SERNA

Curating the Pantheon in Mexico: History and Memory   156
WILLIAM A. BOOTH

Performing Dessalines: State and Popular Appropriations of
Haiti's Founding Father, Jean-Jacques Dessalines   167
ERIN ZAVITZ

Scenes from Hong Kong: Revolution of Our Time, Histories
in Real Time   179
NOAH SHUSTERMAN

The Bastille and the Roundabout: Popular Protest and the
Revolutionary Past of the Gilets Jaunes   194
ANDREW W. M. SMITH

Red, White, and Blood: An Essay on White Terror and
Great Fear, 1789–2021   210
BEATRICE DE GRAAF

Afterword   219
LYNN HUNT

Notes on Contributors   225

Index   229

PREFACE

In 2015, the editors of this volume launched *Age of Revolutions,* or *AoR* (www.ageofrevolutions.com), with the tagline, "We live in an age of revolutions." We live in an age shaped by discourses of revolution, which are often tied to the history of the era (traditionally dated roughly 1775–1848). At its inception, this digital, public-facing, peer-reviewed publication served many purposes. It was an experiment in open-access research publication. In part, we aimed to create a platform for scholars to undergo peer review and publish their work speedily, often while navigating, or in lieu of, the glacial process of traditional academic publishing. Most fundamentally, we envisioned a space for scholars of revolutions, revolutionaries, and the idea of "revolution" itself to share their research with one another *and* with the public. In our view, *AoR*'s digital format mirrors the disruptive and democratizing spirit of the revolutions it explores, making scholarship accessible to a global audience and fostering dialogues that transcend traditional academic boundaries. By its nature, the site has also become a space where researchers bring their expertise to bear on contemporary events in need of historical context. Over the years, contributors to *Age of Revolutions*—which have ranged from early career scholars to established historians, alongside voices from adjacent disciplines—have written about contemporary crises around the globe, fostering a rich interdisciplinary exchange that engages both academic and general audiences. The volume that follows furthers our experiment with a collection of essays, in the shorter-form style of *Age of Revolutions,* that spotlight some of the latest research in the field of revolutionary history.

This book is shaped by the experiences of running the website, coordinating with authors with differing opinions of the revolutionary past and present, editing hundreds of thousands of words, and publishing for a global audience that has grown exponentially each year. Through this work, we have witnessed firsthand how diverse perspectives on revolutions—from political, cultural, and social dimensions—enrich our understanding of their causes, trajectories, and legacies. These experiences have reinforced our belief in the value of public scholarship as a bridge between academic research and broader audiences, fostering critical conversations that extend beyond the confines of our profession. The essays included here reflect this spirit, offering a range of voices and interpretations that challenge conventional narratives and encourage readers to think critically about *revolution*.

This collection is also a testament to the rich and evolving scholarship that defines the field of revolutionary history today. In assembling its essays, we sought to capture not only the range of debates surrounding revolutions but also the array of methodologies, perspectives, and historiographical traditions that have shaped and continue to redefine our understanding of revolutionary movements and their broader implications. This volume was designed to feature concise essays offering a variety of perspectives in the hopes that it will appeal both to those encountering the Age of Revolutions for the first time as well as to seasoned scholars who will appreciate the deliberate diversity of voices and approaches within its pages.

INTRODUCTION

IN HIS TREATISE *Émile; ou, De l'éducation* (1762), Jean-Jacques Rousseau described his eighteenth-century world as one of "inevitable revolutions" that would level class distinctions and topple governments. Rousseau wrote this during the Seven Years' War (1756–63), which itself reordered much of the world and created the "state of crisis and the century of revolutions" that he portended.[1] What followed was the American Revolution, the French Revolution of 1789, the Haitian Revolution, revolutions across Latin America, and beyond. In some sense, the field of scholars who have sought to define the revolutionary era have followed Rousseau by emphasizing the theme of "crisis." David Armitage and Sanjay Subrahmanyam argued that the "World Crisis" model, popular among political scientists, best describes the connective tissue of each revolution. Patrick Griffin's *The Age of Atlantic Revolutions* similarly focuses on world networks that facilitated the movement of revolutionary ideals and what happens when those long used pathways are severed.[2] In doing so, they challenged older models of scholarship that emphasized either a common republican or democratic ethos or foregrounded the social factors that led to both political revolutions as well as workers' revolts against the Industrial Revolution.[3] Still others have focused on the mobility of revolutionaries themselves and the cosmopolitanism of the age, preferring a definition of the revolutionary era that features the individual as much as the increasingly global system.[4]

No single model prevails, nor perhaps *should* one prevail, in part because the revolutionary era was one of constant political expression that appeared as cacophony to those whose privileges and "properties" were challenged. The source and nature of these challenges varied but ultimately emerged out of peripheries, or as Pierre Serna has called them, "colonial" contexts—those spaces and peoples under the weight of the metropole or center of power, largely guided by new liberation ideologies (some republican and others not).[5] In the end, the crisis model advanced by Armitage and Subrahmanyam does not fully consider the power of the variety of *ideas* that drove revolutionary sentiment, and that often produced unintended consequences.

One such idea at the core of this volume and of the digital publication that inspired it (*Age of Revolutions*) is that of "revolution" itself, which was popularized during the French Revolution of 1789 and became a malleable feature of modern discourses on political transformation around the world. "Revolution" underwent a fundamental transition during the eighteenth century from earlier astronomical definitions of the term to new political, social, and economic definitions, all of which promised "progress," as if humans had finally ascended to a new stage of human advancement.[6] And, of course, what constituted "progress" differed greatly from one person or group to another. This evolution in the concept of revolution underscores the central theme of this volume: that revolutionary change is not monolithic but a medley of competing visions and interpretations.

The "Age of Revolutions" serves both as a foundational precedent for modern-day understandings of revolution and as one among many possible historical frameworks for analyzing transformative change. It provides a lens through which the struggles for liberty, equality, and self-determination during the late eighteenth and nineteenth centuries can be understood as shaping modern concepts of political and social upheaval. Yet, our intent is not to reify the Age of Revolutions as a definitive model but to critically examine its legacy and explore how it informs broader revolutionary traditions. By situating the revolutionary era within a wider geographic and temporal context, we hope to highlight its role as one of multiple overlapping narratives of resistance and transformation, and to encourage a more nuanced and expansive understanding of revolution across time and space.

This volume tries to capture the complex nature of revolution and revolutionary change through its content *and* its form, without constraining it to any particular paradigm or set of years but instead recognizing that through debate and even discord, strong commonalities emerge. The book challenges traditional understandings that define the Age of Revolutions as lasting from 1775 to 1848 and occurring within Europe and the Atlantic world, and instead stretches these boundaries from the late seventeenth century through the present day and across the globe. We envision this volume as a collective history because it seizes on the dynamic forms of cultural creativity that William H. Sewell identified in the

French Revolution, making the revolution thinkable, rather than resisting it in the name of advancing a singular paradigm.[7]

Overview

Since launching www.ageofrevolutions.com in 2015, the editors of this volume have published over five hundred articles to date (2025), covering revolutionary activity in North and South America, Africa, Asia, Australia, and Europe—every inhabited continent. This edited volume is a distillation of three of the most prominent themes that have emerged on *Age of Revolutions*, and that historians and other scholars of revolution are grappling with today: What was the Age of Revolutions? Where was the Age of Revolutions? Are we still living in the/an Age of Revolutions? Each of these questions represents a section of this volume.

Part 1, "What Was the Age of Revolutions?" features essays that attempt to define key features of the revolutionary era. In general, two questions permeate the contributions. First, what are the political features of the revolutionary era? Bryan A. Banks argues that the secular character of revolutionary upheaval, if not outright hostile to separation of church and state experiences by revolutionaries, was largely a response to the Wars of Religion and respective harsh policies of intolerance. He explores the political rhetoric of Pierre Bayle, who argued that religious conviction played no role in the English Revolution of 1688 nor in the Siamese Revolution of the same year. Dan Edelstein and Katlyn Marie Carter both explore how issues of political representation were at the heart of the American and French Revolutions and can be viewed as a catalyst for the evolution of natural-rights and human-rights theories. Carter demonstrates how the concept of representative democracy emerged in the late eighteenth century as a way to reconcile the distinct ideas of direct democracy and representative government, either as a practical substitute for direct democracy in large societies or as a superior system that refined the public will through elected officials. Edelstein, meanwhile, explores how the American Revolution sought to establish a balanced constitution based on classical principles, while the French Revolution aimed for historical progress through radical change and centralization, reflecting two distinct concepts of revolution.

The second question examined in part 1 focuses on lived experiences rather than on political ideals. In her panoramic essay, Christy Pichichero advances a global, diasporic, and anticolonial vision of the Age of Revolutions. She contends that our understanding should not only center the experiences of those subjected to dispossession, enslavement, racism, violence, and other forms of subjugation but also acknowledge ongoing struggles for sovereignty and reparations. Denise Z. Davidson draws parallels by foregrounding how the revolutionary era ushered in a revolution in private life, in which women found new ways of advancing their interests and men challenged traditional notions of patriarchy within the family.

Part 2, "Where Was the Age of Revolutions?" compliments part 1 by thinking geographically about the revolutionary era and by identifying places that encourage us to expand or contract what movements are included in the Age of Revolutions. Since ideas move with actors and revolutionaries enact programs that often dislocate individuals, it only makes sense to think in spatial terms. What movements should be added to the canonical Age of Revolutions and why? Cindy Ermus, Junko Thérèse Takeda, Bronwen Everill, and Gideon Fujiwara's pieces encourage the reader to reconceive the revolutionary era. Referring to a "Long Age of Revolutions," Ermus draws our attention to the early eighteenth-century Caribbean, long before the American and French Revolutions broke out, as a means to relocate the origins of the revolutionary era on the periphery of the European empire while a plague outbreak raged in southeastern France. Takeda accomplishes a similar goal but traces imperial tensions across Eurasia. She argues that incorporating Asian political upheavals, such as Siam's 1688 anti-French revolution and Persian "revolutions," into the global Age of Revolutions challenges Eurocentric narratives by demonstrating how these events shaped French revolutionary thought, imperial ambitions, and early modern geopolitics and trade. Similarly, Everill writes about a "West African Age of Revolutions" that centers African agency and calls for us to demarginalize West Africa in the revolutionary epoch. At the same time, Fujiwara looks beyond European empires and asks if the Meiji Restoration in Japan is better understood within the global revolutionary era. Frameworks explored in this section, including those of a "Long Age of Revolutions," a "West African Age of Revolutions," and the expansion of the Age of Revolutions to nineteenth-century Japan and long-eighteenth-century Siam and Persia, significantly broaden our understanding of transatlantic and global revolutionary traditions by challenging Eurocentric narratives and emphasizing global perspectives. Consequently, they help portray revolutions as global phenomena influenced by diverse actors, regions, and temporalities.

How did revolutions force people to rethink their relationships to space? Kate Fullagar's essay focuses on the ways that revolutionary ideals forced people to reconsider their relationships with their spaces. She explores how Cherokees and Indigenous peoples in North America more broadly absorbed certain elements of revolutionary rhetoric to assert their own sovereignty. Laurent Dubois's contribution asks a fundamental question of the field: Should the Haitian Revolution be centered in our discussions of the Age of Revolutions? And if so, how does the Haitian Revolution draw into question the republican and democratic characteristics historians often ascribe to the revolutionary epoch? For Dubois, a history of modern political thought and culture must integrate diverse perspectives, particularly those of marginalized and enslaved peoples, and "Atlantic History," exemplified by the Haitian Revolution, offers a vital framework for challenging traditional Eurocentric narratives and constructing a more inclusive understanding of the past to inform a just future.

Part 3, "Are We Still Living in the Age of Revolutions?" brings the revolutionary era forward to the modern day. Essays in this section argue for essentially two models. First—as described in Naghmeh Sohrabi's piece—perhaps we live in a second Age of Revolutions, better defined by its theocratic and decolonial ideals. In her essay, books, both as physical objects and carriers of ideas, served as crucial tools for politicization, resistance, and network-building among diverse ideological groups in prerevolutionary Iran, playing a central role in the cultural and organizational processes that culminated in the 1979 revolution. Such decolonial ideals had considerable half-lives, as Miguel La Serna evidences in his piece about the many legacies of Túpac Amaru II, the Incan leader who fought the Spanish in the late eighteenth century. La Serna reveals how Túpac Amaru I and II, Andean rebels against Spanish colonial rule, became enduring symbols of resistance, decoloniality, and antiracism, with their legacies inspiring revolutionary movements, cultural expressions, and political struggles across the Americas and beyond for centuries.

La Serna's piece leads us into the second theme, which explores how the Age of Revolutions inspired future generations and has been appropriated by various movements looking to latch onto revolutionary universalist ideals like natural or human rights, in order to foster the rights of self-determination on an individual or national level around the world. A global fascination with the revolutionary era exhibits itself in the political performance of those same ideals in myriad ways. William A. Booth explores how the Mexican Revolution in the nineteenth century continued to shape Mexican politics through the Cold War era, while Erin Zavitz dissects the campaigns of Haitian presidential candidates in 2015–16, who dressed as prominent figures from the Haitian revolutionary era to garner votes. Noah Shusterman examines how protest graffiti in Hong Kong in 2019–20 borrowed from revolutionary symbolism to critique government policing measures as well as an extradition bill. Andrew W. M. Smith explores a similar phenomenon in France, where the *gilets jaunes* protested high gas prices and government reforms and, in the process, adopted revolutionary symbolism to express their political positions. The last piece in the volume is by Beatrice de Graaf, who explores the implications of red and white terror from the French Revolution to the January 6th insurrection in 2021. Lynn Hunt then concludes the conversation with an afterword that considers where we are today in the history of revolutions. In the end, she maintains, the concept of the Age of Revolutions remains relevant despite its broad temporal and spatial range, as it continues to incite diverse reflection and analysis, even when authors challenge its original parameters.

Each section follows a theme, but contributions can and should be read across sections. Themes addressed in part 1 reappear in subsequent essays where they are further validated or complicated. For example, the two essays by Ermus and Fullagar are not merely about the geographic scope of the revolutionary era but also about questions of when, and even who. The editors intentionally sought pieces for each section with such matters in mind, including contributions in all three parts that address, for example, issues of race and gender, as well as the geographical question of the place of Asia within the revolutionary era—a matter traditionally excluded from debates on the Age of Revolutions. In bringing together such a range of voices and approaches, this volume invites readers to rethink longstanding assumptions about revolutions and their global dimensions, both within and beyond traditional temporal and spatial frameworks.

Notes

The editors would like to thank the anonymous readers for their invaluable feedback and suggestions.

1. Jean-Jacques Rousseau, *Émile; ou, De l'éducation*, ed. Pierre Alexandre Du Peyrou and Paul Moultou (Geneva: J. M. Gallanar, 1782), 327.
2. David Armitage and Sanjay Subrahmanyam, *The Age of Revolutions in Global Context, c. 1760–1840* (New York: Palgrave, 2010), xxiii. Wim Klooster offered a similar argument in his *Revolutions in the Atlantic World: A Comparative History* (New York: New York University Press, 2009). Patrick Griffin, *The Age of Atlantic Revolution: The Fall and Rise of a Connected World* (New Haven, CT: Yale University Press, 2023).
3. R. R. Palmer, *The Age of Democratic Revolution: A Political History of Europe and America, 1760–1800* (Princeton, NJ: Princeton University Press, 1959); Eric Hobsbawm, *The Age of Revolution, Europe: 1789–1848* (London: Weidenfeld and Nicholson, 1962). Hobsbawm used a "dual revolution" thesis to tie the origins of the modern world to the French Revolution of 1789 and the contemporaneous British Industrial Revolution.
4. Janet Polasky, *Revolutions with Borders* (New Haven, CT: Yale University Press, 2015).
5. Historian of the French Revolution Pierre Serna asked, "What if, on the eve of the Revolution, France resembled 'colonies' that were geographically bound and politically united? What if the state apparatus had little local power besides the reports that reached Versailles? Were the peripheries and the center not irremediably separated, and the subjects divided, as in a typical colonial society?" Serna followed this series of questions to assert that the French allegiance to their kingdom would be anything but concrete. Categories such as "colony" and "nation" should not be understood as monolithic or self-evident. See Serna, "Every Revolution Is a War of Independence," in *The French Revolution in Global Perspective*, ed. Suzanne Desan, Lynn Hunt, and William Max Nelson (Ithaca, NY: Cornell University Press, 2013), 175.
6. Keith Michael Baker and Dan Edelstein, eds., *Scripting Revolution: A Historical Approach to the Comparative Study of Revolutions* (Stanford, CA: Stanford University Press, 2015).
7. William H. Sewell, "The Concept(s) of Culture," in *Beyond the Cultural Turn: New Directions in the Study of Society and Culture*, ed. Victoria E. Bonnell and Lynn Hunt (Oakland: University of California Press, 1999), 42.

PART 1

WHAT WAS THE AGE OF REVOLUTIONS?

Religious Republican Revolutions in an Age of Confessionalization

Bryan A. Banks

Pierre-Joseph d'Orléans (1641–1698) was a French Jesuit priest who published three books with "revolution" in the title. The first, *Histoire des révolutions d'Angleterre depuis le commencement de la monarchie* (1689), offered an overview of English history, ending with the English Revolution of 1688, which saw the Catholic King James II dethroned and replaced with the Protestant William of Orange (who ruled as William III). The second book, entitled *Histoire de M. Constance, premier ministre du roi de Siam, et de la dernière révolution de cet État*, was published a year later in 1690. This volume, like the one before it, covered the history of the Siamese Ayutthaya Kingdom (now Thailand) up until the 1688 revolution, which saw Phetracha seize the throne and the French Jesuits expelled. The third, *Histoire des révolutions d'Espagne, depuis la destruction de l'empire des Goths, jusqu'à l'entière et parfaite réunion des royaumes de Castille et d'Aragon en une seule monarchie* (1734), appeared in three volumes well after his death. In each of these works, he used the word "revolution" in a stadial sense, referring less to revolutions as political ruptures and more to the successive rise and fall of power.

At the same time that Orléans wrote, others began to refer to revolutions as moments of intense and often violent political change. What drove this semantic shift were confessional conflicts between Catholics and Protestants, who imagined revolutionary rupture in either anarchical or apocalyptic terms. Out of this context of clashing confessions emerged some of the earliest secular arguments for the separation of powers. The idea of an Age of Revolutions around the world came into existence first in the minds of Catholic controversialists who hoped to connect Protestantism and freedom of conscience with republicanism and political radicalism. This argument emerged during the Controverse of the 1670s and 1680s. This essay explores three perspectives on revolutionary politics with respect to religion in what might be referred to as the first Age of Revolutions or a Religious Age of Revolutions.

In his *Histoire du Calvinisme* (1682), the French Jesuit Louis Maimbourg described the "great revolution" that "changed the Religion and the State in Geneva," a revolution of the sixteenth century that Huguenots hoped to commence in France. Following the Edict of Nantes (1598), French Catholics increasingly derided autonomous Huguenot assemblies and southern fortified towns (remnants of the Wars of Religion) as "quasi-republican," representing the Huguenot republican state within the French kingdom. Maimbourg lamented that the "greatest monument of heresy" was that "strangers had introduced into the Kingdom, a republican space established inside the monarchy, and more than a million Frenchmen, who have perished to stop it, received no justice."[1] The body politic of the French absolutist state suffered from a Calvinist republican cancer according to Maimbourg, evidencing the heinous crimes of the other faction (most often drawing from the Wars of Religion). Maimbourg colored the Calvinists as immoral and made the case for intolerance in France.[2]

Catholics used the idea of republican heresy in slanderous ways to promote their expulsion, but the very geopolitics of that expulsion were later taken as evidence of the earlier antirepublican polemics. Louis XIV promulgated the Revocation of the Edict of Nantes in 1685, expelling some 200,000 Huguenots from the country and forcing those communities who remained to worship clandestinely or take up arms, as happened in the infamous Camisard Wars of the early eighteenth century in the southern Cévennes region. Louis XIV remained concerned about the spread of Calvinist republican sentiments—as evidenced by the fact that his chancellor Pontchartrain prevented Huguenots from emigrating to Louisiana, asserting that "the king did not chase the heretics from the kingdom in order to let them form a republic over there."[3] The English Revolution of 1688, or the Williamite coup d'état from the Catholic Church's perspective, only exacerbated the situation. Looking beyond explicit espousals of republicanism like those made by the millenarian Pierre Jurieu, the people who fled settled in established republics—Swiss and Dutch—and in doing so, the so-called republican reformed myth coalesced into a self-fulfilling prophecy. Nowhere was this self-affirming republican argument affirmed more than in the eighteenth-century polemic of the Abbé Jean Novi de Caveirac. In his *Mémoire politico-critique* (1756), Caveirac described how a "tribe of republicans lament their lack of independence" in France and seek refuge in "Holland, England, Switzerland, and the free towns of Germany." Yet, "if they were allowed to return to France, could they be tolerated?"[4] In Caveirac's tract, the republican spirit drove Huguenots into the refuge and abandonment of the French state because of that attachment to republicanism.

Huguenot refugees like the Theologian of Rotterdam, Pierre Jurieu, supported the English Revolution of 1688 and found in the revolution a chance to expound on their republican theories. In his *Apologie pour leurs serenissimes majestés britanniques, contre un infame libelle intitulé le vray portrait de Guillaume Henri de Nassau, nouvel Absçalom, nouvel Herode, nouveau Cromwel, nouveau Neron* (1689), Jurieu argued for a definition of the law that puts forth the safety of the people first and debased the divine will of the king second. As Guy Howard Dodge argued, the English Revolution inspired much discussion of republicanism. Up to 1695, Parisian publishers issued over a dozen histories of the English Revolution alone. Hints can be found in Jurieu's corpus on the rights of resistance as well as in his theological works. In 1677, Jurieu wrote his *Traité de la puissance de l'Eglise*. In it, Jurieu analyzed the power of the Catholic Church. Jurieu's family had been embroiled the previous year in the *Fasciculus epistolarum*, an attack on the ecclesiastical jurisdiction of Jurieu's uncle Louis Dumoulin. At stake was the balance between authority and religious liberty. Jurieu's solution to this conundrum was to reinforce authority by making it accountable to the people. Authority over faith could easily set the stage for the people's authority over politics—Jurieu's republican stance.[5]

Even in the course of debating the ecclesiastical structure within the Catholic Church, Jurieu presented a trinity wherein authority for the Catholic Church might lie—the pope, the bishops and priests, and the people. Immediately, Jurieu noted that the authority of the church for the whole rested on the shoulders of the people, with the ministers and even the pope being held accountable to the spiritual community. The people have the right to elect their leaders, both political and spiritual, according to Jurieu. In both his *Traité de la puissance de l'Eglise* and his later 1683 *Le Janséniste convaincu*, Jurieu insisted on this point. In the latter text, he wrote,

> All peoples of the world have received from God and nature the right to form a government—monarchical or aristocratic—as they please. When this government is established as [the people] see fit, it is not in

their power to disobey. They must obey the kings and magistrates they have installed by law. But if this government comes to a standstill between them, or when kings fail to lead, and their kingdom fails; ... the people ... are entitled to reestablish a new government.... For there are two rights which are inseparable from men; the first is that of the preservation which we owe ourselves before every other after God; the second is to install a leader when one does not exist.[6]

Undergirding the power of the people was the theme of the unity of the people, which Catholics emphasized often to cast Protestants as inefficient spiritual and therefore political advisors. Pierre Nicole's *De l'unité de l'Eglise* (1687) sparked this debate further, leading to Jurieu's response in the form of the *Traité de l'unité de l'Eglise* (1688).

Notably, Jurieu avoided directly sponsoring republican governance before 1688. His opponents only started using the label "republican" in response to texts like *Les soupirs de la France esclave, qui aspire aprés la liberté* (1689). In it, Jurieu associated monarchy with "despotic and arbitrary power" in light of Louis XIV's Revocation of the Edict of Nantes and James II's rule in England.[7] In *Les soupirs de la France esclave*, Jurieu argued for a "reformation of the state" by pointing to the history of republican political and economic expansion. Holland, he noted, was too small for "proper conquest," but other republics in European history had become the most expansive and powerful on the entire continent.[8] Jurieu pointed to the Roman Republic and the republic of Venice, in particular, as examples of republican forms of government capable of uniting to rule over large stretches of territory. Republican governance did not necessarily result in weak authority by his geopolitical calculation. While Holland had not become a traditional landed empire, its people had become "masters of the commercial world." Internal divisions were natural in society, and as such could find political power in republics, but in France, where such divisions existed, according to Jurieu the French monarchy would certainly crumble.

Jurieu emphasized the balance between individual rights and freedoms in relation to collective action intentionally. Republicanism, mobilized as slander, which the last section analyzed, often depended on the idea that Protestant freedom of conscience perpetuated crisis, that only uniformity in faith could hope to bolster a strong state, and that the role of the state was to safeguard the power of the church. For Jurieu, collective action from individuals acting out of their own pursuit of freedom of conscience mobilized the best of each person while safeguarding those from religious persecution. Achieving this balance was key for Jurieu's sense of republicanism. Striking fears of errant and anarchical Calvinist republicans in the hearts of Catholics was the intent of many Catholic writers during the Controverse. But for those in the Huguenot camp, intent on promoting the return of Calvinists to France, Jurieu's republicanism was caustic and casuistic. Pierre Bayle saw Pierre Jurieu as evidence of the Catholic's self-fulfilling prophecy.

Jurieu and Bayle, the Philosopher of Rotterdam, disagreed on the prospects for the Huguenots, and Jurieu's republicanism only strengthened Bayle's opinion that Huguenots needed to disavow republican sentiments and entrench themselves further in the royalist political culture of the late seventeenth century. Bayle was far more moderate than Jurieu when it came to the future of the Huguenot diaspora. Bayle was far more sentimental to the Catholic theological side—having converted to Catholicism for a brief period during his youth—but more importantly, his Pyrrhonian skepticism had already begun forming by the 1680s, leading him to challenge the religious foundations of society and the near religious anthropology that undergirded much of the debates in the Controverse. Like Jurieu, Bayle grew up in the south of France, had been employed at the Academy of Sedan, and chose exile from France rather than endanger himself and his family by remaining in the country. For Bayle, faith was a matter of private conscience, if not articulated in such modern words. No *ipso facto* relationship could exist between Calvinism and republicanism because both were separate choices made by an individual.

In France and later at the École Illustre, Bayle and Jurieu were close acquaintances, but soon a political rift split the two. Shortly after arriving in the Netherlands, Jurieu published a series of tracks justifying Huguenot violence against the state, in prophetic terms as well as preservation ones. Once the English Revolution got underway, Jurieu's millenarianism turned outright republican. In response to his fellow refugee, Bayle anonymously authored his *Avis important aux refugiés* (1690). Historians generally agree that Bayle was the anonymous author, and even those few who remain skeptical argue that the text's arguments were consistent with Bayle's position.[9] It was in this text that Bayle took aim at "a certain republican spirit which introduces anarchy into the world, the greatest scourge of civil society."[10] Calumny became a central feature of Bayle's writings. As Mara van der Lugt has noted, Bayle and Jurieu attacked each other in "near-perfect symmetry," seeing their respective projects as building against a foe that the other embodied: For Jurieu, Bayle stood as the Huguenot driven to moderation and susceptible to conversion.[11] For Bayle, Jurieu stood in the way of his creation of another type of republic.

At the same time that Bayle sought to distance Huguenot refugees from republicanism and revolutionary upheaval through his critique of Jurieu, he appropriated *republique* through his work on the *Nouvelles de la République des Lettres* (1684–1716). Attacking outright republicanism within the Huguenot fold was key, but Bayle also wanted to introduce a new intellectual understanding of republicanism—one that would form the basis of the epistolary Enlightenment in decades to follow. For Bayle, the republic of letters was a powerful political metaphor for "an extremely free state, which only recognizes the empire of truth and reason." In pursuit of intellectual rigor, Bayle swore that his journal would "wage war against anyone. Friends must be on their guard against each other, the fathers against their children, the stepfathers against the sons-in-law; it's like in the Iron Age.... No one is sovereign and justiciable there. The laws of society have not prejudiced the independence of the state of nature from error and ignorance: all individuals have the right of the sword in this respect and can exercise it without ask[ing] permission from those who govern."[12] Bayle's politico-metaphorical "Republic" carried similar undertones to Jurieu's political republicanism. The people held each other accountable. The individual conscience granted the individual the right to engage in the republic of knowledge while also understanding that they themselves would be held accountable to the court of peers for their ideas.

Bayle's use of the political metaphor of a republic in his intellectual work collided with his antirepublican stance toward Jurieu. The two engaged in a heated debate, especially after the publication of Bayle's notorious *Dictionnaire historique et critique* (1697), which far outstretched even the issue of Calvinist republicanism. For Bayle, the errant republican ideology that Jurieu proffered and then staunchly defended presented a direct threat to the metaphorical republic Bayle hoped to foster. The *Jurieu calomniateur* was the living embodiment of a reckless individualism in politics as well as in moral terms for Bayle. Republics breed dissent, and linking republicanism with Calvinist theology reaffirmed the Catholic argument that Calvinists were inherently disloyal. For Bayle, then, the two ideals needed to be staunchly separated and secularized.

If we move forward in time to the nineteenth century, we find a historiography that gave far greater credence to the tumult of the revocation era in the narrative of the revolution in France that came to follow. Jules Michelet, the republican and historian, noted, "What the Revolution was to the eighteenth century, the revocation of the Edict of Nantes [and] the emigration of Protestants was to the seventeenth."[13] In considering what the Age of Revolutions was, accordingly, we need to take into account how the political concept "revolution" before the revolutionary era would leave an imprint on the model ever after.

Notes

1. Louis Maimbourg, *Histoire du Calvinisme* (Paris, 1682), 51, 2.
2. Claims of republican governance within France were not solely limited to the Calvinist population. In 1703, the Duke of Burgundy equally charged the government of Strasbourg with not embracing the absolutist model; instead, "its inhabitants are still gripped by the spirit of republicanism and their hope of returning to their original state has not, as yet, been completely extinguished." Quoted in G. Livet, "Royal Administration in a Frontier Province: The Intendency of Alsace under Louis XIV," in *Louis XIV and Absolutism*, ed. Ragnhild Marie Hatton (London: Macmillan, 1976), 185.
3. Quoted in Arthur Herman, "The Huguenot Republic and Antirepublicanism in Seventeenth-Century France," *Journal of the History of Ideas* 53, no. 2 (April–June 1992): 250.
4. Jean Novi de Caveirac, *Memoire politico-critique, où l'on examine s'il est de l'intérêt de l'Eglise et de l'Etat d'établir pour les calvinistes du royaume une nouvelle forme de se marier. Et où l'on réfute l'écrit qui a pour titre: Memoire théologique et politique sur les mariages clandestins des protestans de France* (N.p., 1756), 183.
5. Pierre Jurieu, *Apologie pour leurs serenissimes majestés britanniques, contre un infame libelle intitulé le vray portrait de Guillaume Henri de Nassau, nouvel Absçalom, nouvel Herode, nouveau Cromwel, nouveau Neron* (The Hague: Abraham Troyel, 1689); Jurieu, *Traité de la puissance de l'Eglise dans lequel on découvre la source de cette puissance* (Rouen: Jean Lucas, 1677); Guy Howard Dodge, *The Political Theory of the Huguenots of the Dispersion* (New York: Octagon Books, 1972), 82, 94f.
6. Pierre Jurieu, *Le Janséniste convaincu de vaine sophistiquerie; ou, Examens des réxions de M. Arnaud sur Le Préservatif contre le changement de religion* (Amsterdam: Henry Desbordes, 1683), 310.
7. Pierre Jurieu and Michel Le Vassor, *Les soupirs de la France esclave, qui aspire aprés la liberté* (1689), 32. On the debate over whether Jurieu was

the author of *Les soupirs* or if Le Vassor had, in fact, authored the piece, see Dodge, *Political Theory of the Huguenots*, 140–46. During the Controverse especially, Jurieu was accused of authoring the piece, and several historians have continued to emphasize that original attribution. Those who argue that Jurieu did not author *Les soupirs* often emphasize the incongruities between Jurieu's usual religious and political positions and those expressed within the text. Jurieu was a Gallican extremist in his arguments that the Bourbon throne's interests conflicted with that of the Holy See, whereas the author of *Les soupirs* appears more ultramontanist. The author of *Les soupirs* also makes a far more critical argument of Bourbon absolutist authority, whereas Jurieu made room for absolute monarchy as long as those absolutist powers did not infringe on freedom of conscience. See Émile Kappler, "Les soupirs de la France ésclave," in *Bibliographie critique de l'œvre imprimée de Pierre Jurieu (1637–1713)* (Paris: Honoré Champion, 2002), 424–35.
8. Jurieu, *Les soupirs de la France*, 187–90.
9. Charles Bastide, "Bayle est-il l'auteur de l'*Avis aux réfugiés?*" *Bulletin de la Société de l'Histoire du Protestantisme Français* 56 (1907): 544–58; Sean O'Cathasaigh, "Bayle and the Authorship of the *Avis aux réfugiés*," *Studies on Voltaire and the Eighteenth Century* 219 (1983): 133–45; H. M. Bracken, "Pierre Jurieu: The Politics of Prophecy," in *Millenarianism and Messianism in Early Modern European Culture: Continental Millenarians: Protestants, Catholics, Heretics* (Dordrecht, Netherlands: Kluwer Academic, 2001), 86–88.
10. Pierre Bayle, *Avis important aux refugiés sur leur prochain retour en France* (Amsterdam, 1690), 11.
11. Mara van der Lugt, *Bayle, Jurieu, and the* Dictionnaire Historique et Critique (Oxford: Oxford University Press, 2016), 116.
12. Pierre Bayle, "Catius," in *Dictionnaire historique et critique*, quoted in Hubert Bost, *Pierre Bayle* (Paris: Fayard, 2006), 233.
13. Jules Michelet, *Histoire de France, nouvelle edition revue et augmentée* (Paris: Marpon, 1879), 15:4.

The Ages of Revolution

Dan Edelstein

In 1775, Benjamin Franklin received a letter from one of his agents in Europe, Charles G. F. Dumas. Dumas, who helped to promote American interests abroad, celebrated the coming conflict with Great Britain in excited terms: "Vices grappling with virtues! The dawn of a total revolution in the world (*une révolution totale dans le monde*)! Seven or eight new states directed by providence to recreate the beautiful ages of Ancient Greece!"[1]

Were one looking for a statement to inaugurate the Age of Revolution(s), Dumas's panegyric is a good candidate. Here was a Frenchman addressing an American on the eve of the American Revolution, already hinting at a massive revolutionary upheaval ("a total revolution in the world") that would usher in a new heroic age. And the Franklin-Dumas connection was of course far from the only Franco-American bond at this time. France would soon enter the war on the side of the Americans, sending men, materiel, and money. In 1789, Thomas Jefferson, author of the Declaration of Independence, advised the Marquis de Lafayette, a former officer in the Continental Army, on the latter's draft Declaration of the Rights of Man. So obvious are the multifarious connections between American and French revolutionaries that historians have long embraced the historical periodization of an "age of revolution(s)." From R. R. Palmer's classic *The Age of Democratic Revolution* (1964) to the present volume, this category has entered the historiographical canon. Scholars may continue to draw contrasts among revolutions, but they are still largely viewed as forming a single revolutionary wave that would subsequently crash into the Caribbean, Central and South America, and eventually back into Europe.

But what if there were in fact *two* waves that converged briefly in the late eighteenth century yet stemmed from different places and traditions? This suggestion might seem churlishly contrarian. Isn't it patently obvious that the American and French Revolutions are intertwined? Consider, however, Dumas's expression once more: "The dawn of a total revolution in the world!" What's odd about this statement is that in 1775, no American would have thought to describe events on the eastern seaboard in these terms. Conversely, there was nothing idiosyncratic about Dumas's choice of words: it was a fairly commonplace observation to make at that time in France. If this was the Age of Revolutions, there was little agreement on either side of the Atlantic about what "revolution" actually meant.

These conceptual differences had major implications for the courses and outcomes of the revolutions themselves. As I argue in this essay (adapted from a recent book), the American Revolution is better understood as the last of "three British revolutions."[2] Like the previous revolutions of 1642–60 and 1688–89, it sought above all to consolidate government under a well-balanced constitution, understood both socially and politically. As Polybius had taught in book 6 of his *Histories*, balancing the constitution was a matter of preventing any single social class, but also any single institution or office, from gaining total supremacy over the others. The payoff of a well-balanced constitution was longevity: the state would not fall prey to internal turmoil. Revolution, from this perspective, was something to be avoided, unless it could deliver what many longed for: a stable constitutional order.

By the mid-eighteenth century, however, a different conception of "revolution" was brewing in France. This conception drew on the modern cosmology of time, which defenders of the Moderns, in their quarrel with the Ancients, had championed.[3] Partisans of the Ancients tended to agree with Marcus Aurelius's observation: "To examine human life for forty years is the same as to examine it for ten thousand years, for what more will you see?"[4] From a classical perspective, history was directionless, capricious, and repetitive. When history was made, it was often at a huge human cost, a point stressed by Thucydides in his history of the Peloponnesian War. The goal of political philosophy, accordingly, was to keep history at bay by preventing revolutions.

The Moderns rejected this pessimistic outlook and championed the doctrine of progress. In their view, history was not one damned thing after another but displayed signs of gradual improvement. As opposed to religious millenarianism, the Moderns did not entrust historical change to a sudden transformation from without.[5] Progress was a matter of *kronos*, not *kairos*.⁶ Eventually, society might progress to the point where reason and justice prevailed in our institutions, as Condorcet imagined they eventually would in his *Esquisse d'un tableau historique des progrès de l'esprit humain* (1794). But this transformation, which could bring about an enlightened age, would result from the gradual, internal perfection of our morals, customs, and knowledge.

While the appearance and success of the doctrine of progress in the eighteenth century has been well studied, its effects on the idea of revolution have mostly gone unobserved. In part, this is because the classical understanding of "revolution" as a disastrous event to be avoided where possible still prevailed for much of the Enlightenment. "Everything is revolution, everything is misfortune," lamented Voltaire in a 1760 letter.⁷ But Voltaire was also responsible for promoting a very different meaning of "revolution." At first, it was a meaning reserved for great cultural advances: Voltaire announced as the subject of his *Siècle de Louis XIV* (1751), "the general revolution that must serve as a lasting testament to the true glory of our country."⁸ Within a decade, he was saluting his own age as launching a "great revolution of the human spirit."⁹ And by the 1770s, he was regularly trumpeting the political efforts of his allies across Europe as the "start of a great revolution."¹⁰

Voltaire was far from alone in adopting this modern meaning of revolution, though he may have played an outsized role in its dissemination. When Dumas cheered Franklin on in 1775, he was simply speaking the late Enlightenment language of progressive revolution. It was a language that Franklin might have understood, or at least heard before, but was a completely foreign idiom compared to what the Americans were saying at the time.

Indeed, for the Americans, there was only one revolution worth emulating and that was the Glorious Revolution. It is even as an analogy with the Glorious Revolution that Americans began to refer to their own actions as a "revolution." This usage, moreover, was quite restricted and took a long time to catch on. Somewhat surprisingly, given his more conservative reputation, John Adams may have first described American resistance to Britain as a "revolution," in 1775. He used the term in a very technical sense: if the Americans (and more particularly the inhabitants of Massachusetts) had adopted what he called "revolution principles," it was because they were reenacting the same script as in 1688. As he wrote in the first issue of *Novanglus*, "If the American resistance to the act for destroying your charter [a reference to the Massachusetts Government Act of 1775], and to the resolves for arresting persons here and sending them to England for trial, is treason, the lords and commons, and the whole nation, were traitors at the revolution," that is, in 1688.[11]

Adams subsequently extended this analogy to events in the other colonies. Shortly after the first meeting of the Massachusetts Provincial Congress (to which he was a delegate), he wrote to Richard Henry Lee to offer guidance on how Virginia might follow Massachusetts in setting up an alternative government: "A single month is sufficient, without the least convulsion, or even animosity, to accomplish a total revolution in the government of a colony."[12] Here was a very different understanding of "total revolution" than the one advanced by Dumas. Adams was using the term in its technical sense of a regime change, making a point to exclude its unfavorable connotations ("without the least convulsion, or even animosity").

There was nothing in this conception of "revolution" that expressed the modern vision of progress. For Adams—who was at this time the only founder even using the term—revolution was simply a matter of rearranging the organs of government. It was not a lengthy or complicated affair, nor did it entail any broader improvement of society. Ten days before Congress issued the Declaration of Independence, Adams informed his former Harvard professor John Winthrop that a few "committees will report in a week or two, and then the last finishing strokes will be given to the politics of this revolution. Nothing after that will remain but war."[13]

That Adams could have spoken of "the last *finishing* strokes ... of this revolution" in June 1776 highlights the extent to which revolution, in his mind, was as much about continuity as change. The purpose and goal of "this revolution" were obvious: "A legislative, an executive, and a judicial power comprehend the whole of what is meant and understood by government," Adams told Lee. "It is by balancing each of these powers against the other two, that the efforts in human nature towards tyranny can alone be checked and restrained, and any degree of freedom preserved in the constitution."[14] If Adams could assure his Virginian friends that their political revolution was just a matter of a single month's work, it was because the proper purpose of a revolution was already well known and could be found in the "revolution principles" derived from the Glorious Revolution.

Adams's interpretation of the American Revolution's purpose may have been somewhat idiosyncratic, but the essential point is that noone else at the time seems to have used the term in relation to American activities.[15] The word is not to be found in Thomas Paine's *Common Sense,* and the *Journals of the Continental Congress* make no mention of revolution until the end of 1777.[16] The few who did almost always drew a parallel with the Glorious Revolution. The year 1688 offered "a precedent which is worthy of imitation. We need no other—we can have no better," argued one pamphleteer in 1776.[17]

It is fairly clear why Americans shied away from branding their own actions "a revolution." Revolutions were still in their minds something in general to be avoided. If Paine did not use the term itself, he did refer to Masaniello, the Neapolitan fisherman who led a popular uprising against the Spanish viceroy in 1647. For Paine, this story served as a warning tale: beware the mob that elevates a demagogue to absolute power, as he will then "sweep away the liberties" of the citizens. Paine likely learned of this incident, directly or indirectly, from Alessandro Giraffi's *Le Riuolutioni di Napoli* ("The Revolutions of Naples"), whose 1650 English translation was very popular (it is found, for instance, in Adams's library).[18] These were the kind of revolutions that gave revolution a bad name.

Americans remained skeptical toward revolutions even after staging a successful one themselves. Adams introduced his *Defence of the Constitutions of the United States*—written in response to the Modern criticism of balanced constitutions by Turgot—with an account of the horrors of ancient revolutions, paraphrasing Thucydides's history of the *stasis* at Corcyra.[19] But Adams was not alone in warning against revolutions. Alexander Hamilton shared his phobia, observing how "it is impossible to read the history of the petty republics of Greece and Italy without feeling sensations of horror and disgust at the distractions with which they were continually agitated, and at the rapid succession of revolutions by which they were kept in a state of perpetual vibration between the extremes of tyranny and anarchy."[20] It was in part because of the fear of renewed revolutions (such as the threat posed by Shays's Rebellion) that the Constitutional Convention sought to draw up a new, "revolution-proof" constitution. James Madison was explicit on this point, reminding the delegates that "the insurrections in Mass[achusetts] admonished all the States of the danger to which they were exposed."[21]

Along with this classical assumption that there was no "greater evil . . . for a city than that which tears it apart and makes it many instead of one," as Plato asserted in *The Republic,* the framers ultimately considered the essential benefit of a revolution to be a constitution that can withstand social and political stress.²² Political sociologists often distinguish between political and social revolutions, typically identifying the American Revolution as an exemplar of the former and the French of the latter.²³ But the Americans also took social differences into consideration when designing the federal Constitution. Madison famously argued that the multiplication of special interests would prevent any single one from assuming majority rule, but he identified one social division as the most critical: "Those who hold and those who are without property have ever formed distinct interests in society. Those who are creditors, and those who are debtors, fall under a like discrimination."²⁴ He made a similar argument at the Constitutional Convention, when defending an upper and lower chamber of the legislature: "In all civilized countries, the interest of a community will be divided. There will be debtors and creditors, and an unequal possession of property, and hence arises different views and different objects in government." If the wealthier class of landowners were not protected from "all classes of people," he warned, the result would be the same as in the late Roman Republic: "An agrarian law would soon take place."²⁵ Many other framers similarly justified the upper chamber in terms of defending the interests of the upper class.²⁶

Historians of the American Revolution who insist on its "modernity" like to claim that the Constitution of 1787 marked (in Gordon S. Wood's expression) "the end of classical politics."²⁷ This claim has been repeatedly challenged by scholars who underscore the many classical references, concepts, and theories that were incessantly invoked during the revolutionary age.²⁸ But even leaving aside this debate, there is no question that the American founders retained the classical skepticism toward revolution (Jefferson's quip about refreshing the tree of liberty with blood standing out as the rare exception). And they clearly believed that only a well-designed constitution, whether based on classical or novel principles, could keep subsequent revolutions at bay.

When the French Revolution broke out, Americans were accordingly quite dumbfounded. To Adams, it offered "a spectacle so novel . . . that I have ever acknowledged myself incompetent to judge of it." But he recognized that it seemed to flow from a different source: "I know that encyclopedists and economists, Diderot and d'Alembert, Voltaire and Rousseau, have contributed to this great event more than Sidney, Locke, or Hoadley, perhaps more than the American revolution."²⁹ As we will see, it was a penetrating insight.

One of the most obvious differences between these two revolutions is that the French celebrated theirs as a "revolution." As Keith M. Baker memorably phrased it, after 1789, revolution became an act, not just a fact.[30] Pamphleteers had been celebrating the calling of the Estates General as a "happy revolution" since 1788.[31] If the revolutionary experience left many participants with lost illusions, most of them began with great expectations. Revolution was no longer just a matter of "balancing each of [the three] powers against the other two," as Adams had put it. For the French, revolution was a historical process, a step up on the ladder of progress. The implications of this changed perception were vast.

Before considering its implications, however, it is worth examining its source. In many regards, Adams was correct. Over the previous thirty years, French *philosophes* had fashioned a new concept of revolution that tied it to the modern doctrine of progress. One of the earliest and most forceful advocates of this new concept was Adams's own antagonist Turgot. As a student, Turgot had delivered a famous lecture at the Sorbonne on the "ongoing progress of the human spirit" (1750), arguing that while progress could be slow and suffer setbacks, in the long run we were always headed toward "ever greater perfection."[32] And this historical vision led Turgot to consider revolutions in a new light as well. In his famous *Encyclopédie* article on "Fondation" (1757), he argued that foundations, through the terms of their endowments, forced future generations to abide by the desires of the past. Not only was this unnatural but it rested on a wrongheaded understanding of history: "Time brings new revolutions," Turgot insisted, "which make [the foundation's] original utility disappear, and can even make it noxious."[33]

When controller-general of finances, Turgot developed the political ramifications of this historical outlook. Drawing on the earlier, modern defenders of progress (such as the Abbé de Saint-Pierre and the Marquis d'Argenson), Turgot composed a "Memorandum on Municipalities," which was ghostwritten by his collaborator (and leading Physiocrat) Samuel du Pont de Nemours. The goal of Turgot's proposed reform was nothing short of perfecting the French political system. Through a layered system of assemblies, stretching from the municipal to the national levels, information would cascade up to the king, who could then make the most rational decisions for the nation. Gone was any talk of a balanced constitution in this model: legislative power would be entirely concentrated "in a single man," the king, who could consider himself an "absolute legislator."[34] As Turgot implicitly acknowledged in his 1778 letter to Richard Price, in this model the king could also disappear, leaving a national assembly to make final decisions in his stead. But in terms of political theory, the more important point was that political power, for the Moderns, was not something to be parceled out among social groups or balanced between organs of government. It should be as concentrated as possible so that the state can become the most efficient motor of progress.

The reforms Turgot sought, alongside related reforms by enlightened monarchs, left the *philosophes,* Voltaire in particular, giddy with optimism. "Many other rulers are making similar changes to the laws of their countries," he gushed to Catherine the Great in 1778. "This revolution will stretch all the way to Rome and the inquisitorial lands. A new century will be born and you will be its creator."[35] But he himself had contributed to making the concept of revolution more palatable, especially to the crowned heads of Europe. In his historiographical writings, Voltaire had turned "revolution" into a marker of periodization. The fall of Rome, the rise of Islam, the fall of Constantinople, the Renaissance, the Reformation—these were all "revolutions" that had brought about great improvements in culture.[36] Voltaire's usage caught on among other authors of enlightened history, including Rousseau and Jean le Rond d'Alembert. By the 1760s, the Enlightenment itself had joined the ranks of these illustrious ages: "There has been a revolution in people's minds," Voltaire wrote to Claude Adrien Helvétius in 1765.[37] Soon, however, Voltaire went from (self-)congratulating the *philosophes* for leading this revolution to applauding the political reform movement sweeping across Europe. After Gustav III of Sweden established royal autocracy in August 1772, Voltaire wrote to Frederick II to congratulate him on his nephew's "lovely revolution in Sweden," which had made him "happy to be alive."[38] Voltaire also sent a cheery letter to d'Alembert, conflating both the Swedish revolution and the expulsion of the Jesuits a decade earlier: "My dear philosophe, doesn't this seem like the century of revolutions, from [the expulsion of] the Jesuits to Sweden, and maybe endless more?"[39]

By 1789, then, many French were primed to embrace the political revolution that swept across their own country. They imagined it would resemble the peaceful revolution described by Louis-Sébastien Mercier (a future member of the National Convention) in his novel *L'An 2440*: the rational transformation of the French state. Where the Americans recognized that different social classes would invariably have different interests, the French cheerily assumed that with time, all reasonable and enlightened people would come to the same rational conclusions. If they didn't, it was because (as Condorcet argued) errors, prejudices, and superstition prevented people from recognizing reason, truth, and justice.[40] Here was the modern revolutionary faith in all its purity: progress will triumph, even if it must crush those who stand in its way.

Not everyone was on board with this modern program, and the French revolutionaries ended up feuding over almost every important question they faced. But after the failure of constitutional monarchy, France moved increasingly in a "modern" direction. The constitution of 1793 did away with the separation of powers, leaving it to the National Assembly to select the twenty-four members of an executive council, which was physically integrated into the legislature (art. 75). This constitution was suspended before it could be enacted, and the National Convention instead proclaimed a "revolutionary government" that acted dictatorially on behalf of the people. A temporary regime, it promised to usher in a new and improved form of government, with a central executive agency that reached into the farthest depths of the state.[41] It was the modern dream of a centralized authority that would leverage the nation's powers rather than balancing them, as Turgot had urged. Ultimately, it was the dream that would be fulfilled by Napoleon.

The modern French understanding of revolution thus encouraged a completely different kind of politics than did the classical interpretation common among Americans. To some extent, the revolutions that followed in their wake exhibited elements of both. A well-balanced constitution remained the goal of many revolutionaries, from Venezuela to Naples. At the same time, few revolutions managed to make their constitutions stick. On the one hand, this led to increasing disenchantment with (what became called) the liberal model, thereby amplifying more progressive ideas. On the other, liberalism often gave way to authoritarianism, following the Napoleonic model (as in Haiti and in Spanish America).

In the long run (i.e., over the next two centuries), the modern idea of revolution triumphed, especially in its Marxist incarnation. Socialism picked up the torch of historical progress, ditching the classical obsession with a balanced constitution. These modern revolutionaries promised democracy but then concentrated power in executive councils and supreme leaders. They promised a better, fairer, more rational future. They did not abide dissent about what this future would bring or how it should come about. "There can be no solution of the social problem but mine," affirms Shigalov, the ideologue of the secret revolutionary society in Dostoevsky's novel *Demons* (also translated as *The Possessed*, 1871–72). "Nothing can take the place of the system set forth in my book, and there is no other way out of it; no one can invent anything else."[42] It was the *reductio ad absurdum* of modern revolutionaries.

If we consider the history of revolution over the *longue durée*, then, what has traditionally been called the Age of Revolution(s) looks much more like the overlapping space between two distinct currents. The Americans were heirs to the classical obsession with constitutionalism, and in particular the English constitution that had been described since Elizabethan times as meeting the Polybian standard of perfection—an ideal balance of monarchy, aristocracy, and democracy.[43] They staged two revolutions on the British Isles to right the balance of this constitution, and then their former colonists staged a third, with a similar goal in mind. The French, by contrast, inaugurated an entirely different current of revolutionary thought, one that downplayed (and sometimes ignored) the importance of constitutionalism and instead portrayed revolutions as the great escalators of history. The first current did not completely die out with the American Revolution and continued to pulse throughout revolutions in the following century. But it would soon be swamped by the modern progressive current that dominated in the twentieth. In this respect, it is more historically accurate and conceptually helpful to identify distinct *ages* of revolution, not to assign moral values to each but to understand why events that we classify under the same name could turn out so differently.

Notes

1. Charles-Guillaume-Frédéric Dumas to Benjamin Franklin, June 30, 1775, in Founders Online, https://founders.archives.gov/documents/Franklin/01-22-02-0049.
2. See John G. A. Pocock, ed., *Three British Revolutions: 1641, 1688, 1776* (Princeton, NJ: Princeton University Press, 1980). For more bibliographical details on this point and others in this essay, see Dan Edelstein, *The Revolution to Come: A History of an Idea from Thucydides to Lenin* (Princeton, NJ: Princeton University Press, 2025).
3. See, e.g., J. B. Bury, *The Idea of Progress* (London: Macmillan, 1920), 109; Hans Blumenberg, *The Legitimacy of the Modern Age*, trans. Robert M.

Wallace (Cambridge, MA: MIT Press, 1983), 33; more recently, Larry Norman, *The Shock of the Ancient* (Chicago: University of Chicago Press, 2011); and Alexander Statman, *A Global Enlightenment* (Chicago: University of Chicago Press, 2023).

4. Marcus Aurelius, *Meditations*, trans. Martin Hammond (London: Penguin, 2006), 65.
5. Hans Blumenberg, "On a Lineage of the Idea of Progress," trans. E. B. Ashton, *Social Research* 41, no. 1 (1974): 5–27.
6. François Hartog, *Chronos* (Paris: Gallimard, 2020).
7. Voltaire to Princess Louise of Saxe-Gotha-Altenburg, August 20, 1760 (D9158). Letter identifiers for Voltaire's correspondence refer to the Theodore Besterman edition, now available online at https://www.e-enlightenment.com/.
8. Voltaire, *Le Siècle de Louis XIV* (Berlin: Chez C.-F. Henning, 1751), 1:4.
9. Voltaire to Denis Diderot, January 8, 1758 (D7570).
10. Voltaire to Frederick the Great, August 10, 1775 (D19599).
11. See John Adams, "Novanglus," in *The Works of John Adams*, ed. Charles Francis Adams (Boston: Little, Brown, 1856), 4:15–16.
12. John Adams to Richard Henry Lee, November 15, 1775, in Adams, ed., *Works*, 4:186.
13. John Adams to John Winthrop, June 23, 1776, in Adams, ed., *Works*, 9:410.
14. John Adams to Richard Henry Lee, November 15, 1775, in Adams, ed., *Works*, 4:186.
15. This claim rests on surveys of databases, including the Early American Imprints, Evans series, http://infoweb.newsbank.com/?db=EVAN, and Founders Online, https://founders.archives.gov/.
16. See *Journals of the Continental Congress* (Washington, DC: U.S. Government Printing Office, 1774–89), 9:987.
17. [Anonymous], *The Alarm; or, An Address to the People of Pennsylvania* (Philadelphia, 1776), 3.
18. Thomas Paine, *Common Sense* (London: Penguin, 1976). See Alessandro Giraffi, *An Exact Historie of the Late Revolution in Naples and of Their Monstrous Successes*, trans. James Howell (London: R. Lowndes, 1650). John Adams owned a 1663 edition of Howell's translation.
19. John Adams, "Preface," in *A Defence of the Constitutions of Government of the United States of America* (1787), in Adams, ed., *Works*, 4:285. Adams had read an English translation of Turgot's letter to Richard Price, which he cited here. See Adam Lebovitz, *Colossus: Constitutional Theory in America and France, 1776–1799* (forthcoming).
20. See James Madison, Alexander Hamilton, and John Jay, *The Federalist Papers*, ed. Isaac Kramnick (London: Penguin, 1987), letter 9, 118.

21. James Madison, June 19, 1787, in *The Records of the Federal Convention of 1787*, ed. Max Farrand (New Haven, CT: Yale University Press, 1911), 1:318.
22. Plato, *The Republic*, in *Complete Works*, ed. John M. Cooper (Indianapolis: Hackett, 1997), 5.462a.
23. See, e.g., Theda Skocpol, *States and Social Revolutions* (Cambridge: Cambridge University Press, 1979).
24. Madison, *Federalist* 10.
25. Madison, June 26, 1787, in Farrand, ed., *Records*, 1:431.
26. See, e.g., Hamilton's speech on June 19 and Gouverneur Morris's on July 2. Farrand, ed., *Records*, 1:299, 512. See Gilbert Chinard's conclusion: "It is clear that in the opinion of several delegates, the executive represented the monarchical power, the senate the aristocratical." Chinard, "Polybius and the American Constitution," *Journal of the History of Ideas* 1, no. 1 (1940): 38–58, 51 (quotation).
27. Gordon S. Wood, *Creation of the American Republic, 1776–1787* (Chapel Hill: University of North Carolina Press, 1969), 606.
28. See especially Dennis Galligan, ed., *Constitutions and the Classics: Patterns of Constitutional Thought from Fortescue to Bentham* (Oxford: Oxford University Press, 2015).
29. John Adams to the Inhabitants of Providence, RI, April 30, 1798; Adams to Richard Price, April 19, 1790, in Adams, ed., *Works*, 9:184, 563.
30. Keith M. Baker, *Inventing the French Revolution* (Cambridge: Cambridge University Press, 1991), 206.
31. See *Le Moniteur*, no. 4 (1788), 1 [Newberry Library], most likely written by Guilaume Saige, available online at https://artflsrv04.uchicago.edu/philologic4.7/newberryfrc1217/. Many of the *cahiers de doléance* also used this phrase (*l'heureuse révolution*).
32. Turgot, *Œuvres de M. Turgot*, ed. Pierre-Samuel Dupont de Nemours (Paris: Delance, 1808–11), 2:52–92. (published posthumously in 1781). See William Max Nelson, *The Time of Enlightenment* (Toronto: University of Toronto Press, 2020).
33. Turgot, "Fondation," in *Encyclopédie, ou dictionnaire raisonné des sciences, des arts et des métiers, etc.*, ed. Denis Diderot and Jean le Rond d'Alembert (1751–72), 7:72–74, available online through the University of Chicago ARTFL Encyclopédie Project (Autumn 2022 edition), ed. Robert Morrissey and Glenn Roe, http://encyclopedie.uchicago.edu/.
34. Turgot, *Œuvres posthumes de M. Turgot, ou Mémoire de M. Turgot sur les administrations provinciales* (Lausanne, 1787). See Gerald J. Cavanaugh, "Turgot: The Rejection of Enlightened Despotism," *French Historical Studies* 6, no. 1 (1969): 31–58.
35. Voltaire to Catherine II, October 28, 1777 (D20862).

36. See especially Voltaire's *Essai sur les mœurs et l'esprit des nations* (1756), ed. Bruno Bernardet al., in *Œuvres complètes de Voltaire* (Oxford: Voltaire Foundation, 2019), vols. 21–27, for details.
37. Voltaire to Claude Adrien Helvétius, June 26, 1765 (D12660).
38. Voltaire to Frederick II, September 15, 1772 (D17911).
39. Voltaire to Jean le Rond d'Alembert, September 16, 1772 (D17913).
40. Condorcet, *Esquisse d'un tableau historique des progrès de l'esprit humain* (Paris: Agasse, 1795), esp. the ninth epoch.
41. Jean-Nicolas Billaud-Varenne, *Rapport . . . sur la théorie du gouvernement démocratique* (Paris: Convention Nationale, 1794).
42. Fyodor Dostoyevsky, *The Possessed*, trans. Constance Garnett (New York: Barnes and Noble Classics, 2005), 402.
43. See Corrine Comstock Weston, *English Constitutional Theory and the House of Lords, 1556–1832* (New York: Columbia University Press, 1965).

The Invention of Representative Democracy

Katlyn Marie Carter

"I know well that in a democracy, it would be the people who would judge the tyrant, because in a purely democratic state, the people do everything themselves; but what we are here [in] France is not a democracy."[1] Jacobin deputy Pierre-François-Joseph Robert made this claim in early 1793, amid debate over whether the National Convention should hold a popular referendum on the judgment of King Louis XVI. Indeed, France was not a democracy; it was something different: a representative republic. Although today we think of representative government as synonymous with democracy, this was not the case when republics were being founded in the eighteenth century.[2] As modern representative democracy was first coming into being, revolutionaries like Robert had a sense of the difference between these two concepts.

Historians debate whether such a distinction predated the founding of republics in the late eighteenth century or was actually a creation of revolutionary attempts to construct new regimes.[3] It was not until the debates over the ratification of the American Constitution in 1787–88, according to historian Willi Paul Adams, that its Federalist supporters suggested a republic (defined by representative government) was different from a democracy. Prior to that, he argued that the terms "democracy" and "republic" were used interchangeably by advocates of popular sovereignty as well as by those who hoped to discredit republicanism by associating it with commonly held reservations about the instability of democracies.[4]

Regardless of when and why the distinction between these concepts came into being, by 1793 making them synonymous, according to Robert, seemed all but impossible. "There is no democracy with national representation," he opined, "and those who wish to adapt all the principles of democratic government to a representative government are either imbeciles who disrupt without knowing it, or rogues who knowingly disrupt in the hope of not losing the fruits of anarchy."[5] Nonetheless, as Mark Philp and Ruth Scurr pointed out in a 2013 volume, the term "representative democracy" came into widespread usage in the 1790s.[6] The concept has since become so familiar that we often fail to remember that it was created at a particular moment in history. But emphatic statements like those issued by Robert should prompt us to interrogate anew R. R. Palmer's characterization of the Age of Revolutions as democratic.[7]

For a crucial, if indeterminate, period of time in the late eighteenth century, political representation and democracy were considered not only distinct but incompatible, before being yoked together as a now naturalized form of government. We would do well to probe the braiding of these concepts—noting how they came together, why they came apart, and how they were united again. Making political representation synonymous with democracy subsumed two distinct visions of representative politics. While some conceived of representation merely as a way to solve for the impossibility of democracy in large polities by making self-government logistically possible, others actually considered it an improvement on majority rule. Nonetheless, this improved vision was labeled "democratic." Recovering these divergent ideas can help illuminate some of the tensions within the concept of democracy today.

DEMOCRACY IN the eighteenth century mainly connoted a form of government exercised in ancient republics wherein the entire citizenry participated in governance. It was generally considered inapplicable in modern societies because they were too large, both in population and geography.[8] Enter political representation.

For some, representative politics was a way to make popular sovereignty possible in a vast and populous polity. Thomas Paine memorably described the ideal of an entire society meeting under a tree to deliberate on "public matters." Once a community became too numerous for this to be possible, he posited the need for representatives who would "act in the same manner as the whole body would act were they present."[9] As scholars have long pointed out, few in the eighteenth-century Age of Revolutions ever argued for direct democracy. Instead, they were advocating for a style of representation that was as democratic as possible, in the sense of providing for popular participation in governance and channeling a public will formed outside government in political decisions.[10] Often erroneously considered an ardent opponent of political representation, even Jean-Jacques Rousseau saw a place for it in the exercise of popular sovereignty, as long as it was properly constructed to ensure the sovereign people retained power over elected officials.[11]

Some of the earliest usages of the phrase "representative democracy" may well have been based on this conception of political representation as a substitute of sorts for classical conceptions of direct democracy. The first English appearance of the phrase in print came in Noah Webster's 1785 *Sketches of American Policy*. His usage appears to confirm that the concept was based on an understanding of political representation as a substitute for direct democracy, in the sense Paine had articulated in 1776: "In large communities, the individuals are too numerous to assemble for the purpose of legislation; for which reason, the people appear by substitutes or agents; persons of their own choice."[12] In short, representation made democratic government possible in a large society, specifically because representatives were elected to act as "agents" of or "substitutes" for the people. It was this conception of how political representation was to work that probably led Paine to characterize the American government as "representation ingrafted upon Democracy" in 1791.[13]

Yet other early uses of "representative democracy" point to tensions within the concept based on variable notions of how political representation was meant to function. Scholars have long considered the phrase's first appearance in English to have been in a letter written by Alexander Hamilton in 1777 in which he mused on the state constitution recently adopted in New York to his correspondent, Gouverneur Morris.[14] "When the deliberative or judicial powers are vested wholly or partly in the collective body of the people, you must expect error, confusion, and instability," Hamilton wrote. "But a representative democracy, where the right of election is well secured and regulated & the exercise of the legislative, executive and judiciary authorities, is vested in select persons, chosen *really* and not *nominally* by the people, will in my opinion be most likely to be happy, regular and durable."[15] A democracy through political representation meant representatives were elected by the people. Yet, it did not necessarily follow that those representatives were merely substitutes for the people. Implied but not directly stated was that representatives could avoid the "error, confusion, and instability" that arose when power was vested in "the collective body of the people." The first use of the phrase "*démocratie représentative*" in print similarly described it as an improvement on direct democracy. In 1788, Philip Mazzei noted that the tumultuous downfall of ancient Greece and Rome was in part because "they did not know the means of combining a representative democracy, wherein there is simultaneously peace and equality."[16]

The tensions that arose when representation was applied as a tool of democracy grew as newly established republics found their footing in North America and France. As democracy became associated with the vision of representatives as substitutes, or agents, of the people, a distinction opened along new lines. Historians have pointed to the way in which the framers of the federal Constitution in the United States viewed an "excess of democracy," in the sense of state legislatures' responsiveness to popular pressure, as a problem to be solved.[17] The term "democrat" in fact became largely pejorative in the early American republic, as it did in France.[18] When they argued against democracy, constitutional framers were really opposing a type of political representation envisioned as a substitute for it. For them, representation was not just a solution to the application of democracy in large countries; it offered particular benefits and corrected for what they considered defects of democracy. Chief among these was the need to rely on the masses and their ability to reason and determine their own best interests—an ability of which many were skeptical. It was in making this point that some opened a new distinction between political representation and democracy. Representative republics were not just an update to direct democracies; they were in fact improvements. And yet, they just as quickly closed this opening by using the terminology of democracy to define a type of political representation that they saw as superior.

In North America, James Madison saw representative government not only as a way to make the exercise of popular sovereignty possible in an extended republic. The extended republic was not the problem; it was actually a solution to challenges posed by democracy. In *Federalist* no. 10, Madison explicitly argued that a republic could avoid the pitfalls of democracy by refining public views through representative institutions. He suggested that a vast republic could endure where others had failed by enlarging the political sphere to elicit the election of "fit characters" who would have enough distance from popular pressure and factional interests to make wise decisions on behalf of the nation.[19] In defending the utility of the Senate, Madison wrote in *Federalist* no. 63 that such a body was necessary to guard against the people's "temporary errors and delusions." The public could be wrong, whether it was because they had fallen victim to "some irregular passion" or been "misled by the artful misrepresentations of interested men." Having a body of "temperate and respectable" citizens to "check" the people until "reason, justice and truth can regain their authority over the public mind," he suggested, was a necessary precaution.[20] Madison clearly distinguished democracy from a republic, and representation was crucial to what made them distinct, an observation Seth Cotlar has also made.[21]

These strains of thinking existed in France as well, even in the most unlikely places. In the midst of the king's trial, Montagnard deputy Jean-Louis Seconds argued against consulting the people on the judgment by laying out the benefits of a representative government. "Among men equal in reason or in enlightenment, the right of every one in the direction of the government and the public good, is equal for all and as a consequence all should govern if it were possible," he declared. However, this would only work if "an entire people could assemble and deliberate simultaneously," and also if the government were not founded partly on "this weakness of the reason of a large number of men on this impossibility and on the contradiction in the government of all." It was thus necessary to select "an elite, and a deliberative, even a guiding minority, who govern the majority" with the aim of determining "truly and really the will and reason of all."[22] In other words, the deputies had to consider the possibility that one reason for allowing representatives to exercise popular sovereignty was simply to guarantee better decisions made by individuals endowed with superior reason.

Yet just as quickly as this distinction between a representative republic and democracy had been opened up, it was closed again. Despite being cast as an improvement on democracy, this vision of representation was defined by its proponents as democratic. In 1794, Maximilien Robespierre declared that the French Revolution aimed to establish "democratic or republican government: these two words are synonyms." Making this claim just a year after Robert's emphasis on the distinction between these regime types, Robespierre undoubtedly had explaining to do. Democracy, he contended, was not "a state wherein the people continually assembled, manage all public affairs by themselves," or even met in groups to decide the direction of society. "Democracy is a state wherein the sovereign people, guided by laws of their own making, does all that it can properly do on its own, and does by delegates all that it cannot do itself."²³ This was nothing short of a redefinition of democracy, specifically to make it compatible, if not interchangeable, with a type representative government that was envisioned as distinct and better than democracy, rather than a mere substitute for it.²⁴

As this passage from Robespierre's oration shows, the invention of modern representative democracy required intellectual labor. By the mid-1790s, it was a wedding of two concepts that had been deliberately separated, and thus it was a marriage that entailed deep paradoxes. Historians have noted this—perhaps most notably Paul Friedland in the context of the French Revolution and Gordon S. Wood in the early American case. "Representative democracy . . . was from its very inception a contradiction in terms, for the basic reason that a true democracy precluded representation," Friedland wrote. "Even while the revolutionaries sang the praises of 'democracy,'" he continued, "they constructed, brick by brick, a political edifice predicated on the exclusion from active political power of the very people in whose name their government claimed to rule."²⁵ Wood suggested the framers of the federal Constitution successfully adopted the language of democratic radicalism to justify an aristocratic system. Sovereignty of the people came to mean that government was derived from their consent but carried out by an elite. This was, by Wood's estimation, the unique invention of the American Revolution and a real innovation.²⁶ In both cases, these authors observed how representative government was couched in democratic terms despite being, in some ways, inherently antidemocratic.

Rather than further debating whether these revolutions were "democratic" or not, we should ask how the governments resulting from them came to be characterized as such. The process by which representative government came to be considered a form of democracy warrants far more scrutiny than it has received. In order to begin understanding it, we need to first ask what made these two concepts distinct to revolutionaries in the 1780s and early 1790s. When the discourse of representative democracy joined these two concepts, some of the salient distinctions were elided and the fault lines papered over. As a result, many of the debates we still have about representative government and how it should work bear the marks of this imperfect (and understudied) intellectual welding.

Notes

1. *Archives Parlementaires de 1787 à 1860* (Paris: Librairie administrative de P. Dupont, 1862–1913), 57:316.
2. Katlyn Marie Carter, *Democracy in Darkness: Secrecy and Transparency in the Age of Revolutions* (New Haven, CT: Yale University Press, 2023), 3.
3. Willi Paul Adams, *The First American Constitutions: Republican Ideology and the Making of the State Constitutions in the Revolutionary Era*, trans. Rita Kimber and Robert Kimber (Lanham, MD: Rowman and Littlefield, 2001), 110, 112. On the ancient origins of the distinction between a democracy and a republic, see Nadia Urbinati, "Competing for Liberty: The Republican Critique of Democracy," *American Political Science Review* 106, no. 3 (August 2012): 607–21.
4. Adams, *The First American Constitutions*, 110, 104–5.
5. *Archives Parlementaires de 1787 à 1860*, 57:316.
6. Mark Philp, "Talking about Democracy: Britain in the 1790s," in *Re-Imagining Democracy in the Age of Revolutions: America, France, Britain, and Ireland, 1750–1850*, ed. Joanna Innes and Mark Philp (Oxford: Oxford University Press, 2013), 101–13; Ruth Scurr, "Varieties of Democracy in the French Revolution," in Innes and Philp, eds., *Re-Imagining Democracy in the Age of Revolutions*, 57–68; Pierre Rosanvallon, "The History of the Word 'Democracy' in France," trans. Philip Constopoulos, *Journal of Democracy* 6, no. 4 (October 1995): 147–53; Raymonde Monnier, "'Démocratie représentative' ou 'république démocratique': De la querelle des mots (République) à la querelle des anciens et modernes," *Annales historiques de la Révolution française*, no. 325 (2001): 1–21.
7. R. R. Palmer, *The Age of Democratic Revolution: A Political History of Europe and America, 1760–1800* (Princeton, NJ: Princeton University Press, 1959–64).
8. Carter, *Democracy in Darkness*, 3; Paul Friedland, *Political Actors: Representative Bodies and Theatricality in the Age of the French Revolution* (Ithaca, NY: Cornell University Press, 2002), 11; Rosanvallon, "The History of the Word 'Democracy' in France," 141–46; R. R. Palmer, "Notes on the Use of the Word 'Democracy,' 1789–1799," *Political Science Quarterly* 68, no. 2 (1953): 203–26; Bernard Manin, *The Principles of Representative Government* (Cambridge: Cambridge University Press, 1997), 2–3. "Democracy" could also be used at the time to connote one segment of a mixed government that was characterized by popular participation and giving voice to the commons.
9. Thomas Paine, *Common Sense*, in *Thomas Paine: Rights of Man and Common Sense*, ed. Peter Linebaugh (London: Verso, 2009), 6–7.

10. Carter, *Democracy in Darkness*, 6–7; Hanna Pitkin, *The Concept of Representation* (Berkeley: University of California Press, 1967), 146; Manin, *The Principles of Representative Government*, 110. For examples of the way historians have equated these different types of representation as more or less democratic, see especially Dana Nelson, *Commons Democracy: Reading the Politics of Participation in the Early United States* (New York: Fordham University Press, 2015); Terry Bouton, *Taming Democracy: The People, the Founders, and the Troubled Ending of the American Revolution* (Oxford: Oxford University Press, 2007); Woody Holton, *Unruly Americans and the Origins of the Constitution* (New York: Hill and Wang, 2007); Gordon S. Wood, *The Creation of the American Republic, 1776–1787* (Chapel Hill: University of North Carolina Press, 1969), 562, 546, 517; Friedland, *Political Actors*, 11; and Yannick Bosc, *Le peuple souverain et la démocratie: Politique de Robespierre* (Paris: Editions Critiques, 2019), 14–15.
11. Richard Tuck, *The Sleeping Sovereign: The Invention of Modern Democracy* (Cambridge: Cambridge University Press, 2016), x.
12. Noah Webster, *Sketches of American Policy* (Hartford, CT, 1785), cited in Tuck, *Sleeping Sovereign*, 7.
13. Thomas Paine, *Rights of Man* (1791), cited in Palmer, "Notes on the Use of the Word 'Democracy,'" 224.
14. Tuck, *Sleeping Sovereign*, 7. Tuck traces this to Gerald Stourzh's 1970 book *Alexander Hamilton and the Idea of Representative Government* (Stanford, CA: Stanford University Press, 1970).
15. Alexander Hamilton to Gouverneur Morris, May 19, 1777, in *The Papers of Alexander Hamilton Digital Edition*, ed. Harold C. Syrett et al. (Charlottesville: University of Virginia Press, 2011), 255.
16. Filippo Mazzei and Jean-Antoine-Nicolas de Caritat, Marquis de Condorcet, *Recherches historiques et politiques sur les Etats-Unis de l'Amerique Septentrionale* (Paris: Chez Froullé, 1788), 1:361.
17. Bouton, *Taming Democracy*, 171; Gordon S. Wood, *Revolutionary Characters: What Made the Founders Different* (New York: Penguin, 2007), 149; Holton, *Unruly Americans*, 5–7; Jack Rakove, *Original Meanings: Politics and Ideas in the Making of the Constitution* (New York: Knopf, 1996), 48; Max Farrand, ed., *Records of the Federal Convention of 1787* (New Haven, CT: Yale University Press, 1911–37), 1:48.
18. Seth Cotlar, "Languages of Democracy in America from the Revolution to the Election of 1800," in Innes and Philp, eds., *Re-Imagining Democracy in the Age of Revolutions*, 13–27; Matthew Rainbow Hale, "Regenerating the World: The French Revolution, Civic Festivals, and the Forging of Modern American Democracy, 1793–1795," *Journal of American History* 103, no. 4 (March 2017): 891–920.

19. James Madison, "Federalist 10," in *The Federalist Papers* (New York: Simon and Schuster, 2004), 65–68; Carter, *Democracy in Darkness*, 82.
20. James Madison, "Federalist 63," in *The Federalist Papers*, 138.
21. Cotlar, "Languages of Democracy in America," 20–21.
22. *Archives Parlementaires de 1787 à 1860*, 56:561.
23. Maximilien Robespierre, "Sur les Principes de Morale Politique qui Doivent Guider la Convention Nationale dans l'Administration Intérieure de la République," in *Robespierre: Textes Choisis, Tome Troisième, aout 1793–juillet 1794*, ed. Jean Poperen (Paris: Editions Sociales, 1958), 110–31, 113 (quotation). This passage is also cited in William Doyle, *The Oxford History of the French Revolution* (Oxford: Clarendon Press, 1989), 272; Scurr, "Varieties of Democracy in the French Revolution," 66–67; Palmer, "Notes on the Use of the Word 'Democracy,'" 214; Carter, *Democracy in Darkness*, 3.
24. Carter, *Democracy in Darkness*, 3–4.
25. Friedland, *Political Actors*, 11; Carter, *Democracy in Darkness*, 106, 114.
26. Wood, *The Creation of the American Republic*, 562–64, 546, 517; Carter, *Democracy in Darkness*, 78.

Gender and the Age of Revolutions in Private Lives

Denise Z. Davidson

One of the most important historical arguments regarding eighteenth- and nineteenth-century society and politics concerns the gendered bifurcation of the public and private spheres and the related rise of domesticity as an ideal for women. Although white middle-class men and women in both Western Europe and North America seem to have largely bought into this ideology, which they then used to criticize those whose material existence did not make it an attainable goal, not all people accepted these definitions of proper behavior. Some women chose to engage in the public world of politics and intellectual pursuits, and some men chose to avoid it. This essay focuses on one Frenchman, Pierre Vitet (1772–1854), who led a largely domestic existence, possibly because of traumatic experiences he lived through during the Revolution. Vitet's life story draws attention to the possibility of middle-class men opting out of public-facing careers. In addition, it suggests that men could feel as attached to home life as their wives. Although separate spheres may have been a powerful ideology, its implementation was far from complete; both men and women could resist such gendered limitations on their life choices.

The increasingly clear distinction between the public and private spheres and its significance as a key component of the modern world has been studied by scholars for decades.[1] Both political developments, such as the French and American Revolutions, and economic ones, such as industrialization, facilitated this separation. Prior to the rise of modern political and economic institutions, these areas of life often overlapped. Courtly politics existed on the border between the two, with royal mistresses, for example, and other family intrigues influencing monarchical decision-making and policies. Among those who worked for their livelihoods, the home was a space for both production and reproduction, with artisans producing goods in home workshops and the peasant household economy requiring the contributions of all family members. As politics and goods-production became viewed as public matters while the family and reproduction became private ones, new ideas about gender and behavior in those spheres emerged. By the early nineteenth century, a full-blown ideology of separate spheres had taken shape. It glorified a purely domestic existence for women and the home as a refuge from the competitive, man-eat-man world of capitalism.

One consequence of historians' attention to the rise of separate-spheres thinking is a tendency to ignore men's roles in the private sphere. While studies of motherhood in this period are quite common, fathers and fatherhood have received less attention, in part because of an assumption that men's energies were devoted to "public" matters: business, politics, and financial dealings. The few existing studies demonstrate that a new image of the father as a nurturing and supportive family member, rather than a fearsome patriarch, emerged in the literature and art of the period.[2] Victorian England is probably the place most associated with domesticity as an ideal for women, even though the majority of the population could never attain it.[3] Despite the power of separate-spheres ideology, many middle-class Englishmen were deeply attached to their home lives and engaged with raising their children, discussing furnishings, and of course managing their properties.[4] Similarly, the rise of Beidermeier culture in the decades following the Napoleonic wars, with its focus on making the home a comfortable and welcoming environment, reflected the German turn toward an idealized family life.[5] This desire to create domestic spaces where men and women alike could find solace had parallels in other parts of Europe as well. Such cultural references suggest that many viewed the private sphere as a refuge from the turbulence and dangers of public life during the revolutionary era.

BY ALL outward appearances, Pierre Vitet should have entered public life like his father (and later his son). The only child of a doctor and professor of medicine, Vitet attended the Oratorian school in Lyon (today the Lycée Ampère), where his classmates were from equally prominent families, including a future prime minister, Casimir Périer, and the intellectual Camille Jordan.[6] With merit replacing birth in determining career paths, the French Revolution and the Napoleonic Empire permitted middle-class men like Vitet to rise through the ranks as never before. While many took advantage of these opportunities, including building illustrious careers in the military, Vitet apparently found such paths unappealing. He led a life focused on quieter pursuits: overseeing the education of his son, socializing with a close circle of family and friends, managing his properties to assure a steady income, and devoting time to his passion for landscape painting.

Traumatic experiences dating from the revolutionary decade may explain his choices. His father, Louis Vitet, served as mayor of Lyon from 1790 to 1792 and then as a deputy to the National Convention from October 1792 to February 1793, where he attended the trial of Louis XVI, voting against the king's immediate execution.[7] Claiming illness, Louis left Paris soon afterward but faced arrest when troops arrived in Lyon that summer to retake control of the city, which had risen in rebellion against the Parisian government. The troops laid siege to the city and eventually took over, installing a Jacobin-dominated municipal government and arresting those deemed counterrevolutionaries, including Pierre's maternal grandfather, who died in jail that fall. After going into hiding for several weeks, Pierre joined his father on a harrowing winter voyage through the mountains and into Switzerland, where they lived in exile from January to July 1794. Pierre later composed a memoir about that time, suggesting how much the experience marked him.[8] Pierre and Louis returned to Lyon after the Terror but not for long, as Louis was elected to the Council of 500, the lower house of the legislature. Pierre joined him in Paris, serving as his secretary and pursuing his studies, including taking some art classes.[9]

In December 1801, Pierre married Amélie Arnaud-Tizon (1785–1860), the daughter of a wealthy Lyonnais textile merchant whose family had relocated to Rouen. Louis transferred his property to Pierre upon his son's marriage, including the building where the couple lived, a former convent located behind the Saint Roch Church that Louis had purchased in 1798.[10] Pierre and Amélie soon had a son, Ludovic, born in October 1802. Twenty years later, they had a daughter whom they named Amélie, like her mother, though they called her Mimi. Soon after marrying, Pierre began to exchange letters on a regular basis with his mother-in-law, Catherine Arnaud-Tizon (1765–1832). The two became close friends and allies, collaborating and strategizing on countless family projects and plans, writing about every five days for over twenty years.[11] Pierre also communicated regularly with many other family members, playing a central role in this vital component of the "work of kinship," one often associated with women.[12]

Thanks to his inheritance, Pierre became what the French labeled a *rentier*, someone who lived off his rents, the income from properties he owned. The goal of being able to afford *not* to work had been a feature of the French bourgeoisie since at least the eighteenth century.[13] Some of Pierre's closest friends were bankers (Jacques Fournel and Vital Roux); his in-laws were textile manufacturers; and one of his childhood friends, Louis Gabriel Suchet, made it to the pinnacle of the Napoleonic military, rising to the rank of marshal. However, Pierre chose *not* to launch a career and instead supported himself and his family by managing his properties wisely.

Capitalism depends on investors using their capital to expand the economy, and one explanation for the slower growth of the French economy in the nineteenth century compared to England and Germany was the disinterest among investors in moving beyond traditional investments and smaller businesses. When an English industrialist profited from his investments, he might have bought a large house and expensive furniture but he also reinvested his profits in other ventures, seeking to make more money. While money certainly interested the French, enjoying the finer things in life seems to have been a higher priority. Regardless of these distinctions, bourgeois life across Europe revolved around building networks and accumulating resources, and while much of this work took place in businesses and stock exchanges, along with other male spaces like clubs and associations, private gatherings and family life, such as marital strategies, were also essential aspects of this work.[14] Instead of investing in industry like his in-laws, whose factory in Rouen produced printed cotton fabric, Pierre's investment strategies resembled those of the old regime, including overseeing agricultural lands, purchasing wooded property, and renting the urban dwellings he inherited from his parents.[15]

While Napoleon was creating and expanding the French Empire, with many Frenchmen taking advantage of the opportunity to build military careers, Pierre's passions lay elsewhere, and he appreciated his quiet lifestyle. In 1815, for example, as Napoleon's attempt to return to power ("the Hundred Days") was coming to an end, Pierre wrote in his journal, "*bonheur de la médiocrité*," comparing his situation to that of Suchet, whose peerage was withdrawn after he sided with Napoleon during the Hundred Days.[16] Throughout his life, Pierre's ambitions seemed focused on others, first his father and then his son, along with other family members.[17] In devoting so much attention to his son's education, his life resembled the model of the good father and husband proposed by Enlightenment thinkers.[18] He and Amélie spent most of their long lives together, socializing and enjoying cultural activities with family and a close circle of mostly Lyonnais friends. It is impossible to know why Pierre chose to lead such a private existence, though it seems likely that his experiences as a young man, watching his father suffer for his political activities, left their mark. The timing of Napoleon's authoritarian regime may also explain Pierre's reluctance to enter public office. His father had resisted the future emperor's 1799 coup d'état, and Pierre's political views seem to have aligned with his father's.

Pierre's engagement with matters that could be defined as "private" included his attention to interior design, his devotion to his son, and his discussions with his mother-in-law about fabric and fashions as well as social gatherings. For example, in the summer of 1809, shortly after his father's death and while Amélie and Ludovic were staying in Rouen, Pierre oversaw some renovations on their apartment. He sent Amélie frequent updates: "The house is horribly filthy. There are traces of the masons and painters on the stairs. Happily, the [stonemasons] have finished their work in the kitchen and elsewhere. Everything looks as I had hoped."[19] In a letter announcing his plans to join her in Rouen, Pierre provided further details: "I ordered the connecting door for your room. . . . It will be installed on Thursday. I would have liked to be there, but in receiving your letter with its request that I return promptly, I am doing so. I will only be able to leave on Thursday, however, because the upholsterer I was counting on for today postponed until tomorrow, and I want to watch him set up the bed on the ground floor. This upholsterer . . . will be able to move the bed that we want to put in our room."[20] In addition to sounding like an accommodating and attentive husband, Pierre's letter makes clear their sleeping arrangements: they each had their own room and a bedroom (and bed) that they shared.

With the work nearly completed, Pierre joined the family in Rouen for a few weeks and asked his friend, the banker Jacques Fournel, to supervise the renovations in his absence. Fournel's updates included advice about interior design: "I visited your apartment. The paint smell is still strong and unpleasant. It will take a good ten days for it to dissipate, and even then, it will be necessary to leave the windows open. Everything else is finished, except for positioning the furniture and hanging the wallpaper. I encourage you to see the apartment of Besson's son, who found some lovely wallpaper."[21] At least in this context and among these families, wallpaper was a perfectly normal topic for middle-class men to discuss.

Although interior design and other family matters occupied his time, Pierre's biggest responsibility was overseeing his son's education. After a failed attempt at sending Ludovic to boarding school when he was nine, his parents made the unusual decision to educate him at home.[22] This choice meant that Pierre needed to ensure that his son received a suitable education, both by teaching Ludovic some subjects himself and by hiring tutors.[23] Pierre's interest in being a "good father" seems to have gone further than most men of this period. He thoroughly embraced this role and developed a close relationship with his son, who thrived and later entered law school where he excelled. Being a *rentier* gave Pierre the time to do this work. He also followed the educational progress of his nieces and nephews, writing long letters offering advice to his sisters- and brothers-in-law on the topic.

Another area where Pierre engaged in matters that one might consider female topics of concern was women's dress. Catherine wrote to him frequently asking that he get a piece of fabric dyed or find a tailor to repair a dress. Pierre's journal includes numerous references to clothing being purchased and mended in Paris and then sent to Rouen for the ladies there. In 1805, Pierre recorded a series of entries about their efforts to help Amélie's family have the right clothes: "Amélie had the crepe dress dyed [and] offered her services for any purchases they need for the upcoming ball." A few days later he wrote to say he had "sent the gray crepe dress and ribbons for Mr. Suchet's ball."[24] In addition to being an attentive father and husband, Pierre was constantly doing favors for his in-laws and other members of his extended family.

Pierre's willingness to help his family included making sure his young wife enjoyed herself. In 1805, Catherine wrote to Amélie, "I am happy to learn that you are satisfied with your ball and that you are amusing yourself. Hopefully your husband isn't too bored. He is so accommodating that I don't think he could get bored when you are having fun. Send him my love and gratitude for all the trouble we have caused him regarding our finances."[25] As a young woman, it is not surprising that Amélie enjoyed these events more than her husband, but he recognized that she relished these moments to dress up and socialize. Pierre sent details on these events, many of which took place during Carnival season (the weeks between Epiphany and Lent), to Catherine who shared her reactions as well.

Catherine's other son-in-law, Jacques Barbet, also enjoyed dances and entertaining:

> Tomorrow a small number of us will be celebrating Mardi Gras at Barbet's. He plans to treat us to ice cream. It is the prelude to a bigger dance that he is planning to host on the second Sunday of Lent. He is going all out. . . . He was obliged to move it to Lent because there were so many parties. It seems the same is true in Paris. You were worried about feeling bored at the homes of high-ranking people where you would find no one you know. My reaction is different from yours; I find that the view of a large gathering is sometimes amusing.[26]

Pierre and Catherine's letters include many discussions regarding social gatherings where men and women demonstrated their good taste by inviting the right kind of people into their homes.

While socializing was a common theme in their correspondence, politics rarely came up until a vocal opposition movement emerged in the 1820s during the Bourbon Restoration. Ludovic Vitet launched a career as a writer, publishing pieces in the liberal newspaper *Le globe,* and helped found François Guizot's oppositional political club, Aide toi, le ciel t'aidera. Some of the women in the family also became avid followers of politics. Amélie Vitet attended meetings of the legislature and sent Pierre commentaries on the speeches she heard when he was out of town.[27] And Ludovic's aunt Amélie Arnaud-Tizon, who resided with her husband at the family's factory near Rouen, wrote impassioned letters to both Ludovic and Pierre regarding political debates and particular politicians.[28] These examples suggest that respectable middle-class matrons could and did involve themselves in politics, at least as spectators. Women sat in the galleries of the legislature during the French Revolution as well, though their disruptive behavior may have contributed to laws banning women's political clubs being passed in 1793 and 1795.[29] Women's political participation is visible in other contexts too, including in the North American colonies and the early United States, where women were central to the boycott movement launched as the colonies moved toward declaring independence from Britain. This example reflects how the domestic sphere could become politicized.[30]

THE REVOLUTIONARY era brought great change around the world: new ideas about politics and economics, about empire and revolution, and about private and public life. Many men took advantage of opportunities to climb the social hierarchy through military service and business ventures, but not all found such activities appealing. Some, like Pierre Vitet, chose to focus on their families and other aspects of private life, thus avoiding the limelight. Why men of his generation, those who experienced the upheavals of revolutionary France firsthand while still too young to participate in politics directly, may have been turned off by politics and other public ventures is difficult to say with certainly.[31] In his case, watching his father suffer and face execution had he not gone into exile, and seeing his grandfather die in jail during the Terror, may have left scars that led Pierre to seek refuge in the domestic realm where he could enjoy the finer things in life and avoid the limelight. Others in France and elsewhere no doubt made similar calculations. The domestic sphere was neither purely private nor purely female.

Notes

1. The classic account of this transformation, which was first published in German in 1966, is by the sociologist Jürgen Habermas, *The Structural Transformation of the Public Sphere: An Inquiry into a Category of Bourgeois Society*, trans. Thomas Burger (Cambridge, MA: MIT Press, 1989). An important study that incorporates gender into its analysis is Joan Landes, *Women and the Public Sphere in the Age of the French Revolution* (Ithaca, NY: Cornell University Press, 1988).
2. See Lynn Hunt, *The Family Romance of the French Revolution* (Berkeley: University of California Press, 1992); Anne Verjus, *Le bon mari: Une histoire politique des hommes et des femmes à l'époque révolutionnaire* (Paris: Fayard, 2010); and Philippe Bordes, *Jacques Louis David: Empire to Exile* (New Haven, CT: Yale University Press, 2005), 144–48.
3. Having a wife who did not need to work for money was a mark of middle-class status. See Anna Clark, *The Struggle for the Breeches: Gender and the Making of the British Working Class* (Berkeley: University of California Press, 1995).
4. Leonore Davidoff and Catherine Hall, *Family Fortunes: Men and Women of the English Middle Class, 1780–1850* (Chicago: University of Chicago Press, 1987), 33; John Tosh, *A Man's Place: Masculinity and the Middle-Class Home in Victorian England* (New Haven, CT: Yale University Press, 1999).

5. Mack Walker, *German Home Towns: Community, State, and General Estate, 1648–1871* (1971; reprint Ithaca, NY: Cornell University Press, 1998), chap. 10; Virgil Nemoianu, *The Taming of Romanticism: European Literature and the Age of Biedermeier* (Cambridge, MA: Harvard University Press, 1984).
6. Paul Sauzet, "Hommage à la mémoire de Ludovic Vitet," *Mémoires de l'Académie des sciences, belles-lettres et arts de Lyon* 26 (1874): 194. As might be expected of a man who avoided attention, the only published biographical information about Pierre Vitet appeared in an obituary of his son.
7. Sauzet, "Hommage," 189–90.
8. Pierre Vitet, *Notes et souvenirs sur quelques-uns des principaux événements de la Révolution, sur la vie politique de mon père, ses malheurs et son exile en Suisse, après le siège de Lyon, 1792–1973 et 1794* (Paris: Renouard, 1932). Pierre Vitet's handwritten memoir, which was probably composed in 1809 and 1810 soon after his father's death, is held in the Fonds Vitet 84II/07, Archives Municpales de Lyon (hereafter AML).
9. Pierre received permission to travel to Paris on 10 Pluviôse an 3 (February 7, 1795) to continue his studies. Laissez-passer, AML 84II/07. The earliest mention of his interest in painting dates from this time: "J'entreprends l'études de la peinture à l'huile." Pierre Vitet Correspondence Journal, AML 84II/07 (hereafter PVCJ), 2 Messidor an 2 (June 20, 1795).
10. Marriage contract, 11 Frimaire an 10 (December 2, 1801), Etude IX, No. 866; Bill of sale, 6 Pluviôse an VI (January 25, 1798), Etude V, No. 962, Archives Nationales, Minutier Central, Paris.
11. Denise Davidson, "A belle-mère idéale, gendre idéale," in *L'étonnante histoire des belles-mères*, ed. Yannick Ripa (Paris: Belin, 2015), 173–80. My book *Surviving Revolution: Bourgeois Lives and Letters* (Ithaca, NY: Cornell University Press, 2025) relies largely on the letters Pierre received from Catherine, most of which are in AML 84II/12 and 84II/13.
12. Micaela di Leonardo, "The Female World of Cards and Holidays: Women, Families, and the Work of Kinship," *Signs* 12 (1987): 440–53. See also John Gillis, *A World of Their Own Making: Myth, Ritual, and the Quest for Family Values* (New York: Basic, 1996).
13. The classic statement on this approach to wealth is George V. Taylor, "Noncapitalist Wealth and the Origins of the French Revolution," *American Historical Review* 72, no. 2 (1967): 469–96. Studies examining bourgeois attitudes include Robert Forster, *Merchants, Landlords and Magistrates: The Depont Family in Eighteenth Century France* (Baltimore: Johns Hopkins University Press, 1980); Christine Adams, *A Taste for Comfort and Status: A Bourgeois Family in Eighteenth-Century France* (University Park: Pennsylvania State University Press, 1999); and Christopher H. Johnson, *Becoming Bourgeois: Love, Kinship and Power in Provincial France,*

1670–1880 (Ithaca, NY: Cornell University Press, 2105). Béatrix Le Wita analyzed such attitudes in more contemporary contexts in *French Bourgeois Culture*, trans. J. A. Underwood (Cambridge: Cambridge University Press, 1994).

14. For a comparative discussion of bourgeois attitudes and practices, see Jerrold Seigel, *Modernity and Bourgeois Life: Society, Politics, and Culture in England, France, and Germany since 1750* (Cambridge: Cambridge University Press, 2012).
15. PVCJ includes countless letters Pierre sent to his business agent in Lyon regarding his agricultural properties and tenants.
16. PVCJ, entry dated July 29, 1815.
17. The Lyonnais lawyer and politician Paul Sauzet described Pierre as choosing to lead "une vie paisible, indépendante, et lettrée.... Il n'eut jamais aucune prétention pour lui-même, et [avec] sa modestie, poussée peut-être à l'excès, partagea sa vie entre le dévouement à son père, qu'il accompagna dans tous ses périls politiques, et l'éducation de son fils, qu'il mit toute sa gloire à rendre digne de son aïeul et de lui." Sauzet, "Hommage," 194–95.
18. Meghan K. Roberts, *Sentimental Savants: Philosophical Families in Enlightenment France* (Chicago: University of Chicago Press, 2016), chap. 4. On childrearing, see Jennifer J. Popiel, *Rousseau's Daughters: Domesticity, Education, and Autonomy in Modern France* (Durham: University of New Hampshire Press, 2008).
19. Pierre Vitet (hereafter PV) to Amélie Vitet (hereafter AV), July 21, 1809, AML 84II/09. (The letter is dated "Friday," but context and PVCJ allowed me to date it.)
20. PV to AV, July 25, 1809, AML 84II/09.
21. Jacques Fournel to PV, September 30, 1809, AML 84II/10.
22. The events that led to this decision are discussed in Anne Verjus and Denise Davidson, *Le roman conjugal: Chroniques de la vie familiale à l'époque de la Révolution et de l'Empire* (Seyssel, France: Champ Vallon, 2011), 101–2.
23. Maurice Parturier, introduction, in *Lettres de Mérimée à Ludovic Vitet*, ed. Maurice Parturier (Paris: CTHS, 1998). In recounting Ludovic's life story, Parturier referred to the fact that "Vitet fut élevé par son père est resta avec lui jusqu'à l'âge de seize ans" (vii).
24. PVCJ, entries dated 26 and 30 Ventôse an 13 (March 17 and 21, 1805).
25. Catherine Arnaud-Tizon (hereafter CAT) to AV, 12 Frimaire an 14 (December 3, 1805), AML 84II/12.
26. CAT to PV, February 6, 1815, AML 84II/12.
27. AV to PV, May 25, [1820], AML 84II/11.

28. Amélie Arnaud-Tizon née Thiébault, letters dating from the mid-1820s, AML 84II/09.
29. On women's political activities, see Dominique Godineau, *The Women of Paris and Their French Revolution*, trans. Katherine Streip (Berkeley: University of California Press, 1998), and Katie Jarvis, *Politics in the Marketplace: Work, Gender, and Citizenship in Revolutionary France* (Oxford: Oxford University Press, 2019).
30. Leora Auslander, *Cultural Revolutions: Everyday Life and Politics in Britain, North America, and France* (Berkeley: University of California Press, 2009), chap. 4.
31. An innovative and wide-ranging analysis of the differing experiences and perspectives of the generations who lived through the revolutionary era appears in Nathan Perl-Rosenthal, *The Age of Revolutions and the Generations Who Made It* (New York: Basic, 2024).

The Global Age of Revolutions
AN ANTICOLONIAL APPROACH

Christy Pichichero

Following Sylvia Wynter, what if we unsettle the coloniality of being/power/truth/freedom in our account of the Age of Revolutions?[1] As postcolonial thinkers like Franz Fanon have argued, the colonial project, especially as pursued by European nations, involved not only the attempted seizure and exploitation of land but also the seizure and exploitation of human beings, both physically and psychologically.[2] Race-making was an essential part of this process and of the Age of Revolutions: the creation of racial categories in multiple domains of discourse and practice (law, science, medicine, philosophy, politics) in order to justify myriad forms of subjugation, violence, and exploitation.[3] As Aníbal Quijano has written, the "idea of race is, in all certainty, the most efficient instrument of social domination invented in the last 500 years."[4] White supremacy and white freedom. The ship. Rape. Disease. Anti-Blackness and anti-Indigeneity. The archive. Literacy. Religion. The plantation. Firearms. Deforestation. The police. Chattel slavery. Capitalism. The whip. These were quintessential technologies of the period's anthropocene, racialized, and colonial necropolitics.[5]

A *de*colonial approach to the Age of Revolutions must involve an epistemic shift that takes forms of refusal: First, a refusal of the colonial gaze and a resistance against the domination of Eurocentric and Global North epistemologies, and second, a refusal of what Sarah Knott has called "history writing for neo-liberal times." The latter modality of empirical history writing is a manifestation of recent "knowledge making in a globalizing present, which appears most often in a socially inclusive but politically quietist narrative form."[6] The academy's simultaneous political correctness and racial capitalism turns histories of the oppressed into a symbolic, tokenistic tableau of diversity or a facile object of white liberal armchair moralism that refuses to acknowledge its own privilege and complicity with those same arrangements of oppression. An *anti*colonial approach to the Age of Revolutions not only exposes and eschews the coloniality of these scholarly politics. It demands epistemic justice beyond racial capitalist representation and demands a radical rethinking and retelling of history. It also insists on the ongoing nature of colonial oppression, exploitation, slavery, and violence. Rather than conveniently and fallaciously cloistering such phenomena into a morally, politically, and economically reprehensible past, an anticolonial approach embraces a radical politics acknowledging and working to advance anticolonial battles for sovereignty, equity, landback, and multiple forms of reparations that remain very real, everyday struggles for colonized peoples around the world, many of whom have been colonized by nations in the Global North since the late fifteenth century.

So, what does the Age of Revolutions look like when we center the geographies, epistemologies, and experiences of peoples who were subjected to—and fought against—racism, dispossession, enslavement, exploitation, and violence by imperial powers? What affects, logics, thematics, and lexicons would shape a vision of the Age of Revolutions from the perspective of those that Fanon would call the "damnés" (damned): the enslaved and indentured; women and children; convicts, sex workers, "sodomites," and "infidels"; the poor, the disabled, the "mad"; planet earth itself?

In approaching such a broad and hallowed subject, this essay adopts a wayward methodology to offer a series of perspectives and provocations that can serve as analytical building blocks for an epistemic reframing of the Age of Revolutions as an anticolonial history from below.[7] New cartographies, figurations, and temporalities are essential to this shift, as is a multiperspectivalism informed by diverse linguistic, cultural, historical, spiritual, and ecological positionalities. Silences in the archives must be addressed while respecting what Édouard Glissant called the "right to opacity" that refuses the colonial drive to "discover," categorize, and thereby control.[8] This essay begins by challenging historiographical traditions in scholarship on the Age of Revolutions, then proposes anticolonial geographic, figurative, and temporal hermeneutics based on primary sources produced by individuals and collectives long silenced or marginalized in the history of this age.

As A point of departure, an effort to unsettle the coloniality of this purported age could begin with dismantling traditional geographical boundaries imposed by historians and imagining new cartographies. The Age of Revolutions was long racially whitewashed as a Global North construct, steeped in Marxist or poststructuralist "linguistic turn" hermeneutics and foregrounding the American and French Revolutions.[9] As Michel-Rolph Trouillot powerfully argued, the Haitian Revolution was virtually ignored by generations of historians, despite its outsized importance and treatment by scholars like C. L. R. James in his classic work *The Black Jacobins* (1938).[10] In the past decades, historians finally began to include the Haitian Revolution into their vision of the Age of Revolutions, though it is still often underweighted on course syllabi and in histories of the era compared to its American and French counterparts. Unequal treatment notwithstanding, this tripartite version of the Age of Revolutions pushed the southern geographical boundary of historical thought just a bit closer to the equator—often still omitting questions of Indigeneity—while settling into an Atlantic history frame.[11]

Yet, the Atlantic Age of Revolutions is also drastically reductive in geographic scale. As David Armitage and Sanjay Subrahmanyam have argued, revolutions and related ideologies did not flow from Europe and North America to the rest of the world but rather intersected in complex ways with "multiple logics of transformation" across the globe.[12] Lisa Lowe has suggested that historians must probe further into what she called "the intimacies of four continents," knowing the interconnections among Africa, Europe, and the Americas that James highlighted long ago and recognizing, as Fernando Ortiz has observed, that "people from all four quarters of the globe" came together as laborers in the plantation capitalist locales such as Cuba.[13] For the Age of Revolutions, this expanding impulse must be accompanied by geological and archipelagic ones, pushing further to include not only all continents but also a plethora of islands, oceans, and other waterways around the globe where revolutionary information, plans, and battles arose or continued. In recent works on jihad in Muslim states of the Sokoto Caliphate, Fuuta Jalon, and Fuuta Toro, and on Tacky's Revolt in Jamaica (1760–61), Paul Lovejoy and Vincent Brown respectively showed the critical place of continuing religious and ethnic wars of West Africa in the exponential rise in slavery as well as in revolts, military operations, and political organizations by enslaved people in the greater Atlantic world.[14] Brown wrote of Tacky's Revolt:

> It was part of four wars at once: it was an extension of wars on the African continent; it was a race war between black slaves and white slaveholders;

it was a struggle among black people over the terms of communal belonging, effective control of local territory, and establishment of their own political legacies; and it was, most immediately, one of the hardest-fought battles of that titanic global conflict between Britain and its European rivals that would come to be known as the Seven Years' War. Each of these four wars introduced different currents that converged and eddied in the Jamaican insurrections of the 1760s. To chart their flows, a new cartography of slave revolt is required—one that combines the histories of Europe, Africa, and America and makes room for new stories of place, territory, and movement.[15]

Viewed as a totality, this multidirectional matrix engenders a new figuration of the Age of Revolutions. Rather than a Global North, Eurocentric "big bang" model indicating a series of explosive forces careening outward from a center point, or a treelike anatomy whose growth extends outward from a central trunk, the Age of Revolutions was ontologically rhizomatic in structure. Flora, fauna, and human beings, along with information, goods, and the aforementioned technologies of oppression, were connected in this rhizome.

Eighteenth-century Bengali Muslim writer Mirza I'tisam al-Din evinced this rhizomatic ontology in the Persian language narrative of his travels from the Indian Subcontinent to England and France, *Shigarf-nama-i vilayet*, or "Wonder Book of England," published in 1785.[16] I'tisam al-Din highlighted the interlinking of natural phenomena (such as effects of oceanic movement and the wind), human movement and technological development (e.g., sea travel with its humanmade instruments including ships and the compass), and Europe's colonial politics of domination. He centered not the colonizer but rather the epistemologies, experiences, and solidarity of the South Asian diaspora. In narrating his visit to the island of Mauritius in the 1760s (then occupied by France), he noted his surprise that Muslim lascars, or South Asian sailors, were living there and had married enslaved women from Bengal, Malabar, and the Deccan. These lascars were generous to I'tisam al-Din, offering advice and even aiding him in purchasing fruits and vegetables typical of summertime in Bengal. These encounters were meaningful to I'tisam al-Din as he contemplated questions of identity, power, and displacement for his people historically and during his lifetime.

I'tisam al-Din's writing illuminates how mobility and immobility—forced or voluntary—constitute key lenses through which to understand experiences in the ever-modulating rhizome. Sovereignty and continued life on traditional lands were, and are currently, long-term battles for Indigenous peoples around the globe. Settler colonialism as well as Indigenous rights and resistance are still too often marginalized in mainstream discussions of the Age of Revolutions, just as they are in modern political debates and reparations. However, histories of settler colonialism and imperial genocides of Indigenous groups, if taken in aggregate globally during the Age of Revolutions, may be one of the most pervasive phenomena of the era in question. Conflicts and competition between European empires drove this violence against Indigenous groups, who sought to simply continue living on their ancestral lands. This was the experience of Aboriginal Tasmanians when their island was taken over by the British in the early nineteenth century. The British invasion at once served the domestic purpose of establishing a penal colony and the geopolitical strategy of blocking republican France and its revolution from expanding into the South Pacific. But for Aboriginal Tasmanians, whose ancestors had inhabited the island for forty thousand years, the arrival of the English nearly annihilated their people as infectious diseases ripped through the population and the genocidal tactics of England's "black war" achieved its aims of almost wiping the Aboriginal Tasmanians off the island and planet. Numerous Indigenous peoples of the Indian and South Pacific Oceans experienced colonization and threats of extermination due to British penal settlements following American independence and the closure of U.S. borders to Britain's convicts. The fight for reparations is ongoing.[17]

The Tasmanian example evokes a triumphalist "Spanish model" of overwhelming conquest by guns, germs, and steel popularized by the Spanish themselves and more recently by Jared Diamond. While this model has dominated the historical imaginary of colonialism, it is largely inaccurate.[18] In the Age of Revolutions and dating back to the fifteenth century, European imperial pursuits in the Americas were deeply impacted and at times strongly dictated by Indigenous politics, power, social-cultural structures, and anticolonial warfare. The Guajiros of current-day Colombia and Venezuela furnish an example in their relationship to the Spanish in New Granada. The Guajiros were the second largest unconquered Indigenous group in the Americas (the Mapuche being the largest) with a population numbering between thirty and forty thousand in the late eighteenth century. Guajiro society was heterogenous, complex, and powerful, making them the dominant force in the region. As historian Forrest Hylton has explained, "Guajiro kinship, law, property relations, trade, and politics dictated the terms, extent, and success of Spanish engagement, missionary as well as martial. Spanish presence was contingent on the goodwill of one or more Guajiro *alaulayus* [leaders], whose power derived in part from the broader Atlantic trade networks in which they participated, and which constrained Spanish imperialism." Indeed, from the time of the first Spanish settlement in 1502, colonial forces never exercised sovereignty over the Guajira region or Guajiro peoples despite repeated military campaigns in 1578, 1616, 1649, and the 1760s to 1770s. Guajiro leaders made clear their objective in their anticolonial military efforts: to be "the sole owners of the land."[19] Further south in Peru, similar demands for sovereignty animated the series of revolts that became collectively known as the rebellion of Túpac Amaru II, named for one of the leaders who was an Incan-descended *cacique*. Dámaso Potosí—brother of Tomás Katari, who led the first major Indigenous insurgency during the period—said that Quechua- and Aymara-speaking Indigenous peoples fought to be "the lords of their own lands and of the fruits they produce, in peace and tranquility."[20]

Inversely, on the side of mobility, experiences and imaginaries of diaspora as well as what Stephanie Smallwood called "anomalous intimacy" formed between captives were hallmarks of the Age of Revolutions.[21] Exemplifying the "common wind" described by Julius S. Scott in his classic work, the wars of independence in Spanish South America, numerous revolts in Cuba in the first half of the nineteenth century, and the 1795 fight for emancipation on the island of Dutch-occupied Curaçao were among the largest enslaved uprisings of the Age of Revolutions. They were motivated and shaped by the Haitian and French Revolutions.[22] Enslaved Curaçaoans largely labored as mariners engaged in the Caribbean's multinational system of ships, ports, trade, and information. In explaining the rationale behind their revolt, Tula, the African-descended general of the self-emancipating army, complained of the abuses of slavery but also offered a savvy political justification: France had abolished slavery and that same law should apply in Dutch territories since France was occupying the Dutch Republic: "We have been badly treated for too long, we do not want to do anybody harm, but we seek our freedom. The French blacks have been given their freedom, Holland has been taken over by the French, hence we too must be free."[23] Tula even called himself "Rigaud" after the mixed-race Haitian revolutionary leader André Rigaud, who led an army in the southern part of colonial Haiti (then the French colony of Saint-Domingue). Louis Mercier, another commander who served under Tula/Rigaud, was from colonial Haiti and adopted the name Toussaint during the Curaçaoan war for freedom.

As the above example of Haitian *noms de guerre* used during a revolt in Curaçao make evident, in the rhizome of the Age of Revolutions, a sense of imagined community animated certain revolutionary actors who perceived themselves to be a part of a heroic and belligerent diaspora of African and African-descended captives fighting for self-emancipation. Solidarities across lines of race, ethnicity, class, profession, chattel slavery, and more were also common in the era's anticolonial and abolitionist militancy. The massive Bahian separatist movement in Brazil that culminated in an armed uprising against Portuguese authority in 1798 (nicknamed the Revolt of the Tailors or Alfaiates) united individuals from many backgrounds.[24] The political manifesto they posted all around the city of Salvador in August 1798 repurposed the main slogan of the French Revolution—liberty, equality, fraternity—in their demand for democracy, the abolition of slavery, absolute racial equality, lower food prices, free trade, and ultimately autonomy from Portugal. Such solidarities—imagined and real—evince the power of diasporic knowledge networks, bonds, and emulation, though factionalism among militant groups along the lines of race, class, and chattel slavery were equally present, as the Haitian Revolution and other examples make clear.

"Anomalous intimacy" between strangers thrust together in holds of slaving and convict ships, on plantations, and in colonial locales elucidate the genesis of ad-hoc political systems and solidarities. Convicts in the British penal system did not only hail from England, Ireland, and Scotland but from all manner of imperial outposts, comprising people from mainland China, Hong Kong, Malaysia, Indonesia, Sri Lanka, and all around the Indian Subcontinent and Africa. As Clare Anderson has shown, across their diverse identities, convicts transported on British vessels came together to fight for their freedom and return home. They ingeniously orchestrated mutinies and planned escape even before boarding the ships, smuggling equipment such as knives, nails, files, and waxed silk thread to cut through their fetters. Women and children also played a crucial role in these mutinies since their greater freedom of movement during the journey overseas—also a characteristic of many slaving vessels traveling from Africa to the Americas—allowed them to reconnoiter information about the locations of arms and any routine movements of the ship's crew.[25]

Unsurprisingly, self-liberating convicts of the Global South devised their own collective politics without any reference to European political discourse. In a bloody and successful mutiny aboard the *General Wood* sailing from Hong Kong to Penang in 1848, the ninety-two convicts, most of whom were pirates from Hong Kong, took over the ship and redirected it to Pulau Laut in the South China Sea. There they separated, with many sailing on to different destinations including Pulau Obi, Thailand, Singapore, and Hǎinán Shěng Island. Anderson inventoried the artifacts seized from twenty-eight of these convicts who were recaptured in Pulau Obi, including a fascinating document written in Mandarin that detailed the group's ideological commitments to unity, solidarity, health, and life:

> If any of us should die, the death of such person is to be made known to the survivors.
> If any of us should succeed in procuring a boat the same is to be made known to all of us.
> None of us are to leave the Island until we have fed and lived well enough so as not to be recognized as convicts when we get to China.
> When I go to China, no one save God will know who I am.
> We are to share alike in every thing, if we procure food we are to share alike.
> If one of us procure[s] a boat the same is to be made known to all of us, that we may go together.
> We all swear to assist and stand by one another to the last.
> God only besides ourselves shall know our actions and what is in our possession.[26]

This and numerous other examples make clear that maritime radicalism during the Age of Revolutions was often caused not by revolutionary ideological fervor but rather by the "borderless maritime world of mutual codes of honour" and the simple quest for freedom.[27]

This leads to an anticolonial postulate regarding scale. Quests for freedom occurred on a grand martial and political scale but also in hyperlocal and personal ways. Enslaved peoples fled plantations, households, ships, docks, and other forced workplaces. Sometimes they left in an attempt to start a new life in a maroon community or another city, sometimes they departed for just weeks or a day to escape the brutalities of their quotidian labors, spend time with kin, and further other pursuits. Women participated in all registers of the fight for freedom: from roles as military officers and soldiers to private family actors exercising what Jessica Marie Johnson has called "Black femme freedom" to protect themselves and their kin.[28] They too entered into the necropolitics of the era, though in an anticolonial orientation, some poisoning their masters and killing their own children to spare the child from the horrors of life under slavery and to deny the reproductive economic logic of the plantation—*partus sequitur ventrem*—by which children born of enslaved women were automatically legally enslaved.[29]

African and African-descended women were also a major spiritual force during this era in which religion—rather than the secular, republican ideology upheld in the American and French Revolutions—was a prevailing force in diasporic solidarities and wars of freedom. In numerous examples, including the 1835 Malê Revolt in Brazil and the Haitian Revolution, religious beliefs, rituals of prayer, sacrifice, song, dance, and spoken word were vital elements in African and African-descended ways of knowing, constructing collective bonds, and approaching wars of self-emancipation from European slaving empires.[30] The gathering of enslaved people at Bois Caïman in northern Haiti on the night of August 14, 1791, often considered the beginning of the Haitian Revolution, was at once a meeting for military planning and a vodou ceremony presided over by *mambo* (female priest) Cécile Fatiman and *oungan* (male priest) Boukman Dutty. The rituals performed there, including the sacrifice of a black pig, were the forces that cemented collective bonds and reinforced their vision of a rightful natural order that legitimized the fight for freedom. According to the account of the ceremony offered by Haitian politician and poet Hérard Dumesle based on oral interviews conducted in the early nineteenth century, Dutty interpreted racial slavery and plantation necropolitics as a clashing between good and evil gods:

> This God who made the sun, who brings us light from above, who raises the sea, and who makes the storm rumble. That God is there, do you understand? Hiding in a cloud, He watches us, He sees all that the whites do! The God of the whites pushes them to crime, but He wants us to do good deeds. But the God who is so good orders us to vengeance. He will direct our hands, and give us help. Throw away the image of the God of

the whites who thirsts for our tears. Listen to the liberty that speaks in all our hearts."[31]

From the hills of colonial Haiti to the revolts in holding facilities at slave ports and aboard slaving vessels that departed from Africa, captives of all manner of geographic, ethnic, cultural, and linguistic backgrounds established "anomalous intimacy" and agreed that freedom or death were the obvious choices.[32]

These last insights generate the final anticolonial postulates of this essay, which include another possible figuration along with a different temporality and chronology of the Age of Revolutions. As Sujit Sivasundaram has pointed out, historians have privileged a single definition of revolution in their analyses, considering the phenomenon as a successful "overthrow or renunciation of one government or ruler and the substitution of another by the governed."[33] Sivasundaram contended that for Indigenous peoples of the Indian and Pacific Oceans—and I would add for individuals and collectives in the African, South Asian, and Asian diasporas of the era—it is more apt to adopt an astrophysical definition indicating the repeated, cyclical motion of celestial bodies rotating on their own axes and orbiting others. "In these decades," wrote Sivasundaram, "European imperial place-making was layered on top of, and in conflict with, indigenous assertions of place, politics, and knowledge. These rival practices of place-making lie at the heart of what is taken here to be the age of revolutions," as are "stand-off[s] between cultures of knowledge, self-hood, war, state-making, and trade."[34] While such conflicts intensified during the Age of Revolutions, a wider chronological lens shows that they were unfurling before and during encounters with European colonizing powers dating back to the fifteenth century.

In this broader geography, chronology, and cyclical temporality of revolution, it is clear that Indigenous, African-descended, South Asian, and Asian peoples did not need eighteenth-century European and European-descended political ideologies to conceive of and fight for their rights and ways of living. For freedom from servitude, mortal exploitation, and abject torture. For religious autonomy and political sovereignty. For land, culture, and a future for their families and people. By the Age of Revolutions, they had battled for these rights over and over again, in some cases for centuries. And for many, their battles went on for centuries thereafter and continue to this day.

Notes

1. Sylvia Wynter, "Unsettling the Coloniality of Being/Power/Truth/Freedom: Towards the Human, after Man, Its Overrepresentation—An Argument," *CR: The New Centennial Review* 3, no. 3 (Fall 2003): 257–337.
2. See Franz Fanon, *Peau noire, masques blancs* (Paris: Éditions du Seuil, 1952). For an English version, see the translation by Richard Philcox: Fanon, *Black Skin, White Masks* (New York: Grove Press, 2008).
3. The list of scholarly works on race, slavery, and early modern European empires is ever expanding. This is a small sample. For France: Sue Peabody, *"There Are No Slaves in France": The Political Culture of Race and Slavery in the Ancien Régime* (Oxford: Oxford University Press, 1996); Sue Peabody and Tyler Stovall, eds., *The Color of Liberty: Histories of Race in France* (Durham, NC: Duke University Press, 2003). For England and America: Ania Loomba and Jonathan Burton, eds., *Race in Early Modern England: A Documentary Companion* (New York: Palgrave Macmillan, 2007); Sean P. Harvey, "Ideas of Race in Early America," in *Oxford Research Encyclopedias of American History*, ed. Jane Dailey (Oxford: Oxford University Press, 2013), https://doi.org/10.1093/acrefore/9780199329175.013.262. For Spain and Portugal: Max S. Hering Torres, María Elena Martínez, and David Nirenberg, eds., *Race and Blood in the Iberian World* (Berlin: Lit Verlag, 2012); Pamela Patton, ed., *Envisioning Others: Race, Color, and the Visual in Iberia and Latin America* (Leiden: Brill, 2015); Manuela Mourao, "Whitewash: Nationhood, Empire, and the Formation of Portuguese Racial Identity," *Journal for Early Modern Cultural Studies* 11, no. 1 (Spring–Summer 2011): 90–124. For Holland and Western Europe more broadly, see D. G. Hondius, *Blackness in Western Europe: Racial Patterns of Paternalism and Exclusion* (New York: Routledge, 2014), especially "Introduction: Long Trends in European Race Relations" (1–14).
4. Aníbal Quijano, "¡Qué tal Raza!," *Ecuador Debate. Etnicidades e identificaciones*, no. 48 (December 1999): 141–52. My translation.
5. Tyler Stovall, *White Freedom: The Racial History of an Idea* (Princeton, NJ: Princeton University Press, 2021).
6. Sarah Knott, "Narrating the Age of Revolution," *William and Mary Quarterly*, 3rd. series, 73, no. 1 (January 2016): 3–36, 21 (quotations).
7. On waywardness, see Saidiya Hartman, *Wayward Lives, Beautiful Experiments: Intimate Histories of Social Upheaval* (New York: Norton, 2019).
8. See Édouard Glissant, *Poetics of Relation*, trans. Betsy Wing (Ann Arbor: University of Michigan Press, 1997), 189. Scholarship problematizing the archive, voice, and writing of history is now vast. Foundational texts include Michel-Rolph Trouillot, *Silencing the Past: Power and the Production of History* (Boston: Beacon Press, 1995); Natalie Zemon Davis, *Women on*

the Margins: Three Seventeenth Century Lives (Cambridge, MA: Harvard University Press, 1995); Michel Foucault, "Lives of Infamous Men," in *The Essential Foucault,* ed. Paul Rabinow and Nikolas Rose (New York: New Press, 2003), 279–93; Saidiya Hartman, "Venus in Two Acts," *Small Axe* 12, no. 2 (2008): 1–14; and Marisa Fuentes, *Dispossessed Lives: Enslaved Women, Violence, and the Archive* (Philadelphia: University of Pennsylvania Press, 2016).

9. On these trends in the context of the French Revolution, see Jack Censer, "Social Twists and Linguistic Turns: Revolutionary Historiography a Decade after the Bicentennial," *French Historical Studies* 22, no. 1 (Winter 1999): 39–167, and "Historians Revisit the Terror—Again," *Journal of Social History* 48, no. 2 (Winter 2014): 383–403.
10. Trouillot, *Silencing the Past*; C. L. R. James, *The Black Jacobins: Toussaint L'Ouverture and the San Domingo Revolution* (London: Secker and Warburg, 1938).
11. For an analysis of the erasure of Indigenous histories from the Age of Revolutions and a further critique of neoliberal history writing, see Michael A. McDonnell, "Rethinking the Age of Revolution," *Atlantic Studies* 13, no. 3 (2016): 301–14.
12. David Armitage and Sanjay Subrahmanyam, "Introduction: The Age of Revolutions, c. 1760–1840—Global Causation, Connection, and Comparison," in *The Age of Revolutions in Global Context, c. 1760–1840,* ed. David Armitage and Sanjay Subrahmanyam (New York: Palgrave Macmillan, 2009), xii–xxxii, xxix (quotation).
13. Fernando Ortiz, *Cuban Counterpoint: Tobacco and Sugar* (Durham, NC: Duke University Press, 1995), 58; Lisa Lowe, *The Intimacies of Four Continents* (Durham, NC: Duke University Press, 2015).
14. See Paul Lovejoy, *Jihād in West Africa during the Age of Revolutions* (Athens: Ohio University Press, 2016), and Vincent Brown, *Tacky's Revolt: The Story of an Atlantic Slave War* (Cambridge, MA: Belknap Press of Harvard University Press, 2020).
15. Brown, *Tacky's Revolt,* 7.
16. Mirza Sheikh I'tesamuddin, *The Wonders of Vilayet: Being the Memoir, Originally in Persian, of a Visit to France and Britain in 1765,* trans. Kaiser Haq (Leeds, U.K.: Peepal Tree Press, 2002). For I'tisam al-Din's biography, see Gulfishan Khan, *Indian Muslim Perceptions of the West during the Eighteenth Century* (Karachi, Pakistan: Oxford University Press, 1998), 72ff. These aspects of I'tisam al-Din's text are highlighted in Sujit Sivasundaram, "Islands and the Age of Revolutions in the Indian and Pacific Oceans," in *Islands and the British Empire in the Age of Sail,* ed. Douglas Hamilton and John McAleer (Oxford: Oxford University Press, 2021), 138.

17. On reconciliation and reparations for Tasmanian Aboriginals, see Maria Rae, "When Reconciliation Means Reparations: Tasmania's Compensation to the Stolen Generations," *Griffith Law Review* 24, no. 4 (2015): 640–56.
18. See Jared Diamond, *Guns, Germs, and Steel: The Fates of Human Societies* (New York: Norton, 1997). Works that debunk this vision of the Spanish model include Mathew Restall, *Seven Myths of the Spanish Conquest* (Oxford: Oxford University Press, 2004); Laura Matthews, *Indian Conquistadors: Indigenous Allies in the Conquest of Mesoamerica* (Norman: University of Oklahoma Press, 2007); and Wayne E. Lee, ed., *Empires and Indigenes: Intercultural Alliance, Imperial Expansion, and Warfare in the Early Modern World* (New York: New York University Press, 2011).
19. See Forrest Hylton, "'The Sole Owners of the Land': Empire, War, and Authority in the Guajira Peninsula, 1761–1779," *Atlantic Studies* 13, no. 3 (2016): 315–44, 316 (quotation).
20. Sergio Serulnikov, *Revolution in the Andes: The Age of Túpac Amaru* (Durham, NC: Duke University Press, 2013), 68. See also Sinclair Thomson, "Sovereignty Disavowed: The Tupac Amaru Revolution in the Atlantic World," *Atlantic Studies* 13, no. 3 (2016): 407–31.
21. Stephanie Smallwood, *Saltwater Slavery: A Middle Passage from Africa to American Diaspora* (Cambridge, MA: Harvard University Press, 2008).
22. Julius S. Scott, *The Common Wind: Afro-American Currents in the Age of the Haitian Revolution* (London: Verso, 2018). See Ada Ferrer, *Freedom's Mirror: Cuba and Haiti in the Age of Revolutions* (Cambridge: Cambridge University Press, 2014), and Gert Oostindie, "Slave Resistance, Colour Lines, and the Impact of the French and Haitian Revolutions in Curaçao," in *Curaçao in the Age of Revolutions, 1795–1800*, ed. Wim Klooster and Gert Oostindie (Leiden: Brill, 2001), 1–22, among others.
23. "Verslag van Pater Jacobus Schinck, 7 September 1795," no. 69, September 10, 1795, Minuut-notulen van de gewone en buitengewone vergaderingen van Directeur (Commissarissen) en Raden, 1791–1804, Oud Archief Curaçao, inv. no. 105, Nationaal Archief, The Hague, cited in Karwan Fatah-Black, "Orangism, Patriotism, and Slavery in Curaçao, 1795–1796," *International Review of Social History* 58, no. S21 (2013): 50. After initial victories, the self-emancipating army was routed within weeks and the leaders were gruesomely punished and executed.
24. For texts in English, see Patrícia Valimm "The Revolt of the *Enteados* and Tailors in Bahia, 1798," in *Oxford Research Encyclopedia of Latin American History*, ed. Ángela Vergara (Oxford: Oxford University Press, 2020), https://doi.org/10.1093/acrefore/9780199366439.013.874, and Kenneth R. Maxwell, *Conflicts and Conspiracies: Brazil and Portugal, 1750–1808* (Cambridge: Cambridge University Press, 1974).

25. See Clare Anderson, "The Age of Revolution in the Indian Ocean, Bay of Bengal, and South China Sea: A Maritime Perspective," in special issue no. 21, "Mutiny and Maritime Radicalism in the Age of Revolution: A Global Survey," ed. Clare Anderson et al., *International Review of Social History* 58, no. S21 (2013): 238. Convicted sailors, soldiers, and pirates were most often responsible for leading these mutinies.
26. Anderson, "The Age of Revolution in the Indian Ocean, Bay of Bengal, and South China Sea," 241; Archival file with inventory, India Office Records (IOR) P/143/21 Bengal Judicial Consultations (BJC), July 12, 1948, British Library, London. This file also contains a letter from Captain George Nibbett (commander of the *Phlegathon*) to Captain P. McQuhae (Senior Officer Straits Settlements) relaying the fact that one of the convicts actually broke the above pact, imputing two fellow convicts for the murder of Captain Stokoe during the original mutiny. In survival and freedom, opportunism trumped ideology.
27. Anderson, "The Age of Revolution in the Indian Ocean, Bay of Bengal, and South China Sea," 242.
28. Jessica Marie Johnson, *Wicked Flesh: Black Women, Intimacy, and Freedom in the Atlantic World* (Philadelphia: University of Pennsylvania, 2020).
29. Jennifer Morgan, *Reckoning with Slavery: Gender, Kinship, and Capitalism in the Early Black Atlantic* (Durham, NC: Duke University Press, 2021). Toni Morrison famously dramatized the practice of infanticide by enslaved mothers in her novel *Beloved* (New York: Knopf, 1987).
30. See João José Reis, *Slave Rebellion in Brazil: The Muslim Uprising of 1835 in Bahia* (Baltimore: Johns Hopkins University Press, 1993).
31. See Hérard Dumesle, *Voyage dans le nord d'Hayti; ou, Revelation des lieux et des monuments historiques* (Les Cayes, Haiti: L'Imprimerie du Gouvernement, 1824), 85–90. Translation from Laurent Dubois and John Garrigus, eds., *Slave Revolution in the Caribbean, 1789–1804: A Brief History with Documents*, 2nd edition (2006; Boston: Bedford/St. Martin's, 2017), 86–88.
32. See Jean Mettas, *Répertoire des expéditions négrières françaises au XVIIIe siècle* (Paris: Société Française d'Histoire d'Outre-Mer, 1978), for documentation on the many uprisings that occurred on French slaving vessels during the eighteenth century.
33. "Islands in the Indo-Pacific region have been historiographically marginalized in the literature on the age of revolutions because of a seeping Euro-Atlanticism and also because of the hold of 'area studies' and continent-focused explanations; yet they were key locales for reconsidering the relationship between territories, cultures, and peoples in this era. . . . Prioritizing them in the narrative of the age of revolutions allows us to begin with the indigenous in the global South and to contend with the

question of why the colonial narrowed the possibilities of the age of revolutions." Sivasundaram, "Islands and the Age of Revolutions," 138. For a discussion of varied meanings of the term "revolution" in historical context, see Reinhardt Kossellek, "Historical Criteria of the Modern Concept of Revolution," in Kossellek, *Futures Past: On the Semantics of Historical Time* (New York: Columbia University Press, 1979), 43–57. For a current dictionary definition of "revolution," see Merriam-Webster Dictionary online, https://www.merriam-webster.com/dictionary/revolution.

34. Sivasundaram, "Islands and the Age of Revolutions," 138.

PART 2

WHERE WAS THE AGE OF REVOLUTIONS?

The Sète Affair of 1721
CRISIS AND RESISTANCE IN THE EARLY EIGHTEENTH-CENTURY FRENCH COLONIES

CINDY ERMUS

IN THE EARLY 1720s, during a virulent epidemic of plague in the south of France, a major scandal broke out on the French colony of Martinique.[1] Over a period of weeks, the upheaval rocked the island, causing its colonial leaders to denounce "the rebellion" and fear for their lives. The Sète Affair is telling of the kind of controversies that unfolded throughout the Atlantic world during the Plague of Provence, or Plague of Marseille, which lasted from 1720 to 1722. It began with the arrival in Martinique of a ship from Sète, a port city in the coastal province of Languedoc on the Mediterranean coast of France, that was suspected of harboring plague as a result of its proximity to the infected neighboring region of Provence. The affair offers an opportunity to reflect on the history of revolt and unrest in the Atlantic world decades before the onset of revolutions in the late eighteenth and nineteenth centuries, and to consider what this history can add to our understanding of the Age of Revolutions as a process rather than a moment, as the label implies. So, what happened?

On the evening of April 25, 1721, a merchant ship named *Les États de Languedoc* from the port city of Sète ran aground as it arrived off the coast of Le Prêcheur near Saint-Pierre, Martinique. The vessel was carrying merchandise destined for the island, including flour, oil, cheeses, wines, eau-de-vie (brandy), anchovies, and other goods, from Languedoc. Soon after the incident, the captain, Jean-Baptiste Bordes, requested two boats to lighten his load so that he could try to set his vessel afloat.[2] Having learned of the ship's arrival, a local merchant named Rieussec, to whom the vessel was addressed, immediately contacted the island's *gouverneur général* and *intendant*, François de Pas de Mazencourt, Marquis de Feuquières (c. 1660–1731), and Charles Bénard (1622–1728), respectively, to see to it that the captain's request was granted.

Now, if the vessel had come from anywhere on France's Atlantic coast, the captain's request for assistance might not have been of much concern, especially since the ship was carrying numerous goods of which the island was in dire need. During the Plague of Provence, however, when much of the world was on high alert against any vessels from southern France or anywhere in the Mediterranean, the arrival in Martinique of this ship from Languedoc launched a weeks-long scandal that temporarily pitted the island's topmost officials against local merchants and residents.

Restrictions against the arrival of vessels from Provence, Languedoc, or any port of the Mediterranean had been in place across the French Atlantic colonies since the previous year, from Cayenne in the south to Quebec in the north.[3] On paper, if not always in practice, all prohibited the entry of vessels from the Mediterranean that were not first granted authorization prior to their arrival. For those ships that *were* granted access to French colonial harbors, ordinances included strict guidelines for anchoring and for the inspection of merchandise and crew by the designated surgeon or physician; quarantines of varying lengths; and the prohibition of movement for the captain, crew, and cargo, as well as restrictions on their ability to communicate with nearby ships and those on land. And for those vessels that nevertheless arrived from anywhere near the infected areas of France *without* authorization, all the colonies had at their disposal the option of burning the ship and cargo. Yet, as the Sète Affair makes clear, the practice could be highly controversial, despite the fact that it would have been done, at least in theory, in the name of public health.

As word quickly spread throughout Martinique that a ship from France's Mediterranean coast was anchored near Saint-Pierre, the entire population of the island was gripped by fear of infection with plague from the French vessel, and on April 30, five days after its arrival, the governor and intendant reported that a large mob had gathered at Fort Royal (today's Fort-de-France) in protest. The people demanded that Captain Bordes and his vessel be forced to depart the coast of the island at once, or else, they threatened, they would burn the entire vessel along with its cargo. Further, they would force the crew to disembark and strip naked, shave their heads, and bathe repeatedly in the ocean. After all, they argued, the owners of the vessel, "who know that the port of Sète is very close to Marseille where the plague has reigned for a long time," should have known that it would not be received in the islands. And if the plague passed to the islands, they feared, the colonies would be quickly depopulated and "lost without resource."[4]

Seeing that the inhabitants of the island would not tolerate *Les États de Languedoc* in Martinique any longer, Governor Feuquières urged Captain Bordes to consider taking his ship and his crew to the French colony of Île-Royale in New France (now Cape Breton Island in Nova Scotia). Promising that he would help with the necessary repairs to get the ship ready for such a journey, Feuquières insisted that Île-Royale would be "the best and most useful thing [Bordes] could do for the owners of the vessel given the unfortunate situation in which he now finds himself. Île-Royale is a cold place where the plague is not to be feared," and unlike Martinique, "it is a newly inhabited island that is not [as] populated." There were also numerous ports where he could quarantine his suspected goods as needed, and his merchandise, Feuquières insisted, would "sell advantageously." The governor even offered to connect Bordes with some of his acquaintances in the colony by writing letters of recommendation for the captain. On the other hand, if Captain Bordes "has an absolute need to *caréner* [repair/refit the vessel]," Feuquières and Bénard saw no other place where he could do so except the island of Saint Lucia, for which he would need to be properly armed because of the possibility of encountering pirates while there. One thing was certain: the inhabitants of Martinique would not easily allow Bordes and his vessel to remain in the island.[5]

On May 2, the "residents and merchants" of Martinique presented a formal statement to Feuquières and Bénard in which they made their case for the expulsion of the Languedocian vessel from the island.[6] Despite the claim that it came from merchants *and* residents, however, the concerns and insider knowledge of the statement make it clear that it was presented primarily at the behest of local merchants. Letters from Feuquières and Bénard in the days that followed complained that the merchants had a vested interest in expelling this ship from Martinique, and to this end were responsible for rabblerousing and intentionally causing alarm among the people of the island.

In the statement, the merchants questioned the credibility of Captain Bordes, who they accused of falsely claiming to be stranded at Le Precheur, "where ships never run aground," in order to have a pretext to stay in Martinique. They argued that even if the plague was not present on *Les États de Languedoc*, a fear of infection and "general desolation" would nevertheless grip the island. This panic would only be intensified with the expected arrival of the *maladie de siam* (yellow fever) on the island—"which begins with foreigners each year around July"—since the residents of Martinique would confuse it for the plague and blame the ship from Sète. Yet, the plague could very well be present on the vessel, "for Provence is currently almost entirely attacked by the contagion . . . and one cannot prep for a trip to the Americas from Sète without help from Marseille." Another danger of allowing the ship from Languedoc to stay was that if news reached the Spaniards, they would close their ports to a number of vessels that already had orders to take their cargo to Cádiz and Bilbao. Moreover, the merchants and residents claimed, "We will be exposed to an avoidable famine and all kinds of miseries because false rumors of contagion would not only prevent the French from giving us much needed help but also the neighboring islands." Allowing the ship to stay at Martinique, even if only to *caréner* for a journey, would expose the islands to no less of a risk than selling its cargo, in part because no ordinance from the governor and intendant—the "pères du peuple" (fathers of the people)—would effectively keep "wretched whites or blacks in search of some gain" from communicating with those on board. For these merchants, the only solution was for Feuquières and Bénard to "order the said captain of the ship from Sète to depart without delay, on pain of death, for the port of Sète accompanied by an armed boat of fifty men who will follow him to *débouquement* [disemboguement]." If these demands were not carried out, they assured that the ship would be burned with its cargo, and its crew—having now been unclothed and freshly shaven—unloaded into a chaloupe to be transported to a designated location for quarantine.[7]

This placed Feuquières and Bénard in an unenviable position. They maintained that since the vessel in question was not in seaworthy condition according to the declaration made to them by Captain Bordes and his crew, they were "unable to send it back whence it came in accordance with the petitioners' request."[8] Although the governor and intendant were more than willing to take reasonable precautions for the preservation of public health, upon review of the letters of health (*lettres de santé*) from the commander in chief and intendant of Languedoc (the Duc de Roquelaure and Louis de Bernage, respectively), they did not, in fact, suspect that the vessel from Sète was infected with plague.[9] Consequently, the proposal from the merchants to burn the vessel and its cargo with no compensation whatsoever seemed nothing short of "violent" to the officials. They also feared that the king and his council would disapprove of the ship's burning, especially given the complaints that the shipowners (*armateurs*) would almost certainly take to the king against the colonial officials.[10]

But there were further reasons for Feuquières and Bénard's wariness. From their perspective, the entire ordeal was being driven not by a genuine fear of infection but by the avarice of a group of merchants who had much to gain from the prohibition of ships from Languedoc and Marseille. On May 8, they reported to the Marine Council in Paris:

> It is best that the Council is informed that the greater part of this terror which is so widely spread among our inhabitants and traders comes only from the insinuation of the merchants of Nantes and Bordeaux established in this island which have always preserved an implacable hatred for the merchants of Marseille and Languedoc, because they wish to have sole rights of commerce in these islands. The Council will easily remember that the trade syndicate of Nantes and Bordeaux did all they could to obtain from his majesty that the Compagnie de Cette [Sète Company[11]] be forbidden to trade in these islands in view of the fact they had permission to go to the Levant, and the just refusal of their request has only served to foment their hatred for this Company.

Feuquières and Bénard argued that these merchants of Bordeaux and Nantes, "who fomented this uproar by the desire to sell their goods at higher prices," should be responsible for the value of any burned property.[12] To the officials, then, the movement on the island to destroy the ship from Sète was not at its core driven by a legitimate concern for public health but by longstanding rivalries between France's Atlantic and Mediterranean ports. These disputes had grown over the previous decades primarily in reaction to Marseille's privilege as a free port and its monopoly over Levantine trade. Now, they were being blamed for the discord that unfolded when ships from these Mediterranean ports arrived in Martinique during the Plague of Provence.

Despite all of this, however, after much deliberation and in consultation with other officials of the island, Feuquières and Bénard ultimately bowed to the demands of the merchants and their supporters, resolving to burn the vessel and much of its cargo "only to appease the noise of the people."[13] But they could not act quickly enough. By now, two weeks after the ship's arrival, the situation in Martinique had escalated to the point that the governor and intendant feared a revolt and even feared for their lives. In May 1721, Feuquières wrote to the head of the Marine Council, Louis Alexandre de Bourbon, of the "ill will, disobedience, and rebellion" that the inhabitants and traders of the island had demonstrated since the arrival of the ship from Sète.[14] "The residents always harbor the idea of revolt," he related, "[and] I have every reason to believe that the current *esprit de sédition* [spirit of sedition] has been suggested to them by the emissaries of merchants from Nantes who cannot suffer that any others trade in these islands, and who . . . do everything in their power to prevent the ships from Sète from coming here."[15] Days later, Feuquières and Bénard even learned of a possible plot in St. Pierre to assassinate them if they did not immediately burn the ship.[16]

Feuquières's fear that the people might rise in revolt was not unfounded. He remembered all too well the events, only three years earlier, that led to his assuming the position as *gouverneur général* of Martinique in the first place. Throughout France's colonial history, the overseas possessions were often left to fend for themselves, since the metropole could not always ensure they were adequately stocked with food and supplies. In part for this reason, colonists engaged in illicit trade with their Spanish, English, and Dutch neighbors outside of the closed system of commerce that France desired to maintain with its colonies.[17] Consequent efforts to clamp down on the unregulated trade, while never fully successful, nonetheless triggered opposition in the colonies, sometimes to the point of revolt.[18] This is what occurred in May 1717, when metropolitan administrators were sent to Martinique to help bring an end to smuggling on the islands.[19] Soon after the arrival of a new governor-general and intendant, Antoine, Marquis d'Arcy de La Varenne, and Louis-Balthazar de Ricouart, Comte de Herouville, respectively, colonial residents began to gather. They protested both the attempts to clamp down on illicit commerce and a four-year-old levy on enslaved people, the *octroi*, that had already incited protests in Guadeloupe two years earlier.[20] The uprising at this time even included calls for independence and the formation of a republic on the island.[21] Siding with the protesters, a group of militia officers and soldiers resolved to arrest La Varenne and Ricouart while they dined in the town of Le Diamant.[22] With the support of the Superior

Council (Conseil supérieur), the island's highest court, the demonstrators promptly placed the two officials on a ship headed back to France with a number of documents explaining their actions.[23] And France barely batted an eye at the insubordination.[24]

This revolt, known as the Gaoulé from a Creole term for "uprising," signified a unity between colonial residents and elites of the island against metropolitan officials. As historian Laurie Marie Wood argued, "It also demonstrated that local elites were not tied to the decisions of the governor and intendant as the sole leaders of the colony." Feuquières, himself a creole notable who had served as governor of Grenada and Guadeloupe before succeeding the ousted La Varenne, knew this history all too well, and often revealed his distrust of the people in letters to Paris.[25] In 1720, for example, a year before the Sète Affair, he related to the Marine Council that the loyalty of the people was "very unsteady."[26] And in May 1721, he wrote, "It is quite sad and even more painful for officers like Mr. Bénard and I, entrusted as we are with the power of his Majesty, to find ourselves exposed to the whims of a wicked people . . . lacking the forces to oppose them or to make them return to their duties."[27]

Accordingly, the primary concern for colonial authorities during the Plague of Provence did not only consist of protecting the colonies from being "lost to the disease" but from being lost to *rebellion*.[28] In fact, conflicts between the French Crown and the Superior Council of Martinique—and its colonies across the eighteenth-century Americas—would arise every so often, prompting its leaders to periodically request help from Paris. In 1726, for example, Pierre Henri Miraillet Du Rieux, the king's lieutenant at Fort Royal, urged the Comte de Maurepas, then the French minister of the marine, "to remedy against [the] independence, and against *the republican and tyrannical spirit* that [the island's Superior Council] wishes to exercise."[29] And in 1721, wishing to prevent "a second rebellion" amid the Sète crisis, Feuquières too called for support from Paris. He wrote,

> I have many times related the absolute necessity that there be stronger garrisons here, and at least two good, well-armed frigates to maintain the authority of the king and contain the inhabitants, [but] since the Council has informed me that this is impossible . . . I had resolved not to speak of it anymore; but the case today is very serious . . . [the King's] interest, the preservation of his colonies, and his authority depend so much on the assistance necessary for the maintenance of both, that as long as we do not

continuously have at least one strong and well-armed vessel, and if a reinforcement of four companies . . . are not sent . . . we will never be able to restrain these people, who are so strongly inclined to disobedience; and supposing that we can avoid with precautions and our temperaments all the insults of which they are more than capable, we can only very weakly assert the authority of the king.[30]

Yet it would take weeks for the Marine Council to receive this renewed request for reinforcements. Indeed, we do not begin to see responses to the Sète Affair from the Conseil until July 12, 1721, two months after the letters requesting support in the matter.[31] And by the time Paris dispatched two armed vessels to Martinique, the entire affair had been over for months. Officials on the island were thus forced to handle the crisis alone, without guidance or assistance from Paris.

The Sète Affair, which unfolded in part because of plague-time regulations that restricted the entry of ships from anywhere near the infected coasts of France, reveals a great deal about how difficult it was to control the colonies in times of crisis, and relatedly, the extent to which the colonies were often left to act on their own in the early eighteenth century. In the French Antilles at least, where the possibility of rebellion seemed ever-present, the real threat exposed by the Plague of Provence was not the loss of the colonies to disease but to revolt.

What, then, does the Sète Affair tell us about the Age of Revolutions? The scandal—much like that of Le Gaoulé and so many other earlier eighteenth-century uprisings in the islands—reveals the "spirit of sedition" and the "republican and tyrannical spirit," to quote various contemporaries, that existed in the overseas colonies many decades *before* the Age of Revolutions, which traditionally dates roughly from the 1770s to 1848.[32] It reminds us that there was an earlier history of resistance, with calls for independence from the metropole that already pointed to an identification with local communities and a perceived disconnect from the mainland and their representatives in parts of the Atlantic colonies. Perhaps the Long Age of Revolutions began much earlier, when it burned in the bellies of those in far-flung colonies who were often forced to manage, and at times survive, with little help or direction from the metropole. We look to the prerevolutionary era to trace the origins of the kind of thinking and conditions that *led* to later revolutions, but perhaps we have not yet paid enough attention to the very uprisings that were already taking place.

Notes

1. This essay is adapted from part of chapter 5 in my book *The Great Plague Scare of 1720: Disaster and Diplomacy in the Eighteenth-Century Atlantic World* (Cambridge: Cambridge University Press, 2023).
2. Marquis de Feuquières and Charles Bénard to the Conseil de Marine, No. 3, Fort Royal, April 25, 1721, Col. F3 252, 43, Archives Nationales d'Outre-Mer, Aix-en-Provence, France (hereafter ANOM).
3. M. Durand-Molard, "Ordonnance sur la peste," in *Code de la Martinique, nouvelle edition* (Saint-Pierre, Martinique: Imprimerie de Jean-Baptiste Thounens, 1807), 1:164–65; John J. Heagerty, *Four Centuries of Medical History in Canada* (Toronto: Macmillan, 1928), 2:25–26.
4. "Memoire pour le Sieur Bordes capitaine commandant le vaisseau de Cete," No. 7, Fort Royal, April 30, 1721, Col. F3 252, 50–52, ANOM. See also "The deputies of the inhabitants and merchants of Saint Pierre" to the Marquis de Feuquières and Charles Bénard, No. 8, Saint Pierre, May 2, 1721, Col. F3 252, 54–57, ANOM; "The deputies of the inhabitants and merchants of Saint Pierre" to the Marquis de Feuquières and Charles Bénard, No. 8, Saint Pierre, May 12, 1721, Col. F3 252, 85–87, ANOM.
5. "Memoire pour le Sieur Bordes capitaine commandant le vaisseau de Cete," No. 7, Fort Royal, April 30, 1721, Col. FM F/3/252, 52–53, ANOM.
6. "The deputies of the inhabitants and merchants of Saint Pierre" to the Marquis de Feuquières and Charles Bénard, No. 8, Saint Pierre, May 2, 1721, Col. FM F/3/252, 54–57, ANOM.
7. "The deputies of the inhabitants and merchants of Saint Pierre" to Feuquières and Bénard, No. 8, Saint Pierre, May 2, 1721, Col. FM F/3/252, 54–55, 56, 57, ANOM. Over the next two weeks, these same representatives would submit additional statements to reiterate these points, confirming that they stood by their demands either to see the vessel sent back to Sète or to destroy the ship and its cargo, and disembark the crew, naked and shaven, for quarantine. See, for example, "The deputies of the inhabitants and merchants of Saint Pierre" to the Marquis de Feuquières and Charles Bénard, No. 8, Saint Pierre, May 12, 1721, Col. FM F/3/252, 85–87, ANOM.
8. "Veu le requette cy dessus a nous presantée par divers habitans et negocians," No. 8, Fort Royal, May 2, 1721, Col. F3 252, 58, ANOM.
9. Roquelaure was Lieutenant Général des Armées du Roi (Lieutenant General of the King's Armies) and *commandant en chef* of the province of Languedoc.
10. "Veu le requette cy dessus a nous presantée par divers habitans et negocians," No. 8, Fort Royal, May 2, 1721, Col. F3 252, 58, ANOM.
11. Sète was developed by financiers from Montpellier in the 1660s in order to provide the province of Languedoc with an adequate port. Some of

these financiers went on to form two Sète trading companies in 1669 and 1676. The latter, which succeeded the former, is the one mentioned in this passage. Initially formed to supply wine and eau-de-vie throughout the Mediterranean, it soon expanded to include trade in the Levant. J. K. J. Thomson, *Clermont-de-Lodève, 1633–1789: Fluctuations in the Prosperity of a Languedocian Cloth-Making Town* (Cambridge: Cambridge University Press, 1982), 149–50.

12. Marquis de Feuquières and Charles Bénard to the Conseil de Marine, Fort Royal, May 8, 1721, Col. C8A 28, ff. 51v–52, 57, ANOM; Feuquières to the head of the Marine Council, Fort Royal, May 9, 1721, Col. F3 26, f. 472, ANOM.
13. Marquis de Feuquières and Charles Bénard to the Conseil de Marine, Fort Royal, May 8, 1721, Col. C8A 28, f. 57, ANOM.
14. S.A.S. (*Son altesse sérénissime*) Louis Alexandre de Bourbon, Comte de Toulouse (1678–1737), was one of the sons of Louis XIV and his mistress Françoise-Athénaïs, Marquise de Montespan. In these letters, he is referred to as "l'amiral" because of his role as *grand amiral de France* (Grand Admiral of France).
15. Marquis de Feuquières to the head of the Marine Council, Fort Royal, May 9, 1721, Col. F3 26, f. 472, 472v, ANOM.
16. Marquis de Feuquières and Charles Bénard to the Conseil de Marine, Fort Royal, May 13, 1721, Col. C8A 28, f. 60v, ANOM.
17. James Pritchard, *In Search of Empire: The French in the Americas* (Cambridge: Cambridge University Press, 2004), 256; Laurie Marie Wood, "Îles de France: Law and Empire in the French Atlantic and Indian Oceans, 1680–1780" (PhD diss., University of Texas at Austin, 2013), 212.
18. As Bertie Mandelblatt has maintained, "While famine and starvation were real problems in French Caribbean colonies throughout this period, they often served to mask the real subject at stake in these commercial debates—colonists' insistence on their right to trade with foreigners and metropolitan merchants' entrenched opposition to this perceived violation of their commercial privileges." Mandelblatt, "How Feeding Slaves Shaped the French Atlantic: Mercantilism and the Crisis of Food Provisioning in the Franco-Caribbean during the Seventeenth and Eighteenth Centuries," in *The Political Economy of Empire in the Early Modern World*, ed. Sophus A. Reinert and Pernille Røge (Basingstoke: Palgrave Macmillan, 2013), 194.
19. The revolt that ensued, called Le Gaoulé, unfolded only weeks after the French Crown issued the *Lettres patentes*, or royal charters, of April 1717, intended to help curtail illicit commerce with foreign merchants. Mandelblatt, "How Feeding Slaves Shaped the French Atlantic," 202–3; "Lettres

patentes du roi portant reglement du commerce dans les colonies françaises," April 1717, Col. A 25, ANOM.
20. In 1715, between four and five hundred colonists took up arms to protest the new *octroi* tax on slaveowners. See Pritchard, *In Search of Empire*, 256. In Saint-Domingue too a revolt broke out beginning in late 1722. In fact, as historian Malick W. Ghachem has observed, "Anti-corporate revolt was already something of an established tradition in the French Caribbean going back to the later 17th century." Ghachem, "'No Body to Be Kicked?' Monopoly, Financial Crisis, and Popular Revolt in 18th-Century Haiti and America," *Law and Literature* 28, no. 3 (2016): 416.
21. See, for example, Pierre Le Bègue, lieutenant of the king at Martinique, to Unknown, September 16, 1717, Col. C8B 4, ANOM. See also Jacques Petitjean Roget, *Le Gaoulé: La révolte de la Martinique en 1717* (Fort de France: Société d'histoire de la Martinique, 1966), chap. 13.
22. Wood, "Îles de France," 218–19.
23. Pritchard, *In Search of Empire*, 257; Wood, "Îles de France," 219. For more on Le Gaoulé, see also Roget, *Le Gaoulé*.
24. Pritchard, *In Search of Empire*, 257. "Conseils in the colonies were created with many of the same personnel and functions as well-respected metropolitan courts like the parlements, like the role of *conseiller*, or magistrate." Wood, "Îles de France," 7.
25. Wood, "Îles de France," 215, 222.
26. Pritchard, *In Search of Empire*, 258.
27. Marquis de Feuquières to the head of the Marine Council, Fort Royal, May 9, 1721, Col. F3 26, f. 473, ANOM.
28. Marquis de Feuquières to the head of the Marine Council, Fort Royal, May 9, 1721, Col. F3 26, f. 473, ANOM.
29. Pierre Henri Miraillet Du Rieux, lieutenant of the king at Martinique, to Jean-Frédéric Phélypeaux, Comte de Maurepas, secrétaire d'État à la Marine, Martinique, April 15, 1726, Col. C8B 9, No. 36, ANOM, emphasis added; Pritchard, *In Search of Empire*, 257.
30. Marquis de Feuquières to the head of the Marine Council, Fort Royal, May 9, 1721, Col. F3 26, f. 473v, ANOM.
31. Marquis de Feuquières to Louis Alexandre de Bourbon, head of the Marine Council, Fort Royal, September 22, 1721, Col. C8A 28, f. 276, ANOM.
32. Marquis de Feuquières to the head of the Marine Council, Fort Royal, May 9, 1721, Col. F3 26, ff. 472, 472v, ANOM; Pierre Henri Miraillet Du Rieux to Comte de Maurepas, Martinique, April 15, 1726, Col. C8B 9, No. 36, ANOM.

Cherokees in the Age of Revolutions

Kate Fullagar

The Age of Revolutions played out in Indigenous country just as surely as it unfurled in European lands and waters. For Indigenous people, however, the central political contest was not between democracy and autocracy, or republicanism and monarchy, but between their rights to sovereignty and imperial efforts to exploit, remove, or replace them. This essay explores the example of the Cherokees in southeast North America during the second half of the eighteenth century. In this period, the Cherokees went from managing multiple dynamic foreign empires to confronting the determined imperatives of one subset of one empire. At first, they had to juggle competing claims on their time, goods, and bodies from a range of French and British colonists, all while trying to preserve essential elements of their culture and economy. As the French gradually ceded imperial space to the British, who in turn faced revolutionary challenges from within, the Cherokees learned that their biggest problem had become how to maintain their very sense of self-definition.

That the latter revolutionary challengers also spoke a language of liberty and consent while plundering Native hunting grounds and towns did nothing to endear the Cherokees to Western notions of equality or popular governance. Worse, it meant that later chroniclers of the American Revolutionary Age were too often distracted by rebellious rhetoric to see how much Indigenous people had paid the price for settler independence. The Cherokees, like most Native American communities, have been overly neglected in histories of the era—not only because their story destabilizes attempts at a triumphalist or celebratory account but also because it makes some of those core debates look half-baked. This essay centers the Cherokee experience of this period in an effort to add back one key group of Native Americans to a well-known field and to reconsider revolutionary ideals in light of unrepentant imperial invasion. It sketches the wide range of ways that the Cherokees faced the conditions of the age—from diplomatic accommodation to violent resistance to an outright refusal to engage. Three men serve here to represent these differing tactics: Attakullakulla (Tsalagi), a long-lived leader from the powerful town of Chota; Dragging Canoe (Tsiyu Gansini), his firebrand son who also identified with the town of Chota; and Ostenaco (Ustanaqua), the *skiagusta*, or Head Man, of Tomotley, near Chota.[1]

Attakullakulla

Attakullakulla was the oldest of the three men, born around 1710. He was originally of the Nipissing peoples located much farther north but had been adopted by Cherokees as a war prize when just an infant. His thorough integration into Cherokee society and unwavering loyalty to them throughout his life demonstrated something of how eighteenth-century Cherokees recognized kin: they belonged to their clans through their maternal lines, but belonging came about either from a mother's blood or from a mother's choice. Attakullakulla had been chosen by his adopted mother, and thus became fully Cherokee.[2]

Attakullakulla's abiding approach to foreign empires was negotiation. He pursued this approach through trade wars, hostage crises, war talks, and revolutionary settlement. This is not to suggest he was always a pushover. His wily ways often bested imperial foes. In those moments when they did not, the outcomes usually spoke more poorly of European attitudes toward diplomacy than they did of Attakullakulla's acumen.

His greatest success was probably his work through the early 1750s trade embargo imposed by British South Carolina on the Cherokees. In 1751, South Carolina governor James Glen ordered an embargo against all Cherokee towns as punishment for their rumored random attacks on British traders. While Glen waited in Charleston for the Cherokees to cave, occasionally entertaining representations from separate Cherokee towns, Attakullakulla traveled to Williamsburg to see if he could start a rival trade with British Virginia. By 1753, he was successful: the Virginian governor Robert Dinwiddie relented to Attakullakulla's argument that Cherokee deerskins, and possible future manpower in any upcoming battles, were worth more than good relations with South Carolina.[3] Glen, needless to say, was irate, suggesting to Attakullakulla that he did not understand how British power worked. Attakullakulla replied coolly that he had British friends other than Glen now to send him over to Britain to verify this claim.[4] Glen had to admit a checkmate, and the Cherokees enjoyed uninterrupted trade, benefiting both them and European colonists, for several further years.

By 1758, however, relations had soured again. The rot had started, in fact, with Virginia, which had recruited hundreds of Cherokee warriors—Attakullakulla among them—to help them fight several battles against French colonists during the Seven Years' War. The Cherokee units served honourably, expecting respect and war prizes in return. When neither eventuated after a failed attack at Fort Duquesne, Attakullakulla was affronted. No less a Virginian leader than Colonel George Washington voiced his concern about offending such an important ally: the Cherokees are "justly fired with the highest resentment," he observed, even though they are "indispensably necessary [to] our interest."[5]

Resentment triggered a backlash, which in turn spurred murderous and rapacious colonial violence. A missionary visiting Cherokee country in 1759 heard Attakullakulla himself "talk bad [and] appear in general disaffected." (The missionary, for the record, thought Attakullakulla justified, for "there is too much truth in what he says.")[6] Tensions boiled over when the next South Carolina governor, William Lyttelton, issued another embargo against the Cherokees. Attakullakulla again went to work, arguing for months for a resumption of relations. But when he was joined by fifty-five other Cherokee delegates, Lyttelton did the unthinkable and locked the whole party (minus Attakullakulla) in his council rooms as hostages. News of this insult traveled quickly to Cherokee townsfolk, who immediately threatened war. At one point Attakullakulla was the only Cherokee left representing peace. He managed eventually to get thirty-three Cherokees freed, but twenty-two remained. Unfortunately, Attakullakulla could not persuade his people to let him keep trying diplomatic efforts. On February 16, 1760, a party of Cherokee warriors surrounded the fort holding the hostages and opened fire. The colonial commander inside apparently screamed to his soldiers to resist retaliation, "but before I could get one to hear or answer me, they laid them all lifeless."[7]

The massacre of twenty-two Cherokees underscored the acuity of Attakullakulla's approach in dealing with Europeans, though being right in this scenario no doubt felt like a hollow achievement. Later, his peacemaking instincts perhaps judged the colonists less well. In 1763, when Pontiac's War exploded in response to the stupefying claims of sovereignty made by Britain in the Paris Peace Treaty, Attakullakulla advised neutrality. Several delegations from a wide range of Native American groups implored the Cherokees to join them in their pan-Indian fight against British usurpation. But Attakullakulla convinced his people that nonalignment was the safer option, given Britain's ever-increasing powers on the continent now that the French had bowed out.[8] Possibly the famed expertise of Cherokee warriors in a pan-Indian force would have helped Pontiac's War make a greater dent on imperial dreams that it did. Certainly it would have prolonged the rebellion beyond its gradual collapse in 1765.

Attakullakulla's implicit hope that neutrality in Pontiac's War would endear the Cherokees to the British was horribly misplaced. Into the late 1760s and early 1770s, British colonists, now freed from the check of French rivalry, pressed the Cherokees into tougher and tougher agreements. As Attakullakulla himself observed by 1770, few of these agreements focused any more on trade: "Now all our talks are about Lands." The talks invariably resulted in unfair exchanges, lands for goods. "The White People get lands that last forever," Attakullakulla saw, "but the goods given us are soon gone." Furthermore, the talks seemed to become more and more lopsided: "The white people . . . are deaf to us and will not hear."[9]

Nevertheless, the goods offered to the Cherokees proved ever more enticing as the group found themselves less and less able to disengage from a global economy of guns and exotic consumables. By 1773, Attakullakulla, ever doubtful about the benefits of violence in such situations, had signed treaties, along with other leaders, that gave away more than 10 percent of Cherokee ground.[10] In 1775, he found himself facing an even more galling proposal. Colonial judge and speculator Richard Henderson gathered five hundred Cherokee men to Sycamore Shoals to offer them up to £4,000 worth of goods in exchange for a giant swathe of their grounds (more than twice what had already been ceded). Confronted with near starvation due to their decreasing hunting area, Attakullakulla felt compelled to take the deal.[11]

The Henderson purchase triggered a split in Cherokee sentiment when revolutionary war eventually arrived in their homelands. Its magnitude had proved too awful to some of the younger Cherokees. When British loyalists came searching for Cherokee allies to help them fight off revolutionary insurgents, these younger bloods were more than happy to seize the weapons proffered. They wanted a chance to fight the "White People," and they did not care on which side of the white-on-white conflict any of them stood.[12] Attakullakulla could only stand back in dismay and watch a newly formed faction of his people go off to fight a newly formed faction of the colonists he knew so well.

The results, as Attakullakulla always feared, were catastrophic. Revolutionary settlers bore down on the Cherokee rebels in a ratio of six to one. Within three months more than two thousand Cherokees were dead. It was a heavy-hearted Attakullakulla who helped draw up the terms of surrender. In May 1777, he signed the Treaty of Dewitt's Corner with the revolutionary states of South Carolina and Georgia, and in July 1777 he signed the Treaty of Long Island with equally new and liberty-spouting North Carolina and Virginia. Each document pledged assurances that the Cherokees would not contest the sovereignty of the latest empire in their world—the United States of America.[13]

Dragging Canoe

One of the rebels who disagreed with Attakullakulla during the Henderson affair was his own son Dragging Canoe. This younger warrior, aged in his thirties at the time, had supported his elders up until this moment. But during the three-day talks, his frustration could not be suppressed. He was said to be very "displeased," explaining that the "white people wanted too much of their Hunting Grounds," and besides, it was "bloody Ground [i.e., contested by other Native groups] dark, and difficult to settle."[14] He walked out of the proceedings.

Thirteen months later, Dragging Canoe was the first to receive the party of British loyalists who came seeking Cherokee assistance. By April 1776, revolutionary war was already raging in other parts of the continent. Whether or not Dragging Canoe understood all the nuanced differences between the loyalists and patriots is unclear. What he wanted to communicate now to John Stuart, heading the visiting British contingent, was that the Cherokee "were almost surrounded by the White People [and] that they had but a small spot of ground left for them to stand upon." Dragging Canoe added that "it seemed to be the Intention of the White People to destroy them."[15]

Stuart thought he could manipulate such feelings into helping Dragging Canoe attack some of the white people in Cherokee Country (revolutionaries) but not target others (loyalists). Specifically, Stuart encouraged Dragging Canoe in his ire yet tried to restrain him until Stuart's side could assemble the right numbers to make a concerted strike on the southern states. In this risky calculation, Stuart failed miserably. One month later, a deputation of mixed Native American groups also arrived in Cherokee Country. They explained to Dragging Canoe that now was the time, while the British usurpers seemed to be fighting each other, to use European weapons to defend all Indian claims. Stuart listened horrified to this deputation's Shawnee leader expound on how "the red people who were once Masters of the whole Country hardly possessed ground enough to stand on," and how "it was plain" that the white people intended "to extirpate them." The Shawnee leader intoned that "it was better to die like men than to diminish away by inches; [and] that now is the time to begin; that there is no time to be lost."[16]

Dragging Canoe, still smarting from the Henderson debacle, was easily convinced. He recruited hundreds of young Cherokee warriors also to paint their faces black and join the motley Native crew. On July 1, 1776, their unit struck at the settlers freshly moved into Sycamore Shoals. For several weeks, the Native rebels held the upper hand, and in some justice to Stuart's horror, they attacked white people "without distinction of party."[17]

As noted, however, the revolutionary backlash was severe. With troops brought in from Virginia, Georgia, and both Carolinas, a force defeated the Native front by October. Attakullakulla was left to sign the two unforgiving peace treaties. What has been too-little noticed in this terrible moment, all the same, is a remarkable piece of intergenerational cooperation in the background. Dragging Canoe knew that one of the terms of the U.S. peace treaties would be for his elders to hand over the rebels who had attacked the revolutionary settlers. Attakullakulla knew that to do so would shatter the last vestiges of Cherokee identity as he understood it. To avoid this impossible situation, Dragging Canoe gathered up his beaten rebels and decamped from Cherokee lands forever. He founded a new subgroup one hundred miles west of their old mountain towns, along the flatlands of Chickamauga Creek. It meant that the remaining Cherokees would not be held responsible for the rebels' actions.[18]

Europeans called the new subgroup the Chickamaugas and treated them like a newly spawned tribe. Dragging Canoe's community, however, called themselves the Ani-Yunwiya—the Real People. The name was not intended as a rebuke to the elders who stayed behind. Instead, it was designed to give hope to all Cherokees: to show that while some had to experience the limitations of assimilation, others could keep the basic contours of their original lifeways alive. Within two years, the Ani-Yunwiya had constructed eleven interlinked new towns, replete with the Cherokees' seven-clan system of governance, central council house, and rules for matrilineal succession. Their resistance to the United States continued unabated. Dragging Canoe led attacks on the ever-advancing front of American citizens for another fifteen years. He died of natural causes in 1792.[19]

It was only in 1794, after every last alliance with other like-minded Native American groups had been smashed, that the Ani-Yunwiya agreed to the Treaty of the Tellico Blockhouse, an act that effectively conceded defeat to so-called republican democracy. Notably, though, it was also in that year that the Cherokee Nation first formally emerged as a recognized legal polity. Its first three leaders were warriors who had served under Dragging Canoe.[20]

Ostenaco

The final exemplary Cherokee man of this era was Ostenaco, nearer in age to Attakullakulla than to Dragging Canoe. Rather more like the son, though, Ostenaco identified through his life primarily as a warrior. By the age of twenty-five he had earned the formal title of Mankiller in his home town of Tellico. After the embargo breakdown of the 1750s, and the consequent rise of the town of Chota, Ostenaco moved to be closer to the new power base. He became the *skiagusta* of the nearby village of Tomotley in 1752.

Ostenaco's life represents a third way that Cherokees approached the incursions of the revolutionary era. He was neither a canny diplomat with Europeans like Attakullakulla, nor was he a violent resister to Europeans like Dragging Canoe. Instead, Ostenaco deployed both approaches at different times, as well as something else besides: by the end of his life he favoured a method that eschewed acknowledging Europeans altogether. He exercised what Mohawk scholar Audra Simpson has theorized as a politics of refusal.[21]

Ostenaco spent most of the 1750s accepting various commissions from colonial Virginia to help them fight off French threats. He always did so for rewards that would benefit the Cherokees as a whole. He fought in the Battle of Sandy Creek in 1756, for example, in return for a fort to protect

Cherokee women and children back home. In 1757, he helped "sort out a mess" in the Ohio Valley in exchange for guns and goods.[22] Virginian governor Robert Dinwiddie noted that Ostenaco had "the Character of a brave officer," while Colonel Washington admitted that his own units could not match Ostenaco's "Indian methods."[23]

As a periodically contracted ally of the British through this decade, then, Ostenaco was much like Attakullakulla. But during the hostage crisis of 1760 the peers parted ways. When Governor Lyttelton caused the death of the twenty-two Cherokee hostages, Ostenaco could not be calmed. "If peace was made even 7 times," he was heard to proclaim, he "would always disregard and break it."[24] Contrary to Attakullakualla's diplomatic approach in this critical moment, Ostenaco now backed the idea of violence. One month after the massacre, as British soldiers from every colony poured into Cherokee country to fight the revenge attacks, Ostenaco helped to lock up a whole garrison of a South Carolina fort. The garrison could do nothing for the next six months except slowly make their way through their rations. By August 1760, the garrison leader capitulated to Cherokee terms and agreed to walk his soldiers home, unarmed, to Charleston. Ostenaco's sense of vengeance, however, was not yet sated. He helped orchestrate an ambush of the garrison on its march. The Cherokees jumped from their positions in the forest and rained arrows down on the shocked party. Estimates vary but it is no accident that in the wash-up it was found that around twenty-two of the soldiers died—startlingly close to the number of Cherokees who Lyttelton had sacrificed.[25]

Through the land cessions of the 1760s and 1770s, Ostenaco was back by Attakullakulla's side, adding his name, dismally but he felt rightly, to the many treaties that gave away Cherokee grounds in exchange for goods and peace. Ostenaco always made decisions according to how he judged historical circumstances at hand.

On the Henderson purchase of 1775, however, his position appeared murky. In a highly unusual move, Ostenaco failed to turn up to the negotiation at all. One colonial observer noted that at this extraordinary meeting, with five hundred Cherokee male leaders, there was "only one principal man left behind." This was Ostenaco. Possibly he was just unwell or otherwise indisposed, and the observer did note that Ostenaco "sent word that what the chiefs agreed to he would abide by."[26] But his absence provides food for thought, especially in light of what happened next.

In the momentous aftermath of Dragging Canoe's 1776 campaign against revolutionary settlers, Ostenaco looked to carve out, at length, a third way of coping with incursion. His name appears on the first of the surrenders, the Treaty of Dewitt's Corner in May 1777. But it is missing from the second surrender at Long Island in July 1777. Ostenaco was certainly expected at the summer meeting that would conclude this second treaty. When revolutionary officials from North Carolina and Virginia turned up to the Holston River they found all the usual Cherokee leaders there bar one. They mentioned that "they were very sorry that [Ostenaco is] not come to the Treaty as we expected." The officials waited ten more days for this influential delegate. Eventually they decided to press on with the signing, since "there are warriors here to represent all your towns [who are] fully authorised . . . to confirm the peace."[27]

Ostenaco's absence from Long Island signaled that he was importantly present elsewhere—namely, among the Ani-Yunwiya at Chickamauga Creek. In between May and July, he had decided to abandon his elder peers and join Dragging Canoe in his efforts to preserve Cherokee culture elsewhere. He was probably the oldest among all the rebels. Critically, however, his move did not signal that he had gone completely over to Dragging Canoe's methods of resistance. Ostenaco lived among the Ani-Yunwiya but did not join their periodic raids on revolutionary settlers. At the same time, his nonviolence did not mean that he was trying to make peace via diplomacy. Ostenaco after 1777 chose to step away altogether from the Europeans' endless lures to engage. This stance confused to no end the whites who knew him. The revolutionaries who saw him as a fierce warrior could not understand his unwillingness to fight (and thus to give them a reason to enact vengeance). The loyalists who remembered him as an accomplished negotiator were befuddled by his reluctance to make new deals (which they might again manipulate in their favour). In his refusal during old age either to attack or to wrangle, Ostenaco sidestepped all the Europeans' ready labels for people like him (ignoble savage, dying Native). His suggestion to them that they were not, after all, the center of his story was the most destabilizing attitude they had ever encountered. It was a behavior so far from the expected that it failed to make headlines in colonial records at all, and consequently became obscured in later histories.

Ostenaco died some time in 1780, surrounded by loving younger Cherokees who respected how he had helped them rebuild their society even while he refused to fight their battles. His peer Attakullakulla died around the same time, back in the old Cherokee mountains, no doubt unreconciled to Ostenaco but perhaps understanding of the choices he had made.

Attakullakulla, Dragging Canoe, and Ostenaco shared the experience of living through the Age of Revolutions as Cherokee men. Their varied approaches illuminate something of the creative ways that Indigenous people did so when the odds were significantly stacked against them.

Notes

1. Much of the research for this essay comes from my book, Kate Fullagar *The Warrior, the Voyager, and the Artist: Three Lives in an Age of Empire* (New Haven, CT: Yale University Press, 2020).
2. On Attakullakulla, see Daniel Tortora, *Carolina in Crisis: Cherokees, Colonists, and Slaves in the American Southeast, 1756–1763* (Chapel Hill: University of North Carolina Press, 2015), 15–16. On women, see Theda Perdue, *Cherokee Women* (Lincoln: University of Nebraska Press, 1998), 42–43.
3. Robert Dinwiddie to Richard Pearis, August 2, 1754, in *The Official Records of Robert Dinwiddie, 1751–1758*, ed. R. A. Brock (Richmond: Virginia Historical Society, 1883), 1:267. And see also John Brown, *Old Frontiers: The Story of the Cherokee Indians* (Kingsport, TN: Southern, 1938), 56.
4. Transcript of July Meeting, 1753, in *Documents Relating to Indian Affairs*, ed. W. M. McDowell (Columbia: South Carolina Department of Archives and History, 1992), 1:433–34. Note that Attakullakulla had in fact already been to see the British king; the South Carolina colony had helped arrange this back in 1730; see Kate Fullagar, *The Savage Visit: New World People and the Imperial Popular Culture in Britain, 1710–1795* (Berkeley: University of California Press, 2012), chap. 3.
5. Washington cited in Tortora, *Carolina in Crisis*, 45. See also Paul Kelton, "The British and Indian War: Cherokee Power and the Fate of Empire in North America," *William and Mary Quarterly*, 3rd series, 69, no. 4 (2012): 763–92.
6. William Richardson, Diary (1758–59), transcribed in S. C. Williams, "An Account of a Presbyterian Mission to the Cherokees, 1757–1759," *Tennessee Historical Magazine* 1, no. 2 (1931): 125–38.
7. Alexander Miln to William Lyttelton, February 24, 1760, in McDowell, ed., *Documents Relating to Indian Affairs*, 2:498–500. See also my extended account in Fullagar, *The Warrior, the Voyager, and the Artist*, 34–38.
8. See Tortora, *Carolina in Crisis*, 138.
9. Attakullakulla cited in "A General Meeting of the Principal Chiefs and Warriors of the Cherokee Nation," Lochaber, October 18, 1770, Colonial

Office (hereafter CO) 5/72, National Archives, Kew, United Kingdom (hereafter NA, UK).
10. See cessions accounts in John Stuart to Lord Hillsborough, June 12, 1772, CO 5/73; Stuart Letters, June 16–August 24, 1773, CO 5/74; Lord Dartmouth to Charles Wright, June 10, 1773, CO 5/662, NA, UK.
11. See *Calendar of Virginia State Papers*, ed. W. M. P. Palmer (Richmond, VA: Walker, 1875), 1:283, 284–85, 291. For a neat account, see also Claudio Saunt, *West of the Revolution: An Uncommon History of 1776* (New York: Norton, 2014), 17–23.
12. Henry Stuart to John Stuart, August 25, 1776, CO 5/77, NA, UK.
13. See Fullagar, *The Warrior, the Voyager, and the Artist*, 124–25.
14. *Calendar of Virginia State Papers*, 1:283, 291.
15. Henry Stuart to John Stuart, August 25, 1776, CO 5/77, NA, UK.
16. Henry Stuart to John Stuart, August 25, 1776, CO 5/77, NA, UK.
17. Cited in Jim Piecuch, *Three Peoples, One King: Loyalists, Indians, and Slaves in the Revolutionary South, 1775–1782* (Columbia: University of South Carolina Press, 2008), 71–72.
18. There is little focused discussion of this group, but see Tyler Boulware, *Deconstructing the Cherokee Nation: Town, Region, and Nation among the Eighteenth-Century Cherokees* (Gainesville: University of Florida Press, 2011), 166–76, and Gregory Evans Dowd, *A Spirited Resistance: The North American Indian Struggle for Unity, 1745–1815* (Baltimore: Johns Hopkins University Press, 1992), 47–57.
19. Boulware, *Deconstructing the Cherokee Nation*, 166–76; Dowd, *A Spirited Resistance*, 47–57. And see Tom Hatley, *The Dividing Path: Cherokees and South Carolinians through the Revolutionary Era* (New York: Oxford University Press, 1995), 225.
20. Dowd, *A Spirited Resistance*, 55, 160.
21. Audra Simpson, *Mohawk Interruptus: Political Life across the Borders of Settler States* (Durham, NC: Duke University Press, 2014), chap. 4.
22. For these two battles, see Fullagar, *The Warrior, the Voyager, and the Artist*, 33–34.
23. Robert Dinwiddie to Richard Pearis, December 15, 1755; George Washington to Dinwiddie, January 1756, in Brock, ed., *Official Records of Robert Dinwiddie*, 2:296–97, 315–16, 322.
24. *South Carolina Gazette* (Charleston), June 21, 1760.
25. See Boulware, *Deconstructing the Cherokee*, 123, and Fullagar, *The Warrior, the Voyager, and the Artist*, 36–38.
26. *Calendar of Virginia State Papers*, 1:291.
27. See a transcript in Alexander Henderson, "The Treaty of Long Island of Holston, July 1777," *North Carolina Historical Review* 8, no. 1 (1931): 74.

French Imperial Failures in Siam and Persia

ASIAN REVOLUTIONS IN THE AGE OF REVOLUTIONS

JUNKO THÉRÈSE TAKEDA

FIFTY MILES UP Chao Phraya or the River of Kings from Bangkok lies a vast collection of ruined buildings. Now turned into a UNESCO World Heritage Center, the city of Ayutthaya, the former capital of Siam, has become a popular destination for tourists renting tuk-tuks and snapping selfies. On Chao Phraya's southeastern bank, across the river from the Portuguese enclave, stands a museum and Japanese garden commemorating the former location of Nihonjin-mura, a Japanese village known in Thai as Ban Yipun. Over a thousand Japanese Catholics, samurai, merchants, and mercenaries made their home there in the seventeenth century after the Tokugawa Shogunate prohibited Christianity and implemented its Sakoku policies. Forty miles upstream along the Lopburi tributary, near King Narai the Great's palace, stands the ruined remains of a stately European-style complex. It housed an ambassador's mansion, Catholic chapel, bell tower, and apartments. This compound is said to have been ordered built by Narai's Greek advisor Constantine Phaulkon, for French King Louis XIV's envoy to Ayutthaya, the Chevalier de Chaumont, in 1685. It subsequently became home to Phaulkon and his Catholic multiethnic Japanese, Indo-Portuguese wife, Maria Yamada Guimar de Pinha, known to the French as Madame Constance and to the Siamese as Thao Thong Kip Ma.

Narai's Siamese kingdom in Southeast Asia has not traditionally appeared in textbooks and lectures about the Age of Revolutions. But perhaps it should. Because in the summer of 1688, as Prince William of Orange planned to invade England to prevent it from becoming a Catholic nation under James II, another anti-Catholic revolution in this Siamese city brought down Narai. James lost the throne to William and Mary just months after Phra Phetracha, Narai's commander of the Elephant Corps, killed the king's family, executed the pro-French Phaulkon, and left Narai to die in detention. England's "Glorious Revolution" has been taught and credited in history classes across the United States for creating a constitutional monarchy, transferring sovereignty to Parliament, and strengthening the lexicon of representative democracy central to the larger narrative of the Age of Revolutions in the Western world. But "the Revolution in Siam" from the same year, which invigorated an anticolonial nationalist current that held strong for centuries, barely receives a mention, if at all. In fact, Asia as a whole tends to remain largely absent in Western, and especially French, historians' current understanding of the Age of Revolutions.

This essay interrogates our Atlantic-centric model of understanding seventeenth- and eighteenth-century political ruptures, and considers how a global Age of Revolutions—from the perspective of French and Francophone history—looks different when we write in Asian empires. Late seventeenth- and eighteenth-century French writers were very attentive to the political earthquakes that they termed "revolutions" occurring contemporaneously across the Asian continent. Siam's was not the only one to attract French curiosity. Nor has it been the only one historians have written out of the canon of revolutions in the Age of Revolutions. Montesquieu noted in *De l'esprit des lois* that China "experienced twenty-two general revolutions [and] infinite particular ones" while southern Asia "continually suffer[ed] very great revolutions."[1] Chinese peasant rebellions, the Manchu conquest, and famine ended Ming rule by 1644. In South Asia, Mughal emperor Aurangzeb began his reign in 1658 with a war of succession that wrested power from Jahan. French observers in the Ottoman Empire characterized dethronements and janissary revolts in 1703 and 1730 as "revolutions."[2] And in Persia, silver drainage, famine, and plague epidemics triggered Mahmud Hotak's Afghan invasion of Isfahan in 1721, the collapse of the Safavid dynasty in 1722, and the rise of Nader Shah Afshar across the 1730s and 1740s. French writers discussed these and other political, social, and imperial perturbances across Asia not in terms of a "fall of gunpowder empires," as historians would qualify them later, but instead as "revolutions."

The following pages foreground some of these "revolutions" less discussed among French historians in an effort to highlight how deeply Asian political ruptures were intertwined with French interventionist projects, proxy wars, and the development of French revolutionary thinking across the long eighteenth century. French ideas about revolutions developed in the context of global competition for access to sea lanes, commodities, and cheap or unpaid forced labor. French activities in Asia were inextricably linked to maintaining or compensating for the Crown's fortunes in the Atlantic and Caribbean worlds. The desire to disrupt first Iberian then English and Dutch trade, arms deals, and military movements prompted French forays across the Mediterranean and Indian Ocean as it did across the Atlantic.

The repertoire of French ideas about revolutions materialized in an interconnected and global world where hostile fiscal military states and empires competed to support an unprecedented rise in global trade in an age of increasing conspicuous consumption.[3] These processes held grave consequences not only for the French *ancien régime* but for Asian empires as well. If we uncouple our understanding of revolutions from the so-called advent of Western democracies and concepts of liberty and rights, and instead see them informed as much by violent contests over imperial power, sea lanes, patronage networks, and market access, we can recognize some deep resonances between Atlantic revolutions and other episodes of violence that erupted halfway around the world. And we can also acknowledge that these revolutions, while offering new ways of expressing and claiming belonging and inclusion for some, in fact inaugurated the loss of independence and political representation for many others.[4]

The revolution that overthrew King Narai of Ayutthaya was an anti-French revolution. Piggy-backing on activities led by the Missions Étrangères de Paris, which sent missionaries in 1662 to found a seminary, minister to Japanese Catholic exiles, and evangelize to the multiethnic population in Ayutthaya, Louis XIV and his controller-general Jean-Baptiste Colbert supported the new Compagnie des Indes' first trading mission to Siam in 1680. Louis pursued multiple projects in Siam to amplify France's reach against his European competitors who had beaten him to South and Southeast Asia. He did so by taking advantage of Narai's pro-French stance developed by Constantine Phaulkon to diminish English and Dutch influence around his kingdom. After the Chevalier de Chaumont's and the Abbé de Choisy's 1685 French embassy to Siam, Kosa Pan brought his embassy from Ayutthaya to Versailles the following year. Subsequently, extraordinary envoy Simon de La Loubère led several Jesuits and General Desfarges's expeditionary force of six hundred soldiers and engineers in a mission to Siam in 1687. They went armed with Secretary of State for the Navy Jean-Baptiste Colbert de Seignelay's secret orders to establish French fortresses and take the ports of Bangkok and Mergui (now Myeik). Their arrival aroused fear among some in Narai's court that the king would convert to Catholicism and allow the French to suppress Buddhism and Siamese political autonomy. These worries prompted Phra Phetracha to take advantage of the old king's failing health, depose him, and order forty thousand troops to besiege the French at Bangkok. Following Phra Phetracha's assassination of the royal family and of Phaulkon, Phaulkon's widow, Madame Constance, who had been promised Louis's protection as a naturalized French subject, sought sanctuary with the French forces.[5] General Desfarges stole her jewels and sent her away. Within four months, he and the French scattered. Phra Phetracha ruled Ayutthaya until his death in 1703.[6] His coup and reign introduced a century of Siamese instability capped by the eventual destruction of Ayutthaya by the Burmese invasion of 1767.

Was the Siamese Revolution of 1688 a revolution? It was according to French contemporaries. "History provides us with few examples of revolutions more tragic than that which occurred in the Kingdom of Siam," Jesuit Marcel de Blanc, one of the French trapped in Bangkok during its siege, wrote in *Histoire de la Révolution de Siam,* published in 1692.[7] François Martin, director of the Compagnie des Indes and governor of Pondicherry, also described the "revolutions he learned about at Siam which are known and public facts" in his *Mémoires*. They were, he argued, the result of Phra Phetracha's "hatred of seeing a foreigner at the head of affairs [Phaulkon] and the French in principal posts." The Siamese, he conceded, despite their reputation for "perfidy and cruelty" as "barbarians and savages," are "intelligent in their treaties, their interests and their government policies in that they do not yield to the nations of Europe."[8] French memoirists—missionaries, architects, and soldiers who witnessed or survived the 1688 siege of their fort at Bangkok—agreed that Phetracha's resistance to French rule lay at the heart of the revolution. And that was the news pitched in the *Mercure Galant* for reading audiences back in France. This "evil" revolution, its December 1689 issue described, saw Phetracha, "the Usurper, proclaimed King, promising the restoration of liberty and the Siamese religion, after which he only thought of routing the French from Bangkok."[9]

These writers described the Siamese revolution in ways consistent with definitions of the term "revolution" at the time. As Keith Baker has shown, "revolution" evolved in France from a word initially used to describe astronomical planetary motion to one used to discuss unfortunate political upheavals.[10] Such usages appeared contemporaneously, for example, in Jean Chardin's and Jean-Baptiste Tavernier's descriptions of "revolutions" shrinking Persia's borders while "despotic governments" deteriorated the empire across the latter half of the seventeenth century. Their assessments were echoed nearly thirty years later, as French consul Etienne Padery noted in 1720 that "we have never seen revolutions so great in Persia as those today."[11] In France, the *Mercure*'s publications between 1722 and 1723 reported on Afghan, Turkish, and Russian invasions related to the fall of the Safavids by coupling "revolutions" with "tyranny," "disorder," and "misfortunes."[12]

Persia's eighteenth-century "revolutions" seen through French eyes, as with Siam's, provide more examples of how French imperial ambitions became entangled with political ruptures, invasions, and conquests across the Caucasus, Eurasia, and the Indian Ocean. As in Ayutthaya, these Persian "revolutions" involved violent dynastic overthrows. French interventionist projects, while not the intended target of the invading Afghans, Ottomans, and Russians in Persia the way they had been for Phra Phetracha in Siam, were nonetheless deeply imbricated with these developments. Following Pierre Victor Michel's first official French embassy under Louis XIV to Shah Soltan Hosayn in 1708, Mohammed Reza Beg arrived at Versailles with his delegation in 1715 to secure a secret weapons and ships deal. The idea for such an agreement dated back to the arrival of some French Catholics dispatched from the Missions Étrangères de Paris at the same time others from the same generational cohort were sent to Siam. Plans for the French to provide ammunitions and naval services to help the Safavids push back the Omani Ya'rubi imams of Muscat in exchange for direct trade privileges constituted one of the shah's last attempts to secure his fragile southern border prior to his dynasty's collapse. And it was, as in Siam, a strategy that the Bourbon monarchy used to override English and Dutch deals already in place.[13]

The Safavid's collapse and the years of political turmoil that followed made Persia an inhospitable environment for sustained diplomatic or commercial engagement with France. But missionaries and merchants embedded in Persia, and armchair philosophers in France, remained attuned to Persian politics. When more positive interpretations of revolutions tied to political and national regeneration began circulating across the mid-eighteenth century, they gravitated toward the figure of Nader Shah, the famous conqueror who led military campaigns against the Ottomans, took back the Caucasus, invaded India, and sacked Delhi while ruling Persia from 1736 to 1747. Some depicted him as a revolutionary who restored a fractured empire. The November 1731 issue of the *Mercure de France* introduced him as a "warrior savior." Excusing his violent conquest of India, authors pitted his masculine power against the effeminacy that Europeans typically ascribed to "oriental despots." Others suggested that he embodied the virtues of republicanism. The brother of French consul Ange de Gardane in Isfahan described Nader's inspirational ascent, chronicling how the humble herdsman became "the restorer of Persia."[14] In *Histoire de Thamas Kouli-Kan, roi de Perse* (1743), André de Claustre, the abbé de Cerceau, described him as a general who "remedied disorders," "relieved poor families," and "judged complaints against governors." Lauding his democratic tendencies, he noted how Nader declined the throne until he "convoked the Estates General" to "freely elect" him king.[15] Authors like Louis, Chevalier de Jaucourt, who qualified Nader as a "usurper" in the *Encyclopédie* still admired the "ambition, courage and activity" of "this extraordinary man."[16]

Writings about Asia and its many revolutions did more than satisfy French orientalist curiosity. They were embedded into foreign policy discussions about interventionist strategies that the Bourbons, French revolutionaries, and ultimately Napoleon Bonaparte could develop around the Levant, North Africa, and western Asia. Particularly after the decisive loss of the French-backed Mirza Muhammad Siraj un-Daulah, nawab of Bengal, to the British at the Battle of Plassey (1757) and the signing of the Treaty of Paris (1763) shortly thereafter, Louis XV's foreign minister Étienne François, the Duc de Choiseul, and secretary of state for the navy César Gabriel de Choiseul, the Duc de Praslin, sought to weaken British influence by instigating proxy Ottoman wars against Russia, considering a conquest of Egypt, and approaching the Zand and Qajar successors of Nader Shah to deliberate over a Franco-Persian invasion of India. The last of these, the idea for a joint Franco-Persian invasion of the Asian subcontinent, was the lifelong project of Jean-François Rousseau, a cousin of the philosopher Jean-Jacques Rousseau born in Isfahan in 1738. Choiseul dispatched Jean-François, then France's trade commissioner in

Baghdad, to Shah Karim Khan Zand in 1768 to boost trade in the Persian Gulf. While neither Louis XV, Louis XVI, nor the Persian Zands had the bandwidth to support an amphibious attack against the British in India, Rousseau's plans piqued the interests of both Napoleon and Persia's Qajar Shah Fath-Ali. Repackaged as a joint Franco-Persian revolution against British rule in India, the plans looked like they might finally materialize at the turn of the nineteenth century. Fantasizing about becoming emperor in Asia, Napoleon corresponded with Fath-Ali, promising aid against Russia and ships in the Indian Ocean in exchange for a Persian-led land assault on the subcontinent. As Napoleon imagined it, his and Fath-Ali's conquest of India, which would unite the "Orient's courage and genius" and Western "military arts and discipline," represented the culmination of both Nader's and France's revolutions.[17] Jean-François Rousseau and his son Joseph submitted a *Tableau général de la Perse* to Talleyrand, outlining plans for French marines to march on Delhi with Persians, Afghans, and Sikhs.[18] The "liberation" of India from British "despotism" would allow Napoleon and his Persian ally to surpass Nader as warrior-revolutionaries of the century.[19]

The Franco-Persian revolution never materialized. After signing the Franco-Persian Treaty of Finckenstein in 1807, Napoleon focused on Eastern Europe and abandoned Fath-Ali. Nonetheless, this abortive revolution offers scholars some historical lessons. Political observations from Isfahan and Baghdad imparted to literary audiences and career bureaucrats in Paris and Versailles the logic of conjoining revolutionary regeneration and imperial expansion. Policymakers recognized that Persia's domestic turmoil and Nader's conquest of India, which they branded as "revolutions," molded a favorable environment for French diplomats and merchants to cut their imperial teeth and stage their own revolution against the British. In the end, it was the British, rather than the French, who were able to capitalize off of them. Nader's "revolution" and conquest of India prepared the ground for European empire-building in the subcontinent.

Both Siam's anti-French revolution and Napoleon and Fath-Ali's Franco-Persian revolution constituted embarrassments for France. The Battle of Bangkok that ended in the expulsion of the French from Siam, and the siege of Delhi that Napoleon never realized bookend over a century of losses, defeats, and miscarriages that highlight France's comparatively weak footprints in Asia. Together, these failures have perhaps suggested to historians of France that there are few stories about eighteenth-century politics, empire-building, or revolution to tell by looking eastward to Asia. Studies of Siam have thus focused largely on cultural exchanges—diplomatic ceremonials and material transfers—between the courts of Versailles and Ayutthaya.[20] Analyses of French observations of Persia have traditionally been framed in terms of literary orientalism or visual culture, and likewise not placed within broader discussions about imperial competition or global trade.

But as I have written elsewhere, failures are great windows into exploring the dynamics of French statecraft and early empire across the global Age of Revolutions.[21] Turning our attention to Siam or Persia and the commercial and military engagements that French administrators, military, diplomats, merchants, and mercenaries pursued therein can allow us to see the importance of Asian geopolitics and political ruptures to the development of France's revolutionary lexicon. If scholars agree for the need to provincialize the "West" in our analyses of this age, one way to do so is by recognizing the roles that Eurasia, South, and Southeast Asia played in the seismic political shifts that occurred across the long eighteenth century, as well as their importance to premodern French statecraft, empire-building, and trade. Such studies would require us to relinquish the kinds of stereotypes about the incompatibility between Asia and democratic, revolutionary experiments that scholars of early modern France have inherited from eighteenth- and nineteenth-century European writers.[22] If we fully abandon their notion that declension, "oriental despotism," Islam, Buddhism, or Hinduism positioned Asia against "Western" individualism, equality, or liberty, we can dismantle Euro- and Atlantic-centric formulations of the so-called advent of modernity. And fight the invisibility and erasure of Asian empires and populations in our historical considerations of revolution.

Notes

1. Montesquieu, "Fatale consequence du luxe à la Chine," *De l'esprit des lois* (Paris: Firmin Didot, 1862), book 7, chap. 7, p. 126.
2. Baron de Tott, *The Memoirs of Baron de Tott Containing the State of the Turkish Empire and the Crimea, during the Late War with Russia* (London: G. G. J. and J. Robinson, 1786), 34.
3. For more on the need to integrate studies of the consumer revolution with analyses of French overseas trade, politics, and imperial competition,

see Michael Kwass, *Contraband: Louis Mandrin and the Making of a Global Underground* (Cambridge, MA: Harvard University Press, 2014), introduction.
4. Kathleen Duval, *Independence Lost: Lives on the Edge of the American Revolution* (New York: Random House, 2015), xxi.
5. Over a decade later, after spending years as a kitchen slave for Phra Phetracha, Madame Constance successfully sued the Compagnie des Indes for 300,000 livres in loans and damages that it had never compensated her late husband. But she did not receive the bulk of that awarded money. For the lawsuit, see "Affaire de Constance Phaulkon," C1 26, Archives Nationales d'Outre Mer, Aix-en-Provence, France. For belated letters of naturalization extended to Phaulkon and his sons by Louis XIV, see *Mercure Galant*, December 1, 1689, 49–54.
6. Michael Smithies, *Mission Made Impossible: The Second French Embassy to Siam, 1687* (Bangkok: Silkworm, 2002).
7. Marcel de Blanc, *Histoire de la Révolution de Siam arrive en l'année 1688* (Lyon: Horace Molin, 1692), http://memoires-de-siam.net/revolution/pereleblanc/pereleblanc01.html.
8. François Martin, *Mémoires de François Martin, Fondateur de Pondichéry*, ed. A. Martineau (Paris: Société de l'Histoire des Colonies Françaises, 1932), http://memoires-de-siam.net/revolution/martin/martin01.html.
9. *Mercure Galant*, December 1, 1689, 39.
10. Keith Baker, "Revolution," in *The French Revolution and the Creation of Modern Political Culture*, ed. Colin Lucas (Oxford: Pergamon, 1988), 2:41–62.
11. Padery, April 15, 1720, CP Perse 5.91, ff. 270–71v; Padery, October 31, 1720, CP 5.105, f. 316, Centre des Archives Diplomatiques du Ministère des Affaires Étrangères, La Courneuve, France (hereafter ADMAE).
12. "Nouvelles étrangères," *Le Mercure de septembre 1722* (Paris: Renaudot, 1723), 159–60; *Le Mercure de juillet 1723* (Paris: Cavelier, Ribou, Cailleau, 1723), 149–50.
13. For more, see Junko Thérèse Takeda, *Iran and a French Empire of Trade, 1700–1808: The Other Persian Letters* (Liverpool: Liverpool University Press, 2020), 91–130.
14. Gardane at Isfahan, March 8, 1730, CP Perse 7.21, ff. 99–100; CP Perse 7.35, ff. 129–31, July 16, 1736, ADMAE. See also Junko Thérèse Takeda, "Persian Wars, the French Republic of Letters, and the Global Age of Revolutions," in Takeda, *Iran and a French Empire of Trade*, 131–68, for a longer discussion of French perceptions of Nader Shah.
15. André de Claustre, *Histoire de Thamas Kouli-Kan, roi de Perse* (Paris: Briasson, 1743), 19, 92, 280–81, 362–63.
16. Chevalier de Jaucourt, "L'empire de Perse," in Denis Diderot and Jean D'Alembert, *Encyclopédie*, ed. Robert Morrissey and Glenn Roe, ARTFL

Encyclopédie Project, Autumn 2022 edition, https://artflsrv04.uchicago.edu/philologic4.7/encyclopedie0922/navigate/12/1637?byte=4354739. See also Takeda, *Iran and a French Empire of Trade,* 153–59.
17. "Bonaparte empereur des Français à Fathali sha emperor des persans," March 1805, CP Perse 8.83, ADMAE.
18. Jean-François Rousseau to Talleyrand, May 1, 1806, CP Perse 9.26, ff. 50–52v, ADMAE.
19. Jean-François Rousseau to Talleyrand, 28 vendémaire an 12, CP Perse 8.64, ff. 182–89v; Rousseau to Talleyrand, 25 ventose an 13, CP Perse 8.89, f.236, ADMAE; Takeda, *Iran and a French Empire of Trade,* 194–201.
20. For some recent works on Siam and cultural representations, see especially Meredith Martin, "Mirror Reflections: Louis XIV, Phra Narai, and the Material Culture of Kingship," *Art History* 38, no 4 (September 2015): 652–67; Ashley Bruckbauer, "Ambassadors and Missionaries, Converts and Infidels: Visualizing the 1686 Siamese Embassy to Versailles," *Journal of the Western Society for French History* 43 (2015): 12–39; and David Irving, "Lully in Siam: Music and Diplomacy in French-Siamese Cultural Exchanges, 1680–1690," *Early Music* 11, no. 3 (2012): 393–420.
21. See Takeda, introduction, in *Iran and a French Empire of Trade.*
22. Ian Coller, *Muslims and Citizens: Islam, Politics, and the French Revolution* (New Haven: Yale University Press, 2020), 4, 240.

Why Haiti Should Be at the Center of the Age of Revolutions

Laurent Dubois

Here is the challenge: to write a history of modern political thought and culture that can simultaneously—and equally—embody and communicate the perspectives of those who arrived in Virginia in the hold the slave ship *São João Bautista,* of Thomas Jefferson and Sally Hemings, of Jean-Jacques Dessalines and Napoleon Bonaparte, of Andrew Jackson and Harriet Tubman. While such a project might seem quixotic, we have to try. That is the political history that we will need in order to construct a future politics that moves beyond the legacies of racial slavery, rather than perpetually dwelling with them. The field of "Atlantic History," which has expanded dramatically in the past decades, is what will enable us to do it.

That the United States was born of a history of conquest and settlement which brought people from Europe and Africa across the Atlantic is, of course, an unavoidable part of the nation's history. More broadly, this is the story of all the Americas, though the particular ways in which European, African, and Native American peoples became intertwined in the process varies greatly from place to place. The questions posed by Atlantic History are about how to tell that story. Who do we place at the center of this history? What categories of analysis should we use, and what social, economic, and institutional structures should we focus on?

It makes good sense that a body of water has become the basis for a questioning of some of our broadest and most cherished historical narratives. Until the invention of the railroad, water was the most important vehicle for movement—of people, goods, rumors, songs, ideas. The world was connected by ports, and in many ways ports came to resemble each other. But if it was a connected world, it was also one in which experiences and perspectives were widely divergent. From whose perspective should we try and reconstruct what the Atlantic world actually looked like?

At the basis of every work of history is a question of positioning. This is also, on some level, an ethical question. Whose history are you telling? And from whose perspective? As the Haitian thinker Jean Casimir likes to put it, when you write the story of Columbus arriving in what the Indigenous people then called Ayiti, you have to make a decision: are you on the boat or on the shore?[1]

Traditionally, the history of the Americas was written largely from perspective of Europeans, the conquerors and settlers. It was their writings, their archives that sustained the history, and in a broader sense European epistemologies and ideologies that undergirded the very sense of what constituted history. In the past decades, historians have struggled to reverse this pattern, telling histories grounded in the perspectives and experiences of Native Americans as well as the Africans and African Americans who were enslaved in the Americas.

There is a dream at the center of a lot of historical work that we can find a balance among all these perspectives—that we can, in fact, be both on the boat and on the shore at the same time, or perhaps floating above, taking notes with equanimity. But while that is at least useful as an aspiration, it is never really that simple. The view from the shore and the view from the boat imply so much else, from the ability to see and understand certain things, to the language spoken and how it is understood. The two perspectives involve deep questions: how does each group think of human history, and their place in it, at the moment of encounter? Casimir, then, is probably right that there are fundamental choices to be made. And while there are few moments in history where the potential for divergent perspectives is quite as radical as it is at the moment of conquest, any historical moment is defined by the differences in perspective—themselves historically constituted—carried by different participants.

That is notably true when we think about how to write the history of slavery, and more particularly of the enslaved themselves and how they experienced, viewed, and at times rebelled against the institution. The Atlantic was the site of one of the most dramatic movements of people in human history: the slave trade, which brought at least 12 million Africans to the Americas between the sixteenth and the nineteenth centuries. The history of the slave ship is at the center of Atlantic history.

About 45 percent of the Africans brought to the Americas came to the Caribbean, a region that has been one of the most generative in terms of both theory and practice surrounding the problem of writing history. The region's intellectuals, writers, visual artists, and musicians have long grappled in particularly rich ways with the question of how to narrate and confront the history of Indigenous genocide, European colonialism, the slave trade, and the plantation, and the rich and layered cultural history that emerged out of this interaction of global and local forces. Historians like C. L. R. James and Eric Williams, whose work has been pivotal in the development of Atlantic history, were part of this broader cultural and intellectual matrix. In the decades since other thinkers—notably the Haitian anthropologist Michel-Rolph Trouillot—have been at the center of discussions about how we write modern history from a perspective rooted in the Caribbean. And at the center of much of this thinking about history and politics in the Caribbean has been one of the most interesting epics in modern history: the Haitian Revolution.[2]

The Haitian Revolution as an Atlantic Revolution

Stretching from 1791 to 1804, the Haitian Revolution was both a local and a global event, a true world-historical moment in ways that are increasingly acknowledged today. One useful way for us to think about the Haitian Revolution is as the most radical (and therefore one of the most important) assertions of the *right to have rights* in human history. Even more so than the American and French Revolutions, with which it was intertwined, the Haitian Revolution posed a set of absolutely central political questions. It did so in a way that was illegible to many and forcibly repressed by others. But any true analysis of modern political history, not only of Haiti but of the world, has to grapple with the implications of this revolution for core concepts surrounding modern politics.[3]

The French colony of Saint-Domingue, the pinnacle of the Atlantic slave system and the richest of the plantation colonies of the Americas, was based on a radical refusal of sovereignty to the majority. Ninety percent of the population of the colony was enslaved—more than half of them African-born, many of them recent arrivals in the colony at the time of the beginning of the revolution in 1791—and were not considered legal or political subjects in any sense. They were chattel property who, through a carefully institutionalized system of laws combined with forms of violent repression, were refused any possibility for self-autonomy. Nevertheless, they carved out spaces of autonomy within the plantation, by cultivating small plots of land and bringing products to market. They also created spaces of cultural and intellectual freedom, crafting political visions that would ultimately find voice in the revolution.

The plantation order was based on racial ideologies that emerged out of and were buttressed by the Atlantic slave system. At the core of these ideologies was a kind of dialectic that enabled the simultaneous celebration of a capacity for free action and sovereignty on the part of certain groups while denying that same capacity to others. The colony's system of racial thinking was based on a set of arguments about the fundamental incapacity of a group that was defined by its skin color to successfully exercise sovereignty over itself. As such, the slave plantation system in Saint-Domingue and elsewhere was one of the most successful mechanisms for the mass denial of human rights in the history of the modern world.

Starting with the 1791 slave insurrection, it is therefore not surprising that those who set about courageously, brilliantly, and systematically destroying this system crafted particularly powerful assertions of human rights. Haiti, not the United States or France, was where the assertion of true universal values reached its defining climax during the Age of Revolutions. Enslaved people who were considered chattel rather than human beings successfully insisted that they had the right to be free and, second, that they had the right to govern themselves according to a new set of principles. Their actions were a signal and a transformative moment in the political history of the world. The Haitian revolutionaries propelled the Enlightenment principles of universalism forward in unexpected ways by insisting on the self-evident—but then largely denied—principle that no one should be a slave. And they did so at the very heart of the world's economic system, turning the most profitable colony in the world into an independent nation founded on the refusal of the system of slavery that dominated all the societies that surrounded it in the Americas.

But crafting an intellectual history of the Haitian Revolution provides a striking challenge, for the vast majority of its key actors did not leave written traces of their political philosophy. That, of course, does not mean they did not have one. It just means that they did not articulate it through writing. In this they were in fact not all that different than the vast majority of actors in the American or French Revolutions, who also depended on conversation and oral transmission of information to shape their thoughts and actions.

Print media was not absent from the Haitian Revolution, but it definitely played a smaller role than it did in the American and French

Revolutions, where the explosion of print was key to the revolutions themselves. Historians of the American and French Revolutions have often depended and focused on the role of print media. But because of the very different circumstances of the Haitian Revolution, namely the fact that slavery itself had prevented most of the event's key actors from gaining access to literacy, we have to use a different method. And in the process, we gain not just insight about the Haitian Revolution but perhaps also new ways of looking at the history of politics more broadly.

Historians depend on texts to do their work. Although historians are increasingly incorporating other materials into their analysis, archives remain largely textual. This can lead to a kind of distortion: because we use texts to access the past, we can sometimes overestimate the centrality of those particular texts within that past. But, as when we study something like the Haitian Revolution, we need to constantly remind ourselves that these texts are mostly traces of a much larger set of conversations that did not take place through writing but rather through speaking, organizing, and debating in the midst of military and political action.

What makes the case of the Haitian Revolution particularly intriguing is that the majority of the people involved were not just enslaved but African-born. They were survivors of the Middle Passage, and they had grown up in a wide range of African societies with their own traditions of political thought. They had, in their minds, examples of different institutions, ways of debating, models of leadership and rule, and cultural and social organizations. In fact, for many of them such reference points would have been far more important than the experiences of slavery and the plantation. In the years before the Haitian Revolution, about 40,000 people were brought to the colony each year on slave ships. That means that at the time of the revolution, as many as 100,000 people or more (out of a slave population of perhaps 500,000) had been in the colony for just a few years.

Most of these recent arrivals, and in fact the majority among the enslaved, were Central African. That means that, as historians John Thornton and more recently Christina Mobley have argued, to write the political history of the Haitian Revolution is necessarily to study and write Central African political history. This represents a profound reorientation: the central organizing principle for most of the writing of the Haitian Revolution, from C. L. R. James on, has been about the relationship between the French and Haitian Revolutions, a reflection on the ways in which that particular set of Atlantic connections became the vector for change and transformation.[4]

The research of scholars like Thornton and Mobley raises many issues about how we can know and interpret the Central African context that so profoundly shaped Haitian history. The diversity and complexity of the region, and the limits of written sources, mean that researchers have to deploy a range of approaches—including wide-ranging archival research, historical linguistics, oral history, and archaeology—to reconstruct the social and political contexts of the region in the seventeenth and eighteenth centuries. There are intense debates, notably around the question of religion: Catholicism was present in the region and embraced by the leaders of the kingdom of Kongo, starting in the sixteenth century, which means that many enslaved people crossing the Atlantic practiced the religion. But Kongolese Catholicism took shape on its own terms, with a complex theology and practice rooted in and connected to local religious and cultural practices.

Figuring out precisely where in the region captives came from before being shipped to Haiti, furthermore, is extremely complicated: registers of slave ships most often indicate ports of embarkation, and sources that do indicate regional or ethnic origins for Africans have to be interpreted with care. We know a great deal, but there is still so much more to learn and discover about these questions. What the remarkable research in this area shows, though, is that to write Haitian history is also to write African history. The opposite, interestingly, is likewise true: the sources of Haitian—and more broadly Caribbean and Afro-Atlantic—history can help us understand African history of the period in new ways.

Historians are still working on understanding the relationship among the Haitian Revolution, Europe, and Africa. How do politics travel? Who creates political ideas? How do they transform into action and institutions? Trying to answer these questions means confronting a knot of issues: reconstructing ideas about and experiences of gender and sexuality in Africa, Europe, and the Caribbean. It also means finding ways to narrate the question of rape and sexual violence while reconstructing the history of reproduction of enslaved people: pregnancy, childbirth, child-rearing. A fuller understanding of the practices of family and community structure is imperative to narrating the political history of slavery and emancipation.

Because gendered ideas have constructed society, they have also shaped the archives. Usually, the archives give us only a fragment of people's lives, so it is important to understand what influences those fragments. In the case of the Haitian Revolution, women participated in military combat and political debate, and led the way to changing labor practices on plantations following emancipation. Women insisted on time and autonomy for themselves, and constructed forms of land tenure, religious life, and family organization to try to move beyond the experience of slavery. There are now exemplary new histories that reconstruct the experiences of enslaved women, like the early chapters in Rebecca J. Scott and Jean Hébrard's *Freedom Papers*. This work expands our understanding of the period and pushes people us to rethink history-telling and its possibilities.[5]

What Is "Atlantic History"?

The example of the scholarship on the Haitian Revolution is just one part of a more "Atlantic" history. What "Atlantic History" actually means, however, depends a great deal on the speaker or historian. Sometimes the term is so vague that it veers toward the meaningless. This problem is not limited to the term "Atlantic." Ask a group of historians at a bar what "Europe" or "Africa" are, and you should be ready to pay for many rounds of drinks and wake up the next morning with a hangover and no clear answer. Are they geographical or political designations? When did people begin to use the terms in question, and what did they mean when they did so? What should be the relationship between categories people used during a given historical period and those categories contemporary historians might use to describe that period?

Still, the politics surrounding calling something "Atlantic" history have a particular valence. Atlantic History tackles a critical question: what is the "West"? The question is, as it has long been, an urgent one. There are few concepts that have been as historically consequential on a global scale. Of course, this term is never really on its own: it exists as part of a concatenation of terms and ideas about race and culture, geography, and the history of ideas.

The geography of Atlantic History approaches relationships among Europe, Africa, and the Americas. Its chronology stretches from the late fifteenth century through the nineteenth century. Its fundamental ethos is to avoid teleological narratives that read nationalist histories back into the colonial period. As a colleague of mine at Michigan State University, Christine Daniels, used to put it when we taught together, we have to get away from the idea that as soon as settlers arrived from England, they began looking at their watches and saying, "I wish I was my grandchild so that I could fight in the American Revolution." None of this, in other words, had to happen the way that it did.

Slavery provides the most powerful place from which to critique triumphalist narratives of American history. Viewed from the slave ship and the plantation, the triumphalist stories many have told about the "West" start to unravel. Thinking about the history of the modern world from the perspective of slavery, and more specifically of the enslaved, compels a different story about almost everything. It also allows a vision of political history that will be particularly meaningful, and helpful, for today's world.

C. L. R. James and Eric Williams, two of the key intellectual touchstones for the approach taken in today's Atlantic History, both came from Trinidad. The titles of their two most renowned books condense the challenge they issued. James's 1938 book *The Black Jacobins,* first written as a play, tells the story of the Haitian Revolution and of the political thought and actions of its key leader, Toussaint Louverture. Eric William's 1944 *Capitalism and Slavery* argues that the plantation complex of the Caribbean was central to the development of industry in Great Britain, and that economic changes rather than ideology spurred on abolitionism in the nineteenth century.[6]

Williams's book spurred the most response. Much of that response attempted to debunk its claims, but important parts of his argument have held up well. James's *The Black Jacobins,* meanwhile, made the story of the Haitian Revolution a subject of debate among historians and provided the foundation for a renaissance in work on Caribbean history. Both remain riveting and inspiring reads, great works in analysis and style.

Not all scholars in the field claim James and Williams as key ancestors. There are other genealogies, built by French and North American historians who starting in the 1960s and 1970s began paying increasing attention to the crossings between Europe and the Americas, especially with regards to the question of political history. R. R. Palmer produced a classic comparative study of the Age of Revolutions, though with what now has come to seem as a startling omission: there is no discussion of the Haitian Revolution. At the same time, historians of the Atlantic slave trade, notably Philip Curtin, began the long process of documenting this history, a project which has culminated in recent years with the production of a remarkable open online database containing essentially all currently known slave trade voyages.⁷

All of this scholarship has given scholars a huge amount of new data. Today, not a month goes by without new articles and books on the connections between different ports, of the lives that transpired between and in them. These stories often challenge received ideas about what American history is, about who Americans are, and therefore about who they might still become. Each historian has to navigate the ethics and challenges of telling these stories, making choices that are at once empirical and ethical.

The past is constantly present in the present—and in its political debates. When Michelle Obama talks about living in a "house built by slaves," she is prompting Americans to consider this history, one that is often obfuscated or distorted because it is not a happy and patriotic story. To understand and confront the present, however, a capacious sense of the past is vital. There is a genealogy linking the Haitian Revolution to abolitionism, the civil rights movement, and the Black Lives Matter movement. Understanding, or even just being aware, of that genealogy can help us all better understand the world in which we live, and to recognize and reach for justice.

The work of history is ongoing, neverending, which is itself a testament to its necessity as a practice. The very fact that so much of the past remains unwritten is also a constant reminder that the future is unwritten as well.

Notes

1. This is something Casimir has said in lectures and in our co-teaching together, rather than in print. But see more generally Jean Casimir, *The Haitians: A Decolonial History*, trans. Laurent Dubois (Chapel Hill: University of North Carolina Press, 2020).
2. Eric Williams, *Capitalism and Slavery* (1944; reprint Chapel Hill: University of North Carolina Press, 1994); C. L. R. James, *The Black Jacobins: Toussaint L'Ouverture and the San Domingo Revolution* (1938; reprint New York: Vintage, 1963); Michel-Rolph Trouillot, *Silencing the Past: Power and the Production of History* (Boston: Beacon, 1995). I draw here and throughout the essay on my book: Laurent Dubois, *Avengers of the New World: The Story of the Haitian Revolution* (Cambridge, MA: Belknap Press of Harvard University Press, 2004).

3. On the "right to have rights," see notably Rebecca J. Scott, *Degrees of Freedom: Louisiana and Cuba after Slavery* (Cambridge, MA: Belknap Press of Harvard University Press, 2005).
4. John K. Thornton, "African Soldiers in the Haitian Revolution," *Journal of Caribbean History* 25, nos. 1–2 (1991): 58–80; John K. Thornton, "I Am the Subject of the King of Congo: African Political Ideology and the Haitian Revolution," *Journal of World History* 4 (Fall 1993): 181–214; Christina Mobley, "The Kongolese Atlantic: Central African Slavery and Culture from Mayombe to Haiti" (PhD diss., Duke University, 2015).
5. Rebecca J. Scott and Jean M. Hébrard, *Freedom Papers: An Atlantic Odyssey in the Age of Emancipation* (Cambridge, MA: Harvard University Press, 2012).
6. Williams, *Capitalism and Slavery*; James, *Black Jacobins*.
7. Robert Roswell Palmer, *The Age of the Democratic Revolution: A Political History of Europe and America, 1760–1800* (Princeton, NJ: Princeton University Press, 1959); Philip D. Curtin, *The Rise and Fall of the Plantation Complex: Essays in Atlantic History*, 2nd ed. (1990; Cambridge: Cambridge University Press, 1998).

Locating West Africa in the Age of Revolutions

BRONWEN EVERILL

IN WHAT IS now northern Nigeria in 1804, Uthman dan Fodio, a cleric and teacher in Gobir, launched his own jihad, which ultimately resulted in the creation of the Sokoto Caliphate, the dominant revolutionary state of nineteenth century West Africa. At the outset, dan Fodio wrote that one part of the justification for his revolution was to end the practice of enslaving Muslims for the Atlantic trade.[1]

Dan Fodio's successful revolution was the culmination of events that had been building over several decades across Islamic West Africa. In 1789, the revolutionary Islamic reformer Fatta set up a new government in Moria, Guinea. He worked with a large maroon community based in the region who had already burned the fields of rice intended for the slave trade. Together, they beheaded former political leaders and slave traders for their lack of observance of the tenets of Islam, including injunctions not to trade Muslims as slaves to non-Muslims. When Fatta's revolution was ultimately crushed by a coalition of neighboring polities in 1791, the British governor of Sierra Leone, down the coast, commented that the revolution and its aftermath mirrored the events he saw happening in Europe.[2]

At the time of Fatta's revolutionary government, the Imamate of Futa Toro, a state along the Senegal River, was undergoing its own revolution. This revolutionary jihad, led by the cleric 'Abd al-Qadr Kane, put a stop to French slave trading in the Upper Senegal and unified the region while implementing a government based on religious principles. Futa Toro's revolution was ultimately unsuccessful, but it sowed the seeds for dan Fodio's victory.[3]

These revolutions were not unknown events outside of Africa. Numerous accounts filtered back to Europe through travel writing and European traders' letters. The French, forced to renegotiate their trading relationship with the revolutionary state of Futa Toro, and the British, keen to trade with the Imamate of Futa Jallon—blocked by Fatta's revolution—and the Sokoto Caliphate, were well aware of the political establishments and revolutionary creeds of these polities. The newly established abolitionist colony in Sierra Leone was an important source of information on these revolutions, as were the proliferation of books about West Africa capturing the public imagination around the Atlantic world.[4]

But if these revolutions were part of a broader Atlantic circuit of information and trade at the time, and subject to scholarly debate among historians of Africa since the 1970s, they have been less important to the historiography of the Atlantic Age of Revolutions until recently. Bringing these well-studied but often historically marginalized West African revolutions into the historiography of the wider Atlantic Age of Revolutions has started to change our understanding of the local and transnational influences on revolutionary actors. The Atlantic slave trade could be both an object of revolutionary concern and a tool for the spreading of ideas of warfare, resistance, and revolution around the Atlantic.

Recent scholarship from people like Christina Mobley and Manuel Barcia has argued alongside John Thornton that other West African political movements and revolutions inspired participants in slave resistance and rebellions in places like Cuba and Brazil, and the revolution in Saint-Domingue.[5] Paul Lovejoy has argued that these West African revolutions were crucial in directing traders away from West Africa and toward West Central Africa as the major source of Atlantic slaves.[6]

Reincorporating West African revolutions has also begun to change our understanding of the wider processes that contributed to a global Age of Revolutions. Joseph Miller and I both use these revolutions, and others, to challenge the idea that the revolutions of the late eighteenth and early nineteenth centuries represented the spread of European values of democracy and Enlightenment, looking instead to wider systemic developments in military-fiscalism, or the emergence of consumer revolutions, which affected the political and economic integration of the Atlantic world.[7]

Why have these revolutions not been accorded a larger place in the historical memory of the Atlantic Age of Revolutions? In part, this was the result of the events of the latter half of the nineteenth century. Race played an important role in framing the historical understanding of the impact of these revolutions, as well as their origins and relationships to the wider Atlantic. By the time of the centennial of the United States' revolution against Britain in 1876, new ideas about a polygenetic racial order were on the rise, and despite the abolition of slavery in most remaining parts of the Americas, an aggressive sense of white racial supremacy was recasting the history of the eighteenth century as a victory for white male governance, rather than an Atlantic-wide moment that incorporated revolutionary activities among enslaved people, Black clerical leaders, and multiracial coalitions.

Similarly, the interesting role of "slavery" in the rhetoric of the revolutionary era was elided with a purely rhetorical, political formulation of the term, whereas in the moment itself it was alternatingly used rhetorically and realistically. And because of the different trajectories of the national projects emerging out the revolutionary era, and the antislavery projects, their overlapping origins were separated out, and antislavery and revolutionary ideologies developed into their own historiographical fields.[8]

At the same time, the decline in Africa's fortunes from the commodity price collapse of the 1873 Great Depression through full "effective occupation" by European states by the end of the nineteenth century signaled to Whiggish historians that the continent was perpetually in need of "civilizing"; it lacked, in their minds, a dynamic history. While the field of professional history was being developed, then, a general sense of white supremacy, civilizational superiority, and neglect of the plethora of historical sources produced in and about Africa—from travel writing, to novels, to personal memoirs, to oral histories, to material artifacts, to European government reports at the time—generated a view of the Age of Revolutions as a story about Europe and its ideas and the reverberation of those ideas as they touched the Americas.

Even after 1938, when C. L. R. James's *The Black Jacobins* extended the story of the revolutionary Atlantic to include revolutionary Saint-Domingue, the impetus for revolution in his Black Atlantic was still European.[9]

As historians began to account for the phenomenon of the Age of Revolutions, the focus in works like Eric Hobsbawm's *The Age of Revolution* or R. R. Palmer's *The Age of Democratic Revolution* was on this proliferation of European ideas of government emerging from the Enlightenment: revolutionary egalitarianism and shifting centers of power and social mobility.[10]

It is true that the West African Age of Revolutions did not inspire specifically democratic change in the polities that were "revolutionized," and that the revolutions' relationships with the practices of the slave trade and slavery were complicated. But if not all of these revolutions were democratic, then maybe it wasn't an age of democratic revolutions at all, which makes the particular cases of democratic revolution interesting in different ways. For instance, how to account for the *economic* revolutions like those explored by Hobsbawm in his pairing of the French political revolution and the British industrial revolution? By incorporating these revolutions into arguments about the origins or implications of this period, it will be possible to see the causes and inspirations of individual polities' economic, political, or moral revolutions in a new light, and to think differently about what might have been the systemic or global causes for this period of political change.

But even more insidiously than ignoring these historical revolutions has been the role they have played in justifying colonial rule. The case of the "Mfecane" in Southern Africa is a case in point. The apparent military revolution of the Zulu in Southern Africa in the 1810s and 1820s—taking over and pushing out Ndebele and other groups as they moved in from the coast—was used as a justification by white settlers in the region in a few different ways. One was to highlight the "barbarity" that the Zulu used in conquering other groups in order to show that the African states were "uncivilized." The second was to justify the suppression and conquest of the Zulu in defense of other groups. And finally, the Mfecane were used to indicate that the Zulu had no natural claim to the territory that white settlers wanted for themselves.[11]

Whether this "revolution" ever actually took place has been called into question in the postcolonial period, but it serves as a useful reminder that the kinds of violence which accompanied revolution and counter-revolution in Africa were incorporated into a narrative that ignored their revolutionary political ideologies purely to cast the continent in terms of endemic warfare, despotism, and slavery as a justification for European political projects from the Age of Revolutions onward. Taking sides in wars between the Fante and Asante, or among Dahomey, Oyo, and Christianized traders in the Bight of Benin, European states helped to pick the winners of the revolutions without fully understanding—or caring about—the implications of their support. In most cases, the invocation of the slave trade was enough to garner support for a group wishing to challenge others with the support of the British anti-slave trade naval squadron. And so the political rhetoric of slavery took on an important role within the continent's politics across the nineteenth century, even as it was slightly different to the political meaning that European states ascribed to it.

But for both the Islamic revolutionary states in West Africa and the Europeans, there was another shared view that united antislavery and revolution: religion. All three of the revolutions that opened this essay linked their change in governance to their religious objections to the form that enslavement was taking under existing regimes, *and* to the establishment of a civilization based on the correct religious confession.

In a book about the slave trade from Madagascar published in London in 1824, the religious and antislavery messages were explicitly linked. This was not particularly surprising, given the evangelical fervor that surrounded the abolition movement in Britain more generally, and the relationship between the anti-slave trade and missionary projects in Africa across the nineteenth century. But what was interesting was the way that the book talked about political change as being attendant on religious change and an embrace of the antislavery cause. *And* that the author ascribed to the anti-slave trade captain Mr Montieth the speech "that those who actively engage in the amelioration of a people, expect too rapid a revolution of habits and manners," calling for a slow and steady image of change, rather than a "revolution."[12]

Christopher Leslie Brown has interpreted the rise of the British abolition movement within the context of a "providential crisis" that washed over Britain in the wake of the loss of the American colonies. Picking up on Boyd Hilton's argument about providentialism at the end of the eighteenth century, Brown argued that abolition was wrapped up with evangelical revival, a sense that Britain had lost its preeminent role in the world order because of its participation in slave trading, and a reaction against the cultural "licentiousness" of the 1770s associated with the excesses of both the East India Company and the West Indies planter class.[13]

This is how Rudolph T. Ware III has interpreted the revolutions of West Africa in this period. For Ware, the revolutions in Futa Toro were primarily driven by a response to the Atlantic slave trade and the concern among devout Muslims along the Senegal River that their leaders were not taking seriously the injunction against trading Muslims into slavery.

Ethics of trade and the perceived failures of the state to protect its citizens were common tropes across the Atlantic Age of Revolutions.

The context of enslavement of Muslims catalyzed a religiously inspired providential crisis that shared much in common with the British slave-trade abolitionists. Ware argued that the revolution in Futa Toro was effectively an evangelical revolution, one led by purists who saw the state failing in its moral obligations to its people and suffering because of its failures to serve God/Allah. The "Walking Qur'an" of Ware's title is embodied in believers, and therefore enslavement is anathema to Allah.[14]

Incorporating West African revolutions into the broader study of the Age of Revolutions helps to frame what role slavery played in the debates about the future of the Atlantic world. The rapid explosion of the slave trade in the second half of the eighteenth century had economic and political consequences, for the states involved in enslaving people and for the enslaved themselves. While the revolutionary states that emerged from this period went in a variety of directions with their rule—dictatorships, oligarchies, counterrevolutions, theocracies, limited-franchise democracies, empires, and emirates—when they succeeded at all, the benefit of bringing West African revolutions into the historiography of this period is the reopening of discussions of the role that ideas of morality played in catalyzing change, and specifically the morality of the state itself in relation to its citizens or subjects.

In 1812, once the initial Sokoto revolution had been secured and Uthman dan Fodio set out to consolidate and justify his government, he wrote a poem for his revolutionaries that outlined the responsibilities of rulers to God and the reciprocal responsibilities of rulers and ruled. It was later translated into Hausa for the wider Caliphate population by dan Fodio's daughter, the poet and philosopher Nana Asma'u. In her telling, the state emanated from the Caliph, but the Caliph was not a law unto himself: "If you are the Caliph, you must act generously, you are warned not to be mean, so you will be trusted by the people: He who is Caliph and acts righteously will be in Paradise Hereafter." The poem lists the punishments in the hereafter that would greet Caliphs who took their position "to devour the people," to "get rich or become powerful" or "allies himself with wrongdoers," or those who oppressed others "in the name of authority." Instead, everyone—Caliph, judges, and everyone else—was exhorted to follow the laws, "seek legal redress," attend to the summons of judges and adhere to their judgments, and "not disregard the law in any respect."[15]

In other words, the morality of the state was the rule of divinely justified law, and that law, as interpreted by dan Fodio's revolution, was meant to protect the people.

The relationship between slavery and citizens' rights, in other words, was more than purely rhetorical in the West African case. The cries of liberty that accompanied the revolutions in Futa Toro, Moria, and Sokoto were expressed by a scholarly class who considered themselves both oppressed by the regime and genuinely in danger of enslavement into the Atlantic trade. Putting their concerns into dialogue with the often more rhetorical understanding of slavery as an inability to have control over oneself and one's property in the North American context, and in dialogue with the revolutions of the enslaved in Saint-Domingue and Jamaica and the American "Black Loyalists" during the American Revolution, fills out a picture that sees slavery as an immoral system that threatened to corrode all relationships between people.

And for what? The trigger in all of these parts of the Atlantic world for linking enslavement to revolution was a sense that the existing government was enriching itself at the expense of the people. The commercial system that the Atlantic slave trade epitomized might have had some benefits initially to those not enslaved, but there was an increasing concern that those it was enriching had ravenous appetites for profit and would not stop with those deemed "enslaveable" but would soon be coming for those who had formerly benefited from the system.

The expansion of the slave trade caused the imperial crises of the Atlantic world in three ways. First, it created an initial bubble of government expansion and expenditure—largely spent on armies backed by credit secured on the booming profits of the plantation complex. Then, when the initial returns on this bubble began to decrease because of the increase in competition over a finite number of enslaved people, the government, asset owners, and merchants all tried to wring out profits where they could. Economic crises hit the different Atlantic regimes at different moments, but there was a general contraction in the 1760s that left many people working hard to keep up. When governments responded to this downturn by increasing taxation on marginal citizens and subjects, owners of certain types of assets—namely enslaved people—were able to continue profiting. Finally, in response to these pressures, with the expansion of slavery and the enrichment of those capturing the windfalls of early investments some people began to question the extent to which a new form of elite domination was beginning to characterize society more widely.

And so, just as the Sons of Liberty emerged among the mercantile class in Boston, dan Fodio found supporters for his cause among "personal disciples, fellow-clerics, and other orthodox Muslims" who shared his concerns at their increasing financial dependency, their inability to hold land, their exclusion from trade and farming, and their dependence on the whims of the ruling class, despite being well-educated elites in their own right.[16]

Notes

1. Paul Lovejoy, *Jihād in West Africa during the Age of Revolutions* (Athens: Ohio University Press, 2016), 214–16; M. Hiskett, *The Sword of Truth: The Life and Times of Shehu Usman Dan Fodio* (Chicago: Northwestern University Press, 1973); Seyni Moumouni, *Vie et oeuvre du cheik Uthman Dan Fodio, 1754–1817* (Paris: Editions L'Harmattan, 2008); Ghislaine Lydon and Bruce S. Hall, "Excavating Arabic Sources for the History of Slavery in Western Africa," in *African Voices on Slavery and the Slave Trade*, ed. Alice Bellagamba, Sandra E. Greene, and Martin A. Klein (Cambridge: Cambridge University Press, 2016), 2:15–49.
2. Macaulay's Journal, June 30, 1793, MSS MY 418, Huntington Library, San Marino, CA; Bruce Mouser, "Rebellion, Marronage and Jihad: Strategies of Resistance to Slavery on the Sierra Leone Coast, c. 1783–1796," *Journal of African History* 48 (2007): 38–39; Ismail Rashid, "Escape, Revolt, and Marronage in Eighteenth and Nineteenth Century Sierra Leone Hinterland," *Canadian Journal of African Studies* 34, no. 3 (2000): 666–70; Ismail Rashid, "'A Devotion to the Idea of Liberty at Any Price': Rebellion and Antislavery in the Upper Guinea Coast in the Eighteenth and Nineteenth Centuries," in *Fighting the Slave Trade: West African Strategies*, ed. Sylviane A. Diouf (Athens: Ohio University Press, 2003), 132–51; Walter Rodney, "Jihad and Social Revolution in Futa Djalon in the Eighteenth Century," *Journal of the Historical Society of Nigeria* 4, no. 2 (1968): 283–84.
3. Rudolph T. Ware III, *Walking Qur'an* (Chapel Hill: University of North Carolina Press, 2014), 129; Dominique Lamiral, *L'Affrique et le people affriquain consideres sous tous leurs rapports avec notre commerce et nos colonies* (Paris: Chez Dessenne, 1789), 174; P. B. Clarke, "Islamic Millenarianism in West Africa: A 'Revolutionary' Ideology?" *Religious Studies* 16, no. 3 (1980): 317–39; Coutumes, AOF 13G1, March 31, 1785, Archives National du Senegal, Dakar; H. F. C. Smith, "A Neglected Theme of West

African History: The Islamic Revolutions of the 19th Century," *Journal of the Historical Society of Nigeria* 2, no. 2 (1961): 174–75.

4. Thomas Winterbottom, *An Account of the Native Africans in the Neighbourhood of Sierra Leone* (London: C. Whittingham, 1803); Adam Afzelius, *Sierra Leone Journal, 1795–1796*, ed. Alexander Peter Kup (Upsala, Sweden: Studia Ethnographica Upsaliensia, 1967), 14; J. Matthews, *A Voyage to the River Sierra Leone* (London: B. White and Son, 1788), 154–55.

5. Christina Mobley, "The Kongolese Atlantic: Central African Slavery and Culture from Mayombe to Haiti" (PhD diss., Duke University, 2015); Manuel Barcia, "An Atlantic Islamic Revolution: Dan Fodio's *Jihād* and Slave Rebellion in Bahia and Cuba, 1804–1844," *Journal of African Diaspora Archaeology and Heritage* 2, no. 1 (2013): 6–18; John Thornton, "'I Am the Subject of the King of Congo': African Political Ideology and the Haitian Revolution," *Journal of World History* 4, no. 2 (1993): 181–214.

6. Lovejoy, *Jihād in West Africa during the Age of Revolutions*, 32–33.

7. Joseph Miller, "The Dynamics of History in Africa and the Atlantic 'Age of Revolutions,'" in *The Age of Revolutions in Global Context, c. 1760–1840*, ed. Sanjay Subrahmanyam and David Armitage (Basingstoke, UK: Palgrave Macmillan, 2010), 101–24; Bronwen Everill, *Not Made by Slaves: Ethical Capitalism in the Age of Abolition* (Cambridge, MA: Harvard University Press, 2020).

8. David Brion Davis, *The Problem of Slavery in the Age of Revolution* (Oxford: Oxford University Press, 1975).

9. C. L. R. James, *The Black Jacobins: Toussaint L'Ouverture and the San Domingo Revolution* (London: Secker and Warburg, 1938).

10. Eric Hobsbawm, *The Age of Revolution, 1789–1848* (London: Weidenfeld and Nicolson, 1962); R. R. Palmer, *The Age of Democratic Revolution* (Princeton, NJ: Princeton University Press, 1964).

11. Julian Cobbing, *The Case against the Mfecane* (Bloomington: Indiana University Press, 1984); John Wright, "Beyond the Concept of the 'Zulu Explosion': Comments on the Current Debate," in *Mfecane Aftermath: Reconstructive Debates in Southern African History*, ed. Carolyn Hamilton (Johannesburg: Wits University Press, 1995), 107–22; Elizabeth Eldgredge, "Sources of Conflict in Southern Africa, c 1800–30: The 'Mfecane' Reconsidered," *Journal of African History* 33, no. 1 (1992): 1–35; J. D. Omer-Cooper, "Has the Mfecane a Future? A Response to the Cobbing Critique," *Journal of Southern African Studies* 19, no. 2 (1993): 273–94.

12. *Radama; or, The Enlightened Africa with Sketches of Madagascar* (London: Harvey and Darton, 1824), 62–63.

13. Christopher Leslie Brown, *Moral Capital* (Chapel Hill: University of North Carolina Press, 2006); Boyd Hilton, *The Age of Atonement* (Oxford:

Oxford University Press, 1986). See also Richard Huzzey, *Freedom Burning* (Ithaca, NY: Cornell University Press, 2012).
14. Ware, *Walking Qur'an*.
15. Nana Asma'u "Be Sure of God's Truth," 1831–32, in *Collected Works of Nana Asma'u, Daughter of Usman 'dan Fodiyo (1793–1864)*, ed. Jean Boyd and Beverly Mack (East Lansing: Michigan State University Press, 1997), 43–57.
16. Marilyn Robinson Waldman, "The Fulani *Jihād*: A Reassessment," *Journal of African History* 6, no. 3 (1965): 341.

(In)forming Meiji
TWO REVOLUTIONS IN NINETEENTH-CENTURY JAPAN

GIDEON FUJIWARA

FROM 2017, AS commemorations began for the 150th anniversary of the Meiji Restoration, new scholarship has emerged that reexamines this period of political and social change in Japan as it transitioned to the modern era. Recent studies have focused on contextualizing the Restoration within global history. Mark Ravina has demonstrated that as Japan had engaged with Tang China from the seventh century, then with East Asia and Europe from the sixteenth through eighteenth centuries, Japan in the Meiji period (1868–1912) engaged with globalization as it thrived to stand alongside Britain and other modern Western nations of the world.[1] In their edited volume, Robert Hellyer and Harald Fuess ranked the Meiji Restoration as a "revolutionary watershed" comparable to the French and American Revolutions.[2] Essays from this volume show that numerous internal factors were shaped through global intersections, that the Japanese overcame military clashes of the 1860s, and that their attempts at national reconciliation achieved some national cohesion by the late 1870s. The Meiji at 150 Project, hosted by the University of British Columbia, defined the Restoration as an "epochal political revolution."[3] From September 2017 through March 2019, this series presented new perspectives on the history of Meiji society on topics ranging from the emperor, poetry, and the environment to urbanism, gender, the military, the Ainu and Japanese settler colonialism, and Japanese immigrants to Canada. Hellyer and David Leheny described this project as "the most comprehensive" among numerous conferences, symposia, and workshops hosted by universities across the world on Meiji's sesquicentennial, thus representing a "global moment" for Japan studies at a time when commemorations in Japan were hosted primarily by local organizations as opposed to the national government.[4]

This essay examines two revolutions witnessed across Japan in the nineteenth century. The first of these, as observed in the above-cited works, was the political revolution of the Meiji Restoration, while the second was the informational revolution. Here I focus on the emergence of one specific form of text called *fūsetsudome*.[5] While it was known previously that communication and cultural network revolutions enabled the spread of information across social classes in early modern Japan, I focus on the emergence of private compilations of political documents called *fūsetsudome*, which scholars across Japan assembled as reproductions of uncensored edicts, memoranda, images, works of literature, and letters issued by the shogun, feudal lords, influential samurai, members of the court, and Western officials.[6] Specifically, I analyze such *fūsetsudome* produced by Hirao Rosen (1808–1880), a merchant-class painter and scholar of ethnographic studies and *kokugaku*, or Japan studies, who lived in Hirosaki, a castle town of northeastern Japan, during a period of rapid change across local society and Japan.

These *fūsetsudome* reveal the pervasive culture of information-sharing between the Japanese elite and commoners. Those with samurai contacts who had political authority gained increasing access to sensitive and uncensored political information. This essay specifically focuses on Rosen's *Meiji nikki*, or *Meiji Diary*, the second of his two *fūsetsudome*.[7] By analyzing this five-volume compilation, I reveal how this scholar commemorated the restoration of imperial rule, including the military-political contributions of his home Hirosaki domain, as well as the sociopolitical landscape of both ally domains who carried out and supported the Restoration and the defeated domains who had backed the Tokugawa shogunate.

Political Information, *Fūsetsudome*, and Rosen's *Meiji nikki*

Japan had a widespread print culture pre-Meiji. Evidence of this can be found in the public media broadsides (*kawaraban*), brocade pictures (*nishiki-e*), and "print material" (*surimono*) produced in especially large volumes following the arrival of U.S. commodore Matthew C. Perry (1794–1858) and his naval fleet to Edo Bay on July 8, 1853.[8] By juxtaposing public media forms alongside the private collections of *fūsetsudome*, we see the far reaches of the informational revolution that indicate both the growing breadth and depth of national political awareness across

Japan. Such developments are especially well-documented in the case of merchant-class painter and *kokugaku* scholar Hirao Rosen, who compiled two *fūsetsudome* to document both Perry's arrival and the Meiji Restoration from the Hirosaki domain on the northern edge of Japan's main island of Honshu.[9]

When he compiled his second *fūsetsudome* in the early 1870s, just following the Meiji Restoration, Rosen not only documented the political and social changes but highlighted contributions of his own domain of Hirosaki to the cause of the Restoration, and celebrated the repositioning of the young monarch and the imperial court to the center of politics.[10] It was not until the late 1870s that the modern newspaper had spread across Japan and become the accessible, preeminent news source for readers of the modern Japanese state. In this sense also, the *fūsetsudome* served a vital function, especially from the 1850s and until well past the Restoration, as it continued to fulfill a sharp demand for uncensored political information and represented rigorous efforts to collect high-quality information with considerable volume and speed.

Let us now examine some examples of the wide range of documents Rosen compiled in *Meiji nikki*. An important document that Rosen features early on in volume 1 of *Meiji nikki* is "Copy of Petition from Shogunal Household" (Shogun ke kenpaku no utsushi), dated Keiō 3 (1867)/3/5, issued by the fifteenth and final shogun, Tokugawa Yoshinobu (1837–1913).[11] Shogun Yoshinobu petitioned to the imperial court to grant approval for the opening of Hyogo port. Following the Japan-U.S. Treaty of Amity of 1854 and the opening of ports at Hakodate and Shimoda to American and subsequently other Western vessels, the two nations agreed to the Japan-U.S. Commercial Treaty in 1858, which led to similar trade agreements with Holland, Russia, England, and France, and resulted in agreements to open additional ports to Western vessels at Kanagawa, Nagasaki, Hyogo, and Niigata.

While the treaties of 1858 required Hyogo port to be opened by 1863, this was delayed due to the surging "Expel the Barbarians" movement, political and economic uncertainty, and concerns regarding this port's close proximity to the imperial capital at Kyoto.[12] In his attempts to convince the imperial court to approve of the opening of Hyogo port, Yoshinobu warned, "If a treaty once agreed upon is changed, trust from all countries will simply be lost." Moreover, he asserted, "the matter of treaties is the basis for relations between various nations, and there are

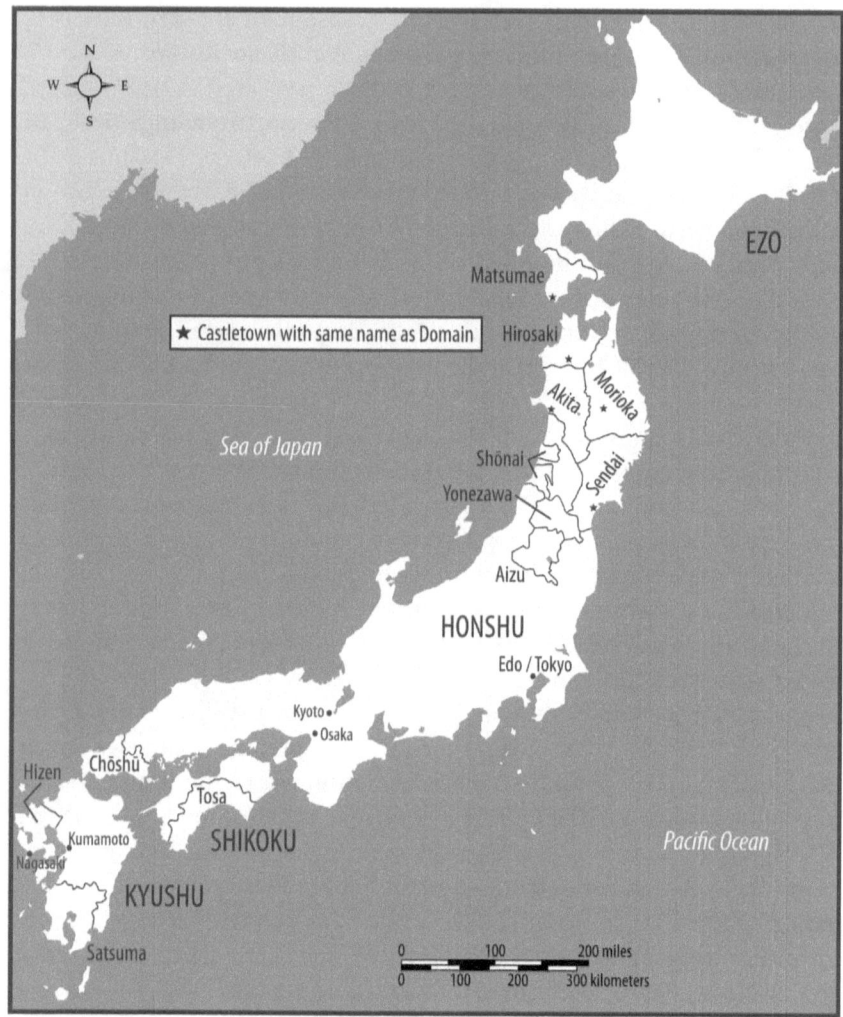

Early modern Japan and Hiroshaki

no rules that remain permanent and so ultimately the strong overcome the weak, and the weak are controlled by the strong." In the years since Tokugawa Japan opened its ports to Western nations and agreed to commercial relations with them, Yoshinobu had increasingly accepted the inevitability of Japan's engaging with the modern world. He asserted, "Thus when the various overseas countries are now opening up and busily move vast distances across neighboring areas, if we alone cling to old practices and do not engage in normal diplomatic relations with all nations, we will revert to the forces determined by nature and will not easily avoid disaster."[13] Yoshinobu's continued advocacy helped to convince the imperial court to decide to open Hyogo port on January 1, 1868.

Immediately following the above petition by Shogun Yoshinobu, Rosen included a pair of political documents issued by Tosa domain in the ninth and tenth months of Keiō 3 (1867) under the category of "Copy of Petition by Tosa Domainal Lord" (Toshū kō kenpaku no utsushi) that were submitted to the Tokugawa shogunate. The set begins with a historical petition issued by Tosa lord Yamanouchi Yōdō (1827–1872), signed Matsudaira Yōdō, dated Keiō 3 (1867)/9, which urges the shogunate to return political power to the imperial court (*Taisei hōkan*). Yamanouchi Yōdō appealed for political change in Japan "to transform the national polity [*kokutai*] of this Imperial nation over several hundred years and to relate with all nations with sincerity," asserting that "this is the sole opportunity to accomplish the work of the Imperial rule of antiquity."[14]

The above petition is accompanied by a second letter dated Keiō 3 (1867)/10 that outlines the details of the petition, signed by Yōdō's vassals, Tosa domainal samurai Teramura Sazen (1834–1896), Gotō Shōjirō (1838–1897), Fukuoka Tōji (1835–1919), and Kōyama Sadae (1829–1909). In this accompanying letter, the Tosa representatives reasserted their petition: "If one desires to build the foundations of restoring the Imperial nation, we must stabilize the national polity [*kokutai*], renew the way of governance, and restore Imperial rule [*Ōsei fukko*], utilizing as the principle those who will not be a shame before all nations for all ages."[15] Earlier that year, in the sixth month, Tosa samurai and "man of ambition" (*shishi*) Sakamoto Ryōma (1835–1867) had drafted his "Eight-Point Plan" (*Senchū hassaku*), which called for the shogunate to return political authority to the emperor as part of a vision of reforms for Japan. Ryōma's draft formed a basis for the eight points outlined in this letter from Tosa. In their renewed form, these eight points assert the imperial court as the source of political authority, propose the creation of a legislative body of upper and lower houses based on elections, promote education, call for reforms in foreign affairs and the legal system, and call for modernizing the navy and army. This historic petition that Tosa domain submitted to the shogunate thus led to Shogun Yoshinobu's officially returning political authority to the imperial court (*Taisei hōkan*) on November 9, 1867, propelling forward the events of the Meiji Restoration.

Next, we turn our attention to the local politics of Hirosaki domain, which were of immediate concern to Hirao Rosen. A key document that provides a Hirosaki perspective on late-Tokugawa politics is "Memorandum (Imperial Palace Gate Incident—Komiyama Tōbei)" or "Oboe (Kinmon no hen no ikken: Komiyama Tōbei)," dated Genji 1 (1864)/7/23 and featured in volume 2.[16] This memorandum was provided by Hirosaki domainal samurai Komiyama Tōbei, who reported on the violent clash just days before, known as the Hamaguri Gate Incident. Chōshū domain, asserting its "Expel the Barbarians" (*jōi*) stance, had become a growing influence on the imperial court but was expelled from Kyoto in 1863, and faced further setbacks in Genji 1 (1864)/6 when Chōshū *rōnin* and their supporters were assassinated or arrested at Teradaya Inn by Shinsengumi forces under shogunal orders. On 7/18, Chōshū forces marched on the imperial palace in Kyoto and clashed at the Hamaguri Gate with shogunal forces led by appointed Protector of Kyoto Aizu Lord Matsudaira Katamori (1835–1893), who was supported by Aizu, Satsuma, and other domains. This battle resulted in deaths and casualties on both sides, large-scale fires at the palace and surrounding district, and the defeat of Chōshū domain.[17]

Komiyama Tōbei's memorandum includes a report on fellow Hirosaki domainal samurai Nishidate Heima (1829–1892), who served his domain as liaison official (*rusuiyaku*) stationed in Kyoto. Tōbei also observed the presence of the Konoe noble family in Kyoto, whose historic ties forged through the efforts of the Tsugaru clan since the late seventeenth century elevated Hirosaki domain's political standing and legitimacy while also playing a crucial factor in Hirosaki eventually shifting their political-military support to the New Government and imperial court in the Boshin War fought from 1868 through 1869.[18] Tōbei reported that on 7/19, a day after Chōshū initiated the conflict at Hamaguri Gate, their forces were defeated and retreated from Kyoto: "On the 19th the defeated army retreated from Kyoto, while some remaining soldiers were apprehended. Furthermore, there are reports of people, unmistakably Chōshū men, who disguised themselves and fled. As aforementioned a major fire burned through Kyoto, north to Nakadachiuri, eastward up to Teramachi road, south to Kamo River and Hori River, to Marutamachi road, and there are even places destroyed by fire past Hori River West."[19] This account provides details of the destruction of this violent confrontation at a time when powerful rivals Chōshū and Satsuma were still enemies, before their historic alliance brokered in 1866 that proved to be a pivotal development leading to the Restoration. The Japanese term that I translate above as "reports," concerning the Chōshū men fleeing in disguise, is *fūsetsu*, which can also be rendered as "news" or "gossip," and makes up the first part of the term *fūsetsudome*. This term *fūsetsu* appears regularly in Tokugawa period documents to refer to various accounts of political and social developments, thus making *fūsetsudome* an appropriate label to refer to this category of collections of a variety of political documents.

Domains and provinces across Japan are characterized in a document titled "Word Flower Resident of Koume Village in the East" or "Higashi naru Koume no sato ni sumeru mono kotoba no hana," contained in volume 4. This piece begins with the southwestern island of Kyushu, stating that this region "possesses the sprouts of revolt," with "an intent to kill, which hints at revolt." Satsuma, a leading domain of the Restoration, boasted landholdings of 770,800 *koku*, and according to this report, "surpasses most in military matters." Tosa domain of the western island of Shikoku was also one of the leaders of the Restoration. In 1866, Tosa samurai Sakamoto Ryōma mediated the Sat-Chō Alliance between Saigō Takamori of Satsuma (1827–1877) and Kido Takayoshi (1833–1877) of Chōshū, uniting two major rival domains toward the cause of the Restoration. Moreover, Ryōma was an influential advocate of "returning political authority to the emperor," or *Taisei hōkan*, which along with his aforementioned "Eight-Point Plan" helped to shape the Restoration and Meiji policy. "Word Flower Resident of Koume Village in the East" provides the following profile: "One, in Tosa martial matters are vigorous. There are many warriors who eat and drink, the previous lord is a hero." In contrast, the report provides a severe assessment on the lord of Kōriyama domain in Yamato Province of Western Japan: "One, The Lord of Kōriyama is young and weak, and this domain does not know the Way of the Warrior [*shidō*]." It also describes the lord-vassal relationship in Hirosaki domain as "weak."[20]

Meiji nikki is textually colorful for the wide array of pieces it features, including "light" satirical pieces such as "Anonymous Jottings from This Time," or "Kono toki no rakugaki," in volume 5, which counter other more "serious" documents.[21] This work includes popular, parodic *tanka* and Chinese poetry that express criticism of the authorities, primarily the last shogun Tokugawa Yoshinobu.[22] The following *tanka* is the first poem cited from this piece:

Satsuma kara	Rice wine
watatta sake no	delivered from Satsuma
atsukan ni	is served hot
atatamerarete	It heats me up
Itami meiwaku	Itami nuisance[23]

Following the convention of five verses of 5-7-5-7-7 syllables, this *tanka* describes the *sake* delivered from Satsuma—a powerful domain leading the Restoration—served hot as *atsukan*. The drinker was warmed up by this sake, and the poet concludes with a pun of "Itami nuisance": Itami, rendered here in its Chinese characters 伊丹, is the name of a town just outside Osaka, famous for brewing sake, while *itami* also means "pain." This verse suggests that this rice wine from Satsuma warmed up its drinkers, but this resulted in painful inconvenience to the drinker(s) for heavy intoxication or to others who were subject to their drunken behavior. These verses resonate with a political and social profile of Satsuma domain cited in "Word Flower Resident of Koume Village in the East" in volume 4, which offers this indictment: "The domain is heroic but has a tendency toward intoxication at the drinking house."[24]

In volume 5, Rosen included a letter that was part of a vital correspondence between the Konoe noble family in Kyoto and Hirosaki's final domainal lord, Tsugaru Tsuguakira (1840–1916). Konoe Tadahiro (1808–1898) and his son Konoe Tadafusa (1838–1873) wrote this letter, "Copy of Lord Konoe's Own Letter" or "Konoe sama gojikan no utsushi," addressed to the Tsugaru major general and lord, dated Meiji 1 (1868)/11/13. This letter follows up on the Konoe's appeal to the Tsugaru family only five months earlier to redirect their political and military allegiance away from the Tokugawa shogunate and toward the New Government and imperial court. In this piece, the Konoe highly praised the Tsugaru lord and his domain for their loyalty to the imperial court, and Tsugaru's honoring of their special "historic roots" with the Konoe house, despite conflicting reports regarding the Boshin civil war: "Repeatedly I say that on this occasion, the thoroughness of your imperial loyalty made for a truly exceptional loyalty. The fact that your command was fully extended to the low ranks is indeed cause for the deep honor of your household, as well as for your joy and peace of mind. From the chief retainers through to the vassals, everyone down to the low ranks demonstrated on this occasion certain loyalty worthy of praise, so I simply pray that you will voice this matter to your vassals without omission."[25] Through the fall of 1868, supporters of the Tokugawa forces across the northeast had surrendered one by one to the New Government Army. Therefore, Tadahiro and Tadafusa were all the more pleased with Tsugaru's loyalty to the emperor and court, and with Lord Tsugaru Tsuguakira's leadership in commanding his chief retainers, all domainal samurai, and even the low-ranking members of Hirosaki domain to support the New Government toward the Restoration. The Konoe urged the Tsugaru household to continue to uphold their support in the ensuing months.

The final document to conclude volume 5, as part of the main volumes of *Meiji nikki* is a letter issued from Edo, dated Meiji 1 (1868)/12/23. This piece identifies twenty-three domains of the Ōu Etsu Domainal Alliance of the northeastern region that remained loyal to the Tokugawa forces and opposed the New Government's imperial army. It outlines these domains, listing their landholdings in *kokudaka* and indicating their political status as enemy households that were defeated by the imperial forces.[26] As a leading domain of the Tokugawa supporters and home to the Protector of Kyoto Matsudaira Katamori, Aizu is listed first, with 200,000 *koku* of land. Its status is simply recorded as *jōchi* (上地), denoting that Aizu was forced to "return its land to the Lord," thus relinquishing its landholdings to the New Government. Second is Sendai, the largest of these domains with 625,600 *koku*, who reportedly had 280,000 *koku* of land confiscated, along with Sendai Castle held in custody. Lord Niwa Nagakuni (1834–1904) of Nihonmatsu domain had 50,000 *koku* of its 100,700 *koku* of land confiscated and held in custody by the Hitotsubashi family. In the case of Lord of Honda Noto of Izumi domain, 2,000 *koku* out of 20,000 *koku* were confiscated, while the daimyo was sentenced to house arrest. This report identifies this penalty of house arrest, or *inkyo*, administered to seven of these domains. The sobering reality of these defeated northeastern domains facing punishments of land confiscation and arrests is laid out through this document. The concluding line states, "Of the total landholdings [*sōdaka*] of these 23 households, the total land 'returned to the Lord' is 707,600 *koku*."[27] This also marks the end of the main volumes of *Meiji nikki*.

Following these main volumes, Rosen concluded *Meiji nikki* with an appendix that features three documents reporting on armies that were loyal to the imperial court through the Restoration. The first of these pieces is titled "Copy of Letter from Tokyo, Tenth Month in Meiji 3" from 1870, which marks the last event chronologically in the collection.[28] This letter reports that on 10/8 the armies of Satsuma, Chōshū, and Tosa performed military demonstrations that were observed by Emperor Meiji (1852–1912). The report goes on to describe the torrential rainfall that interrupted this event and caused flooding that destroyed houses and caused numerous deaths. By concluding *Meiji nikki* with such reports on armies that supported the imperial cause in spite of the tragic flooding, Rosen celebrated the Meiji Restoration as an event through which the forces of the New Government and imperial court succeeded in asserting the emperor's will over the people of Japan.

THESE TWO revolutions of nineteenth-century Japan—the revolution of how sensitive political information was accessed and disseminated, as well as the political revolution of the Meiji Restoration—shaped one another. Criticisms of the Tokugawa regime through print media had previously been suppressed and punishable by death, but from the 1850s the authorities could no longer restrain dissenting opinions that demanded change. While popular print media such as broadsides and the emerging newspapers facilitated the spread of information with great speed and in volume, the private collections of *fūsetsudome* offer glimpses into the quality and extent of uncensored political information that was being accessed even by commoner-class intellectuals such as Hirao Rosen. My analysis of these documents transmitted between the capitals of Kyoto and Edo (later Tokyo) and Hirosaki domain on the northern periphery of Honshu confirms the view that this domain made its fateful decision to redirect allegiance from the Tokugawa shogunate to the New Government primarily based on intelligence of the latter's victories and advances in battles that made up the Boshin War of 1868–69.

My examination of Rosen's *Meiji nikki* sheds light on these two revolutions, as it chronicles the events of the Restoration seen from Hirosaki's perspective on the northern edge of Honshu while also serving as a good example of how sensitive political information was being accessed and shared between samurai and commoners across the archipelago. Further comparisons of these many *fūsetsudome* and their compilers across the archipelago will surely add to our understanding of how the two revolutions (in)formed one another. In turn, the Restoration encouraged public discussion on political and social matters and advanced both the dissemination and accessibility of information.

Notes

The author wishes to thank the editors at both the *Journal of Japanese Studies* and *Age of Revolutions* for permission to publish this essay, with the addition of significant new content and revisions to earlier versions that appeared as the following: "Channeling the Undercurrents: *Fūsetsudome*, Information Access, and National Political Awareness in Nineteenth-Century Japan," *Journal of Japanese Studies* 43, no. 2 (Summer 2017): 319–54, and "(In)forming Meiji: 2 Revolutions in 19th-Century Japan," *Age of Revolutions*, January 8, 2018.

The map "Early Modern Japan and Hirosaki," on page 124, is from my book *From Country to Nation: Ethnographic Studies,* Kokugaku, *and Spirits in Nineteenth-Century Japan*, a Cornell East Asia Series book published by Cornell University Press, © 2021 by Cornell University, and is included by permission of the publisher.

Dates quoted directly from historical sources are rendered according to the Japanese calendar that was used through 1872, and ordered year/month/day (eg., Keiō 3 (1867)/3/5). Other dates have been converted to the Gregorian calendar (e.g., July 2, 1853).

1. Mark Ravina also pointed to the paradox of Meiji Japan's rapid adoption of Western practices while the nation simultaneously asserted its uniqueness rooted in Japan's ancient myth and history. Ravina. *To Stand with the Nations of the World: Japan's Meiji Restoration in World History* (New York: Oxford University Press, 2017).
2. Robert Hellyer and Harald Fuess, eds., *The Meiji Restoration: Japan as a Global Nation* (New York: Cambridge University Press, 2020).
3. The Meiji at 150 Project entailed research presentations, workshops, discussions, and cultural performances from September 2017 through March 2019, hosted by the Centre for Japanese Research (CJR), the Departments of History, and Asian Studies, with the cooperation of the Museum of Anthropology and Asian Studies Library at the University of British Columbia. See Meiji at 150 Project, https://meijiat150.arts.ubc.ca.
4. Robert Hellyer and David Leheny, "Meiji at 150: A Global Moment for Japan Studies, Ambivalent Moment in Japan," *Journal of Japanese Studies* 49, no. 1 (Winter 2023): 117–39. Other notable volumes to appear in recent years include the following: Adam Clulow and D. V. Botsman, eds., *Commemorating Meiji: History, Politics and the Politics of History* (New York: Routledge, 2021); Ayelet Zohar and Alison J. Miller, eds., *The Visual Culture of Meiji Japan: Negotiating the Transition to Modernity* (New York: Routledge, 2021); and Timothy Amos and Akiko Ishii, eds., *Revisiting Japan's Restoration: New Approaches to the Study of the Meiji Transformation* (New York: Routledge, 2022).

5. Gideon Fujiwara, "Channeling the Undercurrents: *Fūsetsudome*, Information Access, and National Political Awareness in Nineteenth-Century Japan," *Journal of Japanese Studies* 43, no. 2 (Summer 2017): 319–54.
6. Mary Elizabeth Berry, *Japan in Print: Information and Nation in Early Modern Japan* (Berkeley: University of California Press, 2007); Eiko Ikegami, *Bonds of Civility: Aesthetic Networks and the Political Origins of Japanese Culture* (New York: Cambridge University Press, 2005); Tokyo Daigaku Shiryo Hensan-jo fūzoku gazō shiryō kaiseki senta, ed., *Fūsetsudome chū gazō shiryō ichiran (kō) fu: Bakumatsu ishinki minshū fūshi mokuroku* (Tokyo: Tokyo daigaku shiryō hensan-jo, March 31, 1999); Miyachi Masato, "Fūsetsudome kara mita bakumatsu shakai no tokushitsu: 'Kōron' sekai no tanshoteki seiritsu," in *Bakumatsu ishinki no shakaiteki seijishi kenkyū*, ed. Miyachi Masato (Tokyo: Iwanami shoten, 1999), 121–54.
7. See Fujiwara, "Channeling the Undercurrents," for my analysis of *Taihei shinwa* or *News of the Great Peace*, the first *fūsetsudome* Rosen compiled in 1855 following Perry's arrival to Japan. This work documents the incursion of Western powers to Japan, the "opening" of Japan's ports, and the challenges of responding to these developments across the country.
8. M. William Steele, *Alternative Narratives in Modern Japanese History* (New York: Routledge, 2003).
9. Gideon Fujiwara, "Rebirth of a Hirata School Nativist: Tsuruya Ariyo and His *Kaganabe* Journal," in *Values, Identity and Equality in Eighteenth and Nineteenth-Century Japan*, ed. Peter Nosco, James Ketelaar, and Yasunori Kojima (Leiden: Brill, 2015), 134–58.
10. Asakura Haruhiko, "The Origins of Newspapers and Magazines in the Bakumatsu and Meiji Periods," in *British Library Occasional Papers 11: Japanese Studies*, ed. Yu-Ling Brown (London: British Library, 1990), 179–87.
11. Tokugawa Yoshinobu, "Shogun ke kenpaku no utsushi," in *Meiji nikki*, ed. Hirao Rosen, Aomori kenritsu toshokan kyōdo sōsho 2, ed. Aomori Kenritsu Toshokan (Aomori, Japan: Aomori Kenritsu Toshokan, 1970), 8–11.
12. "Hyogo kaikō (Kobe kaikō)," "Be Kobe: Kobe no kingendaishi" 兵庫開港（神戸開港）| BE KOBE 神戸の近現代史.
13. Tokugawa Yoshinobu, "Shogun ke kenpaku no utsushi," 9, 10.
14. Yamanouchi Yōdō, "Toshū kō kenpaku no utsushi," in Rosen, ed., *Meiji nikki*, 11–16.
15. Teramura Sazen, Gotō Shōjirō, Fukuoka Tōji, and Kōyama Sadae, "Besshi no hyō," in Rosen, ed., *Meiji nikki*, 13–16.
16. Komiyama Tōbei, "Oboe (Kinmon no hen no ikken: Komiyama Tōbei)," in Rosen, ed., *Meiji nikki*, 107–11.

17. Following the Hamaguri Gate Incident, Emperor Kōmei ordered the shogunate to launch what became the First Chōshū Expedition to suppress Chōshū domain.
18. Hasegawa Seiichi, *Hirosaki han* (Tokyo: Yoshikawa kōbunkan, 2004), 7–11.
19. Komiyama Tōbei, "Oboe (Kinmon no hen no ikken: Komiyama Tōbei)," 109.
20. "Higashi naru Koume no sato ni sumeru mono kotoba no hana," in Rosen, ed., *Meiji nikki,* 198–202.
21. "Kono toki no rakugaki," in Rosen, ed., *Meiji nikki,* 256–57.
22. See Fujiwara, "Channeling the Undercurrents," 340, for analysis of two *tanka* that criticize Tokugawa Yoshinobu.
23. "Kono toki no rakugaki," 256.
24. "Higashi naru Koume no sato ni sumeru mono kotoba no hana," 199.
25. Konoe Tadahiro and Tadafusa, "Konoe sama gojikan no utsushi," in Rosen, ed., *Meiji nikki,* 279–80.
26. One *koku* represents a unit for measuring rice grains, the equivalent of about 180 liters. Land in early modern Japan was assessed not in area but by its agricultural yield. *Kokudaka* refers to this system of land measurement by its agricultural yield in units of *koku*.
27. "Tatsu jūnigatsu nijūsannichi Edo omote yori nanoka buri ni tōchaku shomen hidari no tori," in Rosen, ed., *Meiji nikki,* 292–95.
28. Note that within this document it is dated as the eighteenth day of the ninth month. "Meiji san uma jūgatsu Tokyo yori raijō utsushi," in Rosen, ed., *Meiji nikki,* 299–301.

PART 3

ARE WE STILL LIVING IN THE AGE OF REVOLUTIONS?

The Intimate Life of Books in Iran's 1979 Revolution

Naghmeh Sohrabi

"My father hated books," she said. "He didn't want any books in the house ever." We're sitting in the upstairs section of Café Paul, where the air conditioning is on so high we're both freezing. All around us are students, heads down, reading books and studying. My interlocutor is soft spoken and had been in high school when the 1979 Iranian Revolution happened. She uttered her surprising sentence in answer to a question I began all the interviews I had conducted for my book on the experiences of Iran's 1979 revolutionary generation: How did you become politicized?[1] Her father had a shop in the town of Qazvin across the street from a bookstore, and over the 1970s he had watched the bookseller get hauled away by the feared security service of the monarchy, known as SAVAK, for carrying and selling illegal books. Once, when the bookseller knew that the SAVAK was coming, her father had hidden "those books" for him. This experience had led her father to believe that books, regardless of their content, were dangerous. The best way to keep his children safe was to keep them away from them. "Being politically active allowed [me] to do things [I] normally couldn't do like go hiking and be around boys," she told me. Being political also gave her access to books.[2]

In studies of the 1979 Iranian Revolution, much has been written about the role of mosque networks, clerical networks, and, within it, the role that cassette tapes played in arousing the masses to take part in (or more accurately create) the revolution. A common explanation given for the success of the supporters of Ayatollah Ruhollah Khomeini over other revolutionary groups is the organizational advantages of these ready-made networks.[3] Most famously, cassette tapes of the speeches of Khomeini, who had been in exile since 1964 (first in Iraq and after October 1978 in France), were smuggled into Iran via the pilgrim route between

Iraq and Iran, and later through telephone and travelers' luggage. These audio recordings were then multiplied by activists and distributed among the population.[4] This was not exclusive to Khomeini's sermons from exile. The number of religious sermons on cassettes being sold daily in Tehran rose to an unprecedented forty thousand in the summer of 1978, when during the holy month of Ramadan a number of recording studios who had normally produced music devoted themselves to sermons.[5]

Books as political and politicizing objects (as opposed to the ideas they contain, which has been the focus of the scholarship so far) were similarly crucial in defining political activity and creating revolutionary networks.[6] In fact some of the cassette networks of the late 1970s were networks of book distribution already laid out in the preceding decade. A young religious activist recalled that he and like-minded seminary students would use the legal distribution networks of the nonpolitical religious journal *Maktab-e Islam* to distribute political religious books and cassettes. They would go to mosques to deliver the journal but would also pack up other books that carried political messages and convince the mosque to allow them to set up small libraries in a corner of the prayer hall. "We treated cassette tapes like books," he told me. "Wherever we created a library [literally "book home" in Persian], we'd also create a cassette home."[7]

For students (university or high school) in the 1960s and 1970s who saw themselves as political activists, books quite obviously occupied a singular place. Many of my interviewees named almost the same books that had influenced them in their youth and set them on a path that eventually led to the revolution. Depending on their political leaning at the time, these books included titles such as John Reed's *Ten Days That Shook the World*, Nicolai Ostrovsky's *How the Steel Was Tempered*, Vladimir Lenin's *What Is to Be Done?*, Samad Behrangi's *The Little Black Fish*, and books by Ali Shariati, who famously recast socialist revolutionary thought in Shi'i imagery and discourse.[8] Overall, Iranian leftists mainly looked to Cuban, Chinese, and Russian literature (depending on their leanings: Maoist, communist, armed struggled proponents), while the more religiously inclined to books by Shariati, the collection of sermons by the first Shi'i Imam *Nahj al-balaghah*, and the didactic romance novels of Javad Fazel (who also was a translator of *Nahj al-balaghah*). Regardless of their political leanings, like many across the Global South, young Iranian activists also looked to the Palestinian struggle, the Algerian

Revolution, and the Vietnam War as anti-imperialist revolutions par excellence, and the literatures they produced.

In the mid-1960s to late 1970s, when political repression was at its highest and armed struggled had been born and seemingly crushed in Iran, the owning, reproducing, and distribution of books, particularly illegal and semi-legal ones, defined political action itself. When I asked an interviewee who self-identified as a Marxist-Leninist with Maoist leanings what it meant to be *siyasi,* or political, he said it meant to read illegal books and discuss them. When in Tehran University in the late 1960s he had gotten hold of a book by Lenin (illegal), he set out to make six copies of it by hand using carbon copy paper. As he painstakingly pressed down to make sure all the copies were legible, he realized he couldn't possibly manage to do this alone. This led him to recruit another student whom he knew was also "political" so they could handcopy the entire book faster, with one copying odd and the other even pages simultaneously. "We didn't sleep for two days," he said.[9]

Handcopying books as a form of political activity did not belong exclusively to any one political group. On the other end of the ideological spectrum, a young seminary student and devotee of Khomeini in the 1960s who resided in the holy city of Qom told me about using carbon copy to make three copies of Mahmoud Asgarizadeh's *Economics Made Simple,* an amalgamation of Marxist and Islamist theories, inspired by an older book of economics, which in turn had been a loose translation of *Wage Labor and Capital* among others.[10] *Economics Made Simple* had been a pamphlet laying out the Marxist-Islamist Mujahedin-e Khalq organization's views of economics, yet this seminary student handcopied it for underground distribution alongside Khomeini's speeches reaching him from Iraq.

Handcopying books for underground distribution was not unique to Iran. The height of Iran's print-centered political activity coincided with the samizdat period in the Soviet Union when "self-published" tracts were created and circulated in underground "trusted network[s] of acquaintances." Ana Akhmatova famously called this the "pre-Gutenberg" of the post-Stalin Soviet era due to "the limited technical possibilities for producing and distributing uncensored written material."[11] Like in the Soviet samizdat era, carbon copies reigned supreme in 1960s–1970s Iran as the state monitored and controlled access to typewriters and mimeographs, and much of the oppositional literature was distributed through trust-based distribution networks. Ironically, the samizdat of Iran was often the gosizdat of the Soviet Union: leftist illegal book circulation in Iran included officially sanctioned books in the Soviet Union that were translated into Persian and distributed with Soviet support.[12]

The Pahlavi state was highly sensitive to the possession and distribution of illegal and particularly leftist books. Yet simultaneously, it kept moving the line between legal and illegal books, building an ambiguity into the state/opposition relationship that, counterintuitively, expanded what constituted "the political" in 1970s Iran. In his 1978 report for *Index on Censorship* on the "Perils of Publishing" in Iran, the outspoken writer and intellectual Reza Baraheni used the fate of Ahmad Shamlou's 1973 book of poetry *Abraham in the Fire* to highlight the absurdity of censorship in Iran and the confusion and frustration experienced by writers: The book's first eight reprintings were unproblematic. The ninth one went through the censors only to be confiscated once it was already in bookstores. For the tenth edition, the censors changed some of the words. The eleventh edition containing the censors' word alterations was then banned after it hit bookstores.[13]

As the Pahlavi state expanded and muddied what censorship meant, it also expanded its agents of censorship from state-employed censors to the publishers themselves.[14] Knowing that they would lose money or go to prison if they printed a "subversive book," the publishers became the first line of book censorship and were responsible for rejecting problematic books.[15] One interviewee was encouraged by his advisor to publish his thesis, a translation of a study of the May 1968 events in France. Both his advisor and the publisher who accepted the manuscript had found it innocuous and sent it to the print shop. But SAVAK officials during an inspection of the shop took one look at it and stopped the printing. They then arrested the publisher for a brief period and let him go but imprisoned the author, who had just graduated, handing him a two-year sentence. When I asked him how one was supposed to know which books were legal or illegal, he told me he asked a SAVAK official the same question and was told, "In a pharmacy, selling some types of poison is legal but it doesn't mean everyone has the right to buy it."[16]

What stands out here is how the Pahlavi regime turned ordinary things into subversive objects. When something is legal one day and illegal the next, or when something is legal for some and illegal for others, the range of what is considered political expands, making it, oddly enough, easier to become politicized. Relatedly, resistance becomes defined by this shifting conception of political activity. Politically aware but not active, my interviewee thus became part of organized resistance to the regime once his senior thesis landed him in jail.

Nothing exemplifies this book-centered ambiguity and the politics it engendered more than "white books" or "white covers" as they were interchangeably called. These were books that had been either mimeographed or printed in underground presses with covers that often had no titles, no authors, no dates, and no publishers, the word "white" telegraphing the blankness of ownership: "The standard format consisted of A4 paper folded in half and sometimes the books were simply stapled, resembling more of a booklet, a typescript, or even course notes." As noted by Hannah Darabi and Chowra Makaremi, "What defines this type of publication is not in fact its form, a particular theme or set of political convictions, but rather its method of production and distribution, which was basically under the counter."[17] White books emerged in my interviews as a different category from the pamphlets and hand-copied books of the late 1960s and early 1970s in that they were sold in sympathetic bookstores (such as the one in Qazvin mentioned at the start of this essay) only to people who were trusted. Mahmud Baqeri, who was a book peddler in this period (i.e., he sold books by spreading his wares on sidewalks and not in brick-and-mortar stores), noted that the defining characteristics of white books were that they had some kind of oppositional character (banned religious or leftist books), they had high circulation (over ten thousand copies), and were sold cheaply. The "white" covers in their simplicity reflected the fact that they were printed in secret and often quickly. Baqeri estimated that there were roughly twenty printers in Tehran that produced white books though he only interacted with seven or eight of them.[18]

For some of my interviewees, it was the rise of "white books" to the surface in the fall of 1978 that signaled things had irrevocably changed even though the official victory of the revolution was still months ahead. At that time, white books began to be sold by book peddlers on the sidewalk across the street from Tehran University even though they were still illegal. But unlike a decade earlier, the sellers, buyers, and readers were no longer prosecuted for possessing them, thus giving them even more of a liminal quality. With the victory of the revolution on February 11, 1979, the publication of white books continued, becoming the link between the repression of the Pahlavi era and the Spring of Freedom (the period between February 1979 and the summer of that year when the newly established Islamic Republic began an expanding regime of censorship). Chahla Chafiq, an Iranian sociologist, called the Spring of Freedom "a magical time" for the ways in which "white covers flew off the stands, some were reissued with covers stating their titles and the names of the authors and translators. . . . The fact of being able to buy them was a symbolic act that reaffirmed the end of political repression. However, several of them were quickly banned once again, this time under the pretext that they served the interests of the enemies of the revolution."[19] That the Spring of Freedom is defined by and remembered through books and not, for example, speeches, voting, or pamphleteering only reinforces how central books were in defining the revolution itself.

The ambiguity that engulfed books extended to where they were housed. In addition to the official university libraries, many interviewees spoke of student libraries that were above ground; the universities knew about them and allowed them to function. What separated them from official libraries was that everything—from book selection to operations—was student-run. But some of these libraries had a hidden aspect to them visible only to those in trusted circles: they housed illegal pamphlets and white books. One interviewee, when asked what Tehran University was like when she attended in 1973, said, "At the time there were two types of students: the Islamic students who occupied the upper floor of the library and the Leftist students who occupied the lower floor where they would secretly read Lenin and Che Guevara. On the upper floor, they'd secretly exchange books by Shariati, which at the time were banned and having them carried a two-year sentence." Mirroring the ever-changing line of legal/illegal books, sometimes the student libraries would function with no problems and sometimes SAVAK would crack down on them, leading one religiously inclined student to reminisce years later how they would move the illegal stash from student library to student library when they would get wind of the raids.[20]

These small libraries were connected to university-sanctioned student clubs that were manifestations of *mahfils,* or "circles of friendships," that profoundly shaped student political activity in the years preceding the revolution. *Mahfil* was frequently used by my interviewees as a way of distinguishing their political activities from formal organizations, or *tashkilat.* In fact, many of them were adamant that they were not *tashkilati* as a way of underscoring their independence of thought and actions. For university students, *mahfils* were connected to university-funded *sinfs* (literally guilds) that functioned as university clubs, like hiking clubs, cinema clubs, or book clubs. These above-ground university clubs sometimes, though not always, acted as a cover for political discussions and mobilization among students.[21] The hiking club of the Polytechnique Institute, for example, was known for its leftist leanings, where club members would discuss political ideas and books as they hiked the mountain trails on the northern edges of Tehran. As one member told me in jest, "It was where the ideology of the body and mind came together." It wasn't only secular leftist students who were engaged in this type of *sinfi-siyasi* activity. Nosratollah Tajik, the former ambassador to Jordan for the Islamic Republic, recalled how when he first entered the university in 1972 as a religious, politicized student, he was part of the *sinfi* activities of his university even though it was dominated by leftist secular students. But by 1975, the religious nonleftist students had managed to have their own clubs and their own student library where they also housed both legal and illegal religious books.[22]

The financial and human capital of student libraries, housing the spectrum of legal/illegal books, were connected to university-funded clubs, which in turn were responsible for numerous university strikes from the mid-1960s onward and at least two citywide protests in Tehran: one in 1968 on the occasion of the death of Iran's beloved Olympic gold medal winner Gholamreza Takhti that turned into an anti–United States, anti-Shah protest, and another in March 1970 to successfully protest the increase in city bus ticket prices.[23] The experience of and with books thus gives us insights into informal networks of political activity that have not left behind obvious archival footprints or organizational structures, since after all, while organizations leave paper traces, circles of friendship rarely do.

Books as revolutionary objects are at the core of the shared experience of prerevolutionary activity across ideological thought. They linked religious networks and leftist ones to each other, a linkage that came to define the revolution, when in the fall of 1978, after decades of parallel activity, the various groups joined forces to successfully oust the monarchy by early 1979. How communist, Marxist-Leninist, nationalist, Islamic-Marxist, and secular forces aligned themselves to a religious coalition with which they had little in common on the level of ideas is a question that has occupied every scholar of the Iranian Revolution. Answers have ranged from the left was duped to everyone was naive, to the cunning of the religious groups, to the tragedy of the left, to no one but the Islamists ever really mattered. The answer, I would suggest, might lie with a book.

Notes

1. For more information on these interviews and the question of memory, see "Muddling through the Iranian Revolution," *Perspectives on History*, November 1, 2015, https://www.historians.org/research-and-publications/perspectives-on-history/november-2015/muddling-through-the-iranian-revolution.
2. Interview with PB, Paris, October 2014.
3. For in-depth discussions on the role of religion and clerical networks in the revolution, see Michael M. J. Fischer, *Iran: From Religious Dispute to Revolution* (Cambridge, MA: Harvard University Press, 1980); Michael M. J. Fischer and Mehdi Abedi, *Debating Muslims: Cultural Dialogues in Postmodernity and Tradition* (Madison: University of Wisconsin Press, 1990); and Roy P. Mottahedeh, *The Mantle of the Prophet: Religion and Politics in Iran* (Oxford: Oneworld, 2000). For a critical historiography of the 1979 revolution, see Naghmeh Sohrabi, "The Problem Space of the Historiography of the 1979 Iranian Revolution," *History Compass*, November 2018.
4. Annabelle Sreberny and Ali Mohammadi, *Small Media, Big Revolution: Communication, Culture, and the Iranian Revolution* (Minneapolis: University of Minnesota Press, 1994), 120.
5. "Forty Thousand Religious Tapes Are Sold Daily in Tehran," *Kayhan*, 5 Shahrivar 2537/1357, 5 (in Persian).
6. I use the word "object" here in its surface meaning as a "thing" and without recourse to the rich debates within the fields of cultural studies and material history. The drawbacks to this use have been discussed in Kusha Sefat, *Revolution of Things: The Islamism and Post-Islamism of Objects in Tehran* (Princeton, NJ: Princeton University Press, 2023).
7. Interview with AR, London, March 2015.
8. See Asef Bayat, "Shariati and Marx: A Critique of an 'Islamic' Critique of Marxism," *Alif: Journal of Comparative Poetics* 10 (1990): 19–41. For a biography of Shariati, see Ali Rahnema, *An Islamic Utopian: A Political Biography of Ali Shari'ati* (London: I. B. Tauris, 1998).
9. Interview with FR, Paris, 2014.
10. Interview with HE, Bonn, 2016.

11. Ann Komaromi, "The Material Existence of Soviet Samizdat," *Slavic Review* 3 (Autumn 2004): 598–99.
12. For a succinct overview of Soviet-sponsored publications in Iran and the Pahlavi attempts at stopping them, see Mahdi Ganjavi, *Education and the Cultural Cold War in the Middle East: The Franklin Book Programs in Iran* (London: I. B. Tauris, 2023), 68–72.
13. Reza Baraheni, "Perils of Publishing," *Index on Censorship* 7, no. 5 (September 1978): 15.
14. For a comprehensive survey of Pahlavi state tools to prevent the dissemination of illegal books and institutions involved in book censorship, see Kamran Arvan, "Pahlavi Government Tools to Prevent the Publication, Distribution, and Study of Illegal Books from 1963–1979," *Historical Studies Quarterly* 17, no. 66 (Autumn 2019): 46–66 (in Persian).
15. In the fascinating *An Oral History of Publishing in Iran* (Tehran: Qufnus, 2003), Abdulhusayn Azarang and Ali Dehbashi talked to several publishers about the minutiae of censorship, the push and pull of book publishing and selling, and the Pahlavi state's monitoring and punishment of their business.
16. Interview with BB, Paris, September 2014.
17. Hannah Darabi (with texts by Chowra Makaremi), *Enghelab Street: A Revolution through Books: Iran, 1979–1983* (Leipzig: Spector, 2019), 13, 289.
18. Azarang and Dehbashi, *An Oral History of Publishing in Iran*, 186–188.
19. Darabi, *Enghelab Street*, 339.
20. Interview with ZH, Paris, 2014.
21. For a detailed discussion on *mahfil* political activism and its significance for the Iranian revolution, see Naghmeh Sohrabi, "Remembering the Palestine Group: Global Activism, Friendship, and the Iranian Revolution," *International Journal of Middle Eastern Studies* 51, no. 2 (April 2019): 281–300.
22. "Nosratollah Tajik Speaks about the Student Movement before the Revolution," *Khabar Online*, December 17, 2014, https://www.khabaronline.ir/news/388882 (in Persian).
23. For more on these protests see Arash Davari and Naghmeh Sohrabi, "'A Sky Drowning in Stars': Global '68, the Death of Takhti, and the Birth of the Iranian Revolution," in *Global 1979: Itineraries of the Iranian Revolution*, ed. Ali Mirsepassi and Arang Keshavarzian (Cambridge: Cambridge University Press, 2021), 213–44.

Two, Three . . . Many Túpacs
THE ENDURING AFTERLIFE OF AN ANDEAN REBEL

Miguel La Serna

THE IMAGE REMAINS etched in the memory of a nation whose citizens never witnessed the event. There lay José Gabriel Condorcanqui, the Andean rebel known as Túpac Amaru, hands and feet stretched out in four opposing directions, each limb bound to a rope. Horses tugged at the end of each rope in an effort to rip the rebel limb from limb—yet, they could not tear him apart. This was not an uncommon outcome for such an unscientific execution, but it would do wonders for the insurgent's mystique: Túpac Amaru, more powerful than four horses; Túpac Amaru, the Inca incarnate with supernatural strength; Túpac Amaru, the anticolonial hero who refused to die. This defiance was short-lived of course. The executioners promptly beheaded and quartered their victim, displaying his severed head and limbs throughout the areas of rebel activity as a reminder of the fate that awaited colonial subjects who resisted Spanish rule.[1]

The way in which Túpac Amaru met his untimely demise, limbs stretched in opposing directions, is an apt metaphor for the ways in which his legacy fueled revolutionary politics in the twentieth and twenty-first centuries. Like the horses that sought to dismember Túpac Amaru, state and nonstate actors in Peru and beyond have engaged in a symbolic tug-of-war over his name, likeness, and memory, pulling him in different directions to lend a sense of revolutionary authenticity to their own causes.

The Shining Serpent

These modern-day actors were merely continuing a revolutionary tradition of symbolic appropriation that Condorcanqui himself had begun two hundred years earlier. Before taking up arms, Condorcanqui had been a *kuraka*, or ethnic lord (also known as a *cacique*), from the province of Canas y Canchis in the highlands of Cuzco.[2] A literate muleteer who spoke both Quechua and Spanish, Condorcanqui claimed to be the direct descendent of the Inca monarch Túpac Amaru. This first Túpac Amaru, whose name means the "Shining Serpent" or "Royal Serpent" in Quechua, reigned over Vilcabamba, an Inca kingdom-in-exile, before leading a doomed Indigenous rebellion against the Spanish colonizers in 1572. After capturing the rogue Inca later that year, Spanish authorities beheaded Túpac Amaru before a crowd of onlookers in the main square of Cuzco, the former Inca capital. His death spelled the end of the resistance, the Incan epoch dying with him on that crowded colonial square.[3]

Nearly two hundred years later, Condorcanqui led his own rebellion against Spanish authorities in Peru. His first act of rebellion involved the public execution of Antonio de Arriaga, a Spanish administrative and judicial official, or *corregidor*, with a reputation for abuse of the Indigenous population of his jurisdiction of Tinta, Cuzco. Shortly after sending Arriaga to the gallows on November 4, 1780, Condorcanqui declared open rebellion and encouraged all Peruvian-born whites, Mestizos (people of mixed European and Indigenous ancestry), Blacks, and Indigenous people to take up arms against their oppressors. Condorcanqui claimed, without offering definitive proof, to be a direct descendent of Túpac Amaru, adopting the Inca's name to cement his royal claims and earn legitimacy in the eyes of his Quechua-speaking followers. This second Túpac Amaru promised a return to Inca rule even while professing fealty to the Spanish Crown and Catholic Church. Above all, Túpac Amaru II fought to preserve Peru for Peruvians—regardless of color—and end the abuses of European-born Spaniards who governed there.[4]

The call to arms produced the desired effect, and within weeks the rebellion had spread throughout the Andes, bringing as many as seventy thousand rebels into its orbit and posing a serious threat to the colonial order.[5] The following year, however, Spanish forces captured Túpac Amaru, his wife and rebel commander Micaela Bastidas, and other members of his family, putting them on trial and sentencing them to death. In a cruel twist of historical fate, Túpac Amaru's captors brought him back to the same square where his Inca namesake had met his end two centuries prior. After torturing and executing Bastidas and other family members, the executioners killed Túpac Amaru on May 18, 1781.[6] The rebellion lived on after his death, with new leaders continuing the struggle throughout the Andes. It died down by 1783, after royal officials had captured and killed its major leaders and conspirators.[7]

A Decolonial Icon

According to legend, Túpac Amaru II made one final promise before he was beheaded: "I will return and I will be millions." This version of the story became a prophecy of sorts, with Túpac Amaru reemerging in the twentieth century as a decolonial and antiracist icon from California to Argentina.

In Peru, everyone from leftist guerrillas to military dictators invoked the Indigenous martyr. The Revolutionary Left Movement (MIR), a predominantly Mestizo guerrilla organization, christened columns and camps in Túpac Amaru's name. Then, after General Juan Velasco Alvarado led a military coup in 1968, his left-leaning Revolutionary Government of the Armed Forces (GRFA) positioned itself as the embodiment of Túpac Amaru, deploying his image as the foremost symbol of the regime. The GRFA used Túpac Amaru's name and likeness in everything from government propaganda to speeches, memorials, and social reforms in an effort to rebrand the state as his true revolutionary heir.[8] Túpac Amaru continued to occupy state discourse even after the GRFA took a right turn. After installing the conservative Francisco Morales Bermúdez as president in 1975, the GRFA rebranded Túpac Amaru as a reformist. Moralez Bermúdez's principal legislation, El Plan Túpac Amaru, undid many of Velasco's social welfare programs in the name of the revolutionary icon.

Some on the left saw the appropriation of Túpac Amaru by a conservative military government as a betrayal. In the following decades, armed insurgents sought to pull him back to the left. Peru's Shining Path and the Túpac Amaru Revolutionary Movement (MRTA), two guerrilla groups active in the 1980s and 1990s, situated their own armed struggles within a longer national history that went back to the Túpac Amaru Rebellion. Although Shining Path, the armed Communist Party headed by Abimael Guzmán, emphasized its origins in Marxism-Leninism-Maoism, it nevertheless conceived of itself as existing within a longer revolutionary tradition that included the rebellion.[9] And while Guzmán and other leaders do not appear to have explicitly acknowledged the coincidence of their historical timing, it is worth noting that their insurgency marked the two-hundred-year anniversary of Túpac Amaru's 1780 rebellion, and the date they chose to launch it—on the eve of the May 18 presidential election—coincided with the date of Túpac Amaru's death. If Shining Path acknowledged Túpac Amaru II's contributions to Peru's revolutionary tradition, the MRTA openly embraced them. This group of mostly Mestizo insurgents, which carried out its first armed action in 1982 before initiating a full-fledged guerrilla struggle two years later, sought to reclaim Túpac Amaru's name, image, and legacy for the Peruvian people once and for all.[10]

But the allure of Túpac Amaru went beyond his native land. In the 1960s, while Peru's MIR and GRFA were reappropriating the Andean hero for their respective causes, Uruguayan rebels reclaimed the term *tupamaro*—formerly used by Spanish authorities to refer to treasonous insurgents—as a badge of honor, christening their guerrilla movement the Movement of National Liberation–Tupamaros. Made up almost entirely of white and Mestizo militants, the Tupamaros waged urban warfare from the streets of Montevideo, staging kidnappings, Robin Hood actions, and other headline-grabbing stunts designed to capture the popular imagination. In particular, the Tupamaros targeted symbols of U.S. imperialism, which they saw as a major impediment to Uruguayan sovereignty and economic independence.[11]

As far north as New York City, members of the Black Panther Party learned about the history of Túpac Amaru I and II. The Panthers created a transnational solidarity network with Uruguay's Tupamaros, finding common cause with the South American rebels.[12] Through these and other means, some Panthers drew parallels between the anticolonialism and antiracism of the Peruvian Túpacs and their own liberation struggle against white oppression. One of these Black Panthers, Afeni Shakur, named her son Tupac Amaru. Shakur had been a member of the so-called Panther 21, a group of Black Panthers falsely accused—and later acquitted—of plotting attacks against a number of targets throughout New York City. Shakur, who despite not having a law degree represented herself for the 1970 trial, gave birth during this turbulent period of her life. "I chose his name," Shakur said, "because I wanted my son to understand that African Americans are not the only people that this [racial oppression] has happened to."[13]

That boy grew up to be the world-famous rapper Tupac Shakur, better known as Tupac or 2Pac. Tupac the rapper understood the broader significance and general origins of his name, even as he was unclear about some of the details of his namesake's life and death. "I was named after this Inca chief from South America whose name was Túpac Amaru," he explained to MTV News's Tabitha Soren. "But it's a lot of people named Túpac Amaru. . . . And I think the tribal breakdown means 'Intelligent Warrior' or something like that. [Túpac Amaru was] a deep dude."[14] Tupac appreciated his mother's decision to give him a unique and meaningful name. "If you have a name that no one else has, you have to repeat it twice," he told one interviewer. "You gotta say it with extra feeling the second time. It builds character. Well, you know, that's why my mother gave it to me."[15] Like the Túpac Amarus before him, the rapper's own life and career would be defined by rebellion, antiracism, tragedy, and martyrdom.[16]

In the twenty-first century, Túpac Amaru remains a powerful symbol of resistance, decoloniality, and antiracism. The political career of Hugo Chávez, perhaps the most recognizable leftist of twenty-first-century Latin America, has long been intertwined with the rebel moniker. Since the 1980s, radical urban youth became known as Tupamaros. Following Chávez's failed 1992 coup and subsequent arrest, he formed a political alliance with the Tupamaro Revolutionary Movement, a far-left group that took Túpac Amaru II as their namesake. That alliance would span the rest of the Bolivarian leader's life and aid in his ascendency to the presidency of Venezuela in 1999.[17] After surviving a short-lived coup in 2002, Chávez called on his supporters to defend his political revolution from a hostile right-wing takeover. Members of the Tupamaro Revolutionary Movement heeded the call, serving as a kind of armed community watch organization (some would call it a paramilitary squad) and working with the Chávez administration to organize social programs and mobilize voters. At the same time, some Tupamaros threatened and committed acts of violence against alleged criminals and Chávez's political opponents. In doing so, they represented a new form of symbolic appropriation of the Túpac Amaru marker, turning to vigilantism as a method for supporting a revolutionary state. They remained an important ally of Chavismo even after Chávez's 2013 death.

If Túpac Amaru represented militarized Chavismo in Venezuela, he became a symbol of grassroots organizing among the poorest, Brownest communities in Argentina. In 1999, Milagro Sala, an Indigenous woman from the northwestern slums of San Salvador de Jujuy, formed the Túpac

Amaru Neighborhood Association, an organization that offered housing, employment, textiles, and other social services to the shantytown's mostly Brown-skinned residents.[18] From the outset, Sala's organization adopted an antiracist, Indigenist ideology. In the first decade of the twenty-first century, Sala's star rose along with that of her organization, earning her both the adulation of Argentina's Indigenous populations and the consternation of dominant white society. In 2015, Gerardo Morales, the newly elected governor of Jujuy and a political opponent of the association, alleged that Sala had embezzled millions of dollars from the association, starting a political and legal campaign that led to its dismantling and Sala's arrest. In 2019, Sala was sentenced to thirteen years in prison for extortion, later serving out part of her sentence on house arrest. Throughout her trial and imprisonment, the Indigenous leader maintained her innocence, claiming that the charges were as preposterous as they were racially motivated. "I am dark skinned and I am a colla [Indian]," Sala told Radio Mitre, "but I'm not an idiot."[19]

Túpac Amaru has also inspired anti-imperialist and decolonial artists in North America. In 2003, Latine artist-activists Jesus Barraza and Favianna Rodriguez founded the Taller Tupac Amaru, a screen-printing collective for Bay Area artists that, through artistic expression, called attention to issues impacting Latine, Chicane, and migrant communities. The artists sought to illuminate how "racism, hate, and economic exploitation . . . transcend lines on maps or demographic classification." Naming the artist collective after the Inca Túpac Amaru I was an obvious choice, given the antiracist and decolonial scope of the artists' work. "We take [on the name of] Túpac Amaru because he embodies the history of rebellion as well as [Rodríguez's] Peruvian lineage," Barraza explained.[20] The Puerto Rican rapper Residente honored both Túpac Amaru II and the late rapper Túpac Shakur in his 2022 hit "This Is Not America." The song and accompanying music video are decolonial on multiple levels, with references to Spanish conquest, genocide, Indigenous survivance, racialized police brutality, and the violence of U.S. imperialism. At one point in the video, Residente reminds listeners that "*2Pac se llama Tupac, por Túpac Amaru del Perú / América no es solo USA, papá*" [2Pac is named Tupac, after Túpac Amaru of Peru / America isn't only USA, *papá*], while modern-day police attempt to rip an Indigenous man limb from limb, just as the Spaniards attempted to do to Túpac Amaru II. Elsewhere in the video, Black and Brown people with dismembered and disfigured bodies stand, sit, and lay defiantly before the camera, stubbornly refusing to be killed, until they finally pepper the pavement, encircled by a line of police in riot gear—a configuration of human corpses spelling out the word "America."

The Recoiled Serpent

Addressing the attendees of the 1966 Tricontinental Conference in Havana, Che Guevara famously called on the people of Africa, Latin America, and Asia to create "two, three, many Vietnams" in their struggle against U.S. imperialism.[21] Following his death the next year, Guevara became a martyr in his own right, his image, words, and likeness invoked by everyone from athletes to artists to leftists the world over.[22] While few—if any—historical figures match the global appeal and endurance of Che, he nevertheless joins a pantheon of twentieth-century martyrs who have been reclaimed as global icons. Other one-word names like Frida, Marley, Marilyn, Mao, and even the rapper Tupac come to mind.[23] To be sure, Túpac Amaru does not begin to approach the Zeitgeist associated with these other figures. Yet, what makes the Andean rebel so significant is precisely what sets him apart from the rest of the herd. He is a figure that preceded mass media, the video camera, the record player, and the photographic lens. He also preceded the civil rights movement, the U.S. Civil War, the Latin American nation-state, and the very concepts of antiracism, anti-imperialism, the left, and decoloniality with which he has been associated. What makes Túpac Amaru such a unique icon in the modern era is that he was never a figure of the modern era to begin with. In this sense, Túpac Amaru I and II join a small handful of historical figures whose causes predated the nation-state yet continue to resonate with audiences across the Americas. The history of Túpac Amaru's long afterlife speaks to the icon's propensity for rebirth, reappropriation, and reinvention more than half a millennia after the death of the last Inca who bore his name. As long as the legacies of colonialism and racism prevail in the Americas—as long as there is a revolutionary cause to champion—Túpac Amaru lays in waiting, recoiled like a serpent ready to strike.

Notes

1. The literature on the Túpac Amaru Rebellion is too vast to list here. For a general introduction, see, for example, Boleslao Lewin, *La rebelión de Túpac Amaru y los orígenes de la independencia Hispanoamericana* (Buenos Aires: Sociedad Editora Latino Americana, 1967); Daniel Valcárcel, *La rebelión de Túpac Amaru* (Lima: Fondo de Cultura Económica, 1970); Alberto Flores Galindo, ed., *Túpac Amaru II–1780: Sociedad colonial y sublevaciones populares* (Lima: Retablo de Papel Ediciones, 1976); Scarlett O'Phelan Godoy, *La gran rebelión en los Andes: De Túpac Amaru a Túpac Catari* (Lima: PETROPERU CPC, 1995); Lillian Estelle Fisher, *The Last Inca Revolt* (Norman: University of Oklahoma Press, 1966); and Charles F. Walker, *The Tupac Amaru Rebellion* (Cambridge, MA: Harvard University Press, 2016).
2. For more on the world in which Condorcanqui came of age, see Ward Stavid, *The World of Túpac Amaru: Conflict, Community, and Identity in Colonial Peru* (Lincoln: University of Nebraska Press, 1999).
3. See John Hemmings, *The Conquest of the Incas* (San Diego: Harcourt, 1970), and Kim MacQuarrie, *The Last Days of the Incas* (New York: Simon and Schuster, 2007).
4. See Walker, *The Tupac Amaru Rebellion*.
5. See Sergio Serulnikov, *Subverting Colonial Authority: Challenges to Spanish Rule in Eighteenth-Century Southern Andes* (Durham, NC: Duke University Press, 2003); Sinclair Thomson, *We Alone Will Rule: Native Andean Politics in the Age of Insurgency* (Madison: University of Wisconsin Press, 2002); and Nicolas A. Robins, *Genocide and Millennialism in Upper Peru: The Great Rebellion of 1780–1782* (Westport, CT: Praeger, 2002).
6. Walker, *The Tupac Amaru Rebellion*, 165.
7. For more on the scope of Andean insurrections during this period, see, for example, Walker, *The Tupac Amaru Rebellion*; Serulnikov, *Subverting Colonial Authority*; Thomson, *We Alone Will Rule*; and Robins, *Genocide and Millennialism*.
8. Charles F. Walker, "The General and His Rebel: Juan Velasco Alvarado and the Reinvention of Túpac Amaru II," in *The Peculiar Revolution: Rethinking the Peruvian Experiment under Military Rule*, ed. Carlos Aguirre and Paulo Drinot (Austin: University of Texas Press, 2017), 49–72; Raúl H. Asensio, *El Apóstol de los andes: El culto a Túpac Amaru en Cusco durante la revolución velasquista (1968–1975)* (Lima: Instituto de Estudios Peruanos, 2017); Christabelle Roca-Rey, *La propaganda visual durante el gobierno de Juan Velasco Alvarado (1968–1975)* (Lima: Instituto de Estudios

Peruanos, 2016); Enrique Mayer, *Ugly Stories of the Peruvian Agrarian Reform* (Durham, NC: Duke University Press, 2009), 43.

9. Segunda Conferencia Nacional del Partido Comunista Peruano (SL), Group A, Box 2, Folder 2, PCP-SL, July 1982, 3, Documenting the Peruvian Insurrection, Davis Library, University of North Carolina at Chapel Hill.
10. For a political history of the MRTA, see Mario Miguel Meza, "El Movimiento Revolucionario Túpac Amaru (MRTA) y las fuentes de la revolución en América Latina" (Doctoral thesis, El Colegio de México, 2012), and Miguel La Serna, *With Masses and Arms: Peru's Tupac Amaru Revolutionary Movement* (Chapel Hill: University of North Carolina Press, 2020).
11. Pablo Brum, *The Robin Hood Guerrillas: The Epic Journey of Uruguay's Tupamaros* (Self-published, 2014).
12. Lindsey Churchill, *Becoming the Tupamaros: Solidarity and Transnational Revolutionaries in Uruguay and the United States* (Nashville, TN: Vanderbilt University Press, 2014).
13. Quoted in Allen Hughes, *Dear Mama*, Episode 1, "Panther Power" (FX Productions, 2022).
14. "You Had to Be There: MTV News Spends a Day with Tupac at Venice Beach," MTV News, 1995, https://www.youtube.com/watch?v=GpPbYGJRgoQ.
15. Tupac Shakur, Interview in *New Generations 2.0 Hip-Hop Magazine TV Show*, 1993, https://www.youtube.com/watch?v=cbzINgweVac.
16. See Jeremy Prestholdt, *Icons of Dissent: The Global Resonance of Che, Marley, Tupac, and Bin Laden* (Oxford: Oxford University Press, 2019), chap. 4.
17. "Los Tupamaros, el brazo armado del chavismo," *Infobae*, February 13, 2014, https://www.infobae.com/2014/02/13/1543408-los-tupamaros-el-brazo-armado-del-chavismo/. According to George Ciccariello-Maher, the radical Venezuelan youth groups known popularly as the "Tupamaros" date back at least to the mid-1980s. See Ciccariello-Maher, *We Created Chávez: A People's History of the Venezuelan Revolution* (Durham, NC: Duke University Press, 2013), 67–87.
18. Melina Gaona and Andrea López, *Género, comunicación y cultura en dos organizaciones sociales de San Salvador de Jujuy* (San Salvador de Jujuy, Argentina: Universidad Nacional de Jujuy, 2013); Santiago Battezzati, "La Tupac Amaru: Intermediación de intereses de los sectores populares informales en la provincia de Jujuy," *Desarrollo económico* 52, no. 205 (April–June 2012): 147–71.
19. "Yo soy negra, coy colla, pero no soy pelotuda," *Clarín*, June 20, 2011, https://www.clarin.com/politica/negra-colla-pelotuda_0_HJ3FR6xTvXg.html.

20. Matthew Harrison Tedford, "Taller Tupac Amaru," May 4, 2013, http://www.mhtedford.com/taller-tupac-amaru.
21. For more on Che's revolutionary vision at the Tricontinental Conference, see Michelle D. Paranzino, "Two, Three, Many Vietnams: Che Guevara's Tricontinental Revolutionary Vision," in *The Tricontinental Revolution: Third World Radicalism and the Cold War*, ed. R. Joseph Parrott and Mark Atwood Lawrence (Cambridge: Cambridge University Press, 2022), 276–303.
22. See Michael J. Casey, *Che's Afterlife: The Legacy of an Image* (New York: Vintage, 2009), and Prestholdt, *Icons of Dissent*, chaps. 1, 6.
23. Prestholdt, *Icons of Dissent*; Julia Lovell, *Maoism: A Global History* (New York: Knopf Doubleday, 2019).

Curating the Pantheon in Mexico
HISTORY AND MEMORY

William A. Booth

> Heaven is just up there; one can see it and dream about it. Up there are the fruits of the Mexican Revolution, the heroes of the fatherland, the nationalized nation, the *ejidos* of the agrarian reform, popular culture, the expropriation of foreign oil companies, social security, rescued indigenous traditions, the murals of Diego Rivera.
>
> —Roger Bartra, "Missing Democracy"

As we see in the essay by Erin Zavitz in this volume, the revolutionary general and Haiti's first head of state, Jean-Jacques Dessalines, was erased from official national ideology only to be appropriated once the futility of such erasure in the face of popular adoration was recognized. This century-long process has echoes in a similar series of developments in Mexico. Both the independence struggle (ca. 1810–ca. 1821) and the Mexican Revolution (1910 onward, with little consensus on when it ended) brought forth their own galleries of heroes, sanitized, appropriated, and remolded to fit the purposes of their political successors. As Roger Bartra notes above, this national-revolutionary pantheon is only a part of the superstructure that kept the postrevolutionary regime in power for seven decades, yet it is a crucial one.

The first time I was in Mexico for Independence Day celebrations—in 2001, a few days after the 9/11 attacks, in fact—some friends took me to hear the local mayor read the *grito*. The *grito*, in which a cryer wishes long life to a list of heroes before climaxing in three cries of *¡Viva Mexico!*, is one of the most clearly defined expressions of the pantheon. The modern version is not quite as stirring as the purported original *Grito de Dolores* made by Father Miguel Hidalgo in 1810—"death to the corrupt government" is the last thing modern Mexican regimes have wanted after all—but it does hark back in evocative fashion to a popular, anti-imperialist insurrection. Usually, as a starting point, it goes as follows:

> ¡Mexicanos!
> ¡Vivan los héroes que nos dieron patria!
> ¡Viva Hidalgo!
> ¡Viva Morelos!
> ¡Viva Josefa Ortiz de Domínguez!
> ¡Viva Allende!
> ¡Viva Aldama!
> ¡Viva la independencia Nacional!
> ¡Viva México!, ¡Viva México!, ¡Viva México!

The events of each September 15 are not precisely Independence Day celebrations but rather a rebranding of the birthday of prerevolutionary dictator Porfirio Díaz, in combination with the anniversary (a day after) of the *Grito de Dolores*. Independence was actually declared on September 28, 1821, eleven years later, but the manner in which Mexico achieved independence and the form of the new state do not sit easily with the official national narrative.[1] Two radical priests played fundamental roles in the early independence movement. Father Hidalgo was a priest and scholar who in the late eighteenth century settled in the parish of Dolores. There he left formal religious duties to his underlings while he turned his hand to artisanal and agricultural innovations, aiming to improve the lives of the local *campesinos* and to endow them with a degree of economic autonomy. He eventually fell foul of the authorities, who jealously guarded the market for tariff-protected goods. After a debilitating drought raised tensions in New Spain, Hidalgo made his famous "Cry of Dolores," and the uprising began in earnest. The following summer he was captured and executed, and for the next four years his successor—Father José María Morelos—led a guerrilla campaign against the royalists. The popular, multiethnic uprisings of Hidalgo and Morelos terrified both the colonial authorities and, over time, the local creole elite. Morelos was killed in 1815, and after six further years of conflict, the creoles made common cause with Agustín de Iturbide, a high-ranking royalist officer who turned his coat to lead the final charge toward independence. Having done so, he declared himself emperor and consigned himself to infamy.[2]

That particular September 15, I was staying in Tlalpan, in the south of Mexico City, and we walked down to the square to hear the *grito*. After the first few names, the mayor shouted "*¡Viva Villa!*" to some consternation; Pancho Villa's standing as a hero is ambiguous at best, and his legacy is pretty hard to sanitize.[3] This was my first inkling that the pantheon had a set of unspoken criteria for entry: dead Mexicans who had popular ideas or undertook momentous acts, able to be repackaged to appeal to some elements of all social classes. Villa does not quite tick those boxes, despite his reinterment in the Monument to the Revolution in 1976 (see below). As one who consistently reserved the right to rebel against the state, Villa is still seen as too much of a bandit for some to stomach.

The Mexican ambassador to the United Kingdom Diego Gomez-Pickering slipped up with the *grito* in 2015. Standing on the balcony of the Victoria and Albert Museum in London, he rattled through the list, left off two "canonical" names, and included Porfirio Díaz and Emiliano Zapata. As many commented at the time, the inclusion of leaders from long after the independence era was unorthodox, though it is hardly unknown—I have heard Zapata included on many occasions, for instance—but Díaz in particular was seen as a step too far. People wondered why Gomez-Pickering had not also included Iturbide or Maximilian I, the unfortunate Hapsburg transplanted from Austria to the Mexican throne on behalf of Napoleon III.[4]

This reveals the basic function of the pantheon: as a progressive, popular cloak, worn to conceal the essentially authoritarian body politic. For instance, the hero of oil nationalization, Lázaro Cárdenas, enacted policies that ran counter to almost everything Mexican governments have done since the Second World War, yet he has been consistently lauded and revered. So, Hidalgo, Morelos, Josefa Ortiz de Domínguez, Ignacio Allende, and Juan Aldama were elevated to the figurative pantheon, and their remains were placed under the Angel of Independence monument in 1925, save Ortiz de Domínguez, who had been reinterred in her home city of Querétaro. Iturbide, by attempting to install himself as emperor, is denied a place in the pantheon: his remains are to be found in the Metropolitan Cathedral, though I am not sure how many people go looking for them.

The pantheon goes far beyond the *grito*, encompassing heroes of the Reform Wars and liberation from French occupation, and later of the revolution. It would also reach back, linking modern rule to that of the

Cuauhtémoc Memorial, Mexico City. (Photo by Alejandro Linares García, Wikimedia, Creative Commons Attribution Share-Alike 3.0)

pre-Hispanic *Tlatoque,* or emperors. We can find the faces and names of the chosen ones in murals, on the metro map, in the names of streets and public institutions, and of course in monuments such as that to Cuauhtémoc in Mexico City. Lázaro Cárdenas named his son Cuauhtémoc; the latter remains an important figure on the Mexican left.

Zapata, unquestionably a national hero today, was killed in 1919 by the (briefly) victorious Carranza regime; later his image, and implicit approval, was used by successive postrevolutionary governments to give a powerful sheen (and, in fairness, some substance) to their agrarian policies. Sanitizing Zapata was dangerous though. From 1943 to 1962, followers of Rubén Jaramillo—who as a teenager had risen through the ranks of Zapata's forces—successively rebelled against Mexican governments in pursuit of overtly *zapatista* goals. Each time an amnesty was negotiated it broke down, and Jaramillo was eventually murdered (along with his family) by federal police.[5] More famously, in 1994 a rural, largely Indigenous group—the Ejército Zapatista de Liberación Nacional (EZLN)—seized part of Chiapas state in Zapata's name.[6] How does a pantheon of appropriation respond to its members being seized back by popular challenge? Such risky absorptions continue; in 1999, a Metro B station was named after the anarchist Ricardo Flores Magón, an antiauthoritarian hailed as a national hero by both government and dissidents for many decades.[7] Perhaps, like Dessalines, long enough had passed in the afterlife of this radical pamphleteer and campaigner for his image to safely adorn a piece of infrastructure, but Flores Magón's name and legacy are invoked in current struggles against the government in Oaxaca and elsewhere.

What was this all for? The salience of both the "imagined community" and the "invention of tradition" are now well digested, if not universally accepted, though both concepts are crucial to understanding the motivations of elite Mexican decision-makers from a wide range of ideological positions and across more than one hundred years.[8] Alan Knight has argued that "images and allegiances drawn from a (partly mythic) past helped shape discourse, policy, and political affiliation, and did so across a wide ideological spectrum.... Radicals like Adalberto Tejeda were at pains to place themselves within old historical traditions: in this case, the liberal tradition of Lerdo, Juárez, and Ocampo."[9] By creating one lineage running from the Aztec Triple Alliance to independence, through the Liberal period thence to the revolution, the pantheon would absorb a great swathe of ideological and ethnic identities. Octavio Paz talks of "distinct and contradictory phases of one continuing effort to break free," and the Partido Revolucionario Institucional (PRI, the party that ruled, essentially, from 1929–2000, then again from 2012–18) placed themselves as the logical culmination of that effort.[10]

A more concrete expression of the pantheon is the Rotunda of Illustrious Persons, a special section of Mexico's largest cemetery, the Panteón de Dolores. Here one can find the graves of many of those mentioned previously, as well as a host of others including oft-imprisoned painter and

Rotunda of Illustrious Persons, Panteón de Dolores, Mexico City. (Photo by Leigh Thelmadatter, Wikimedia, Creative Commons Attribution Share-Alike 3.0)

communist (and would-be assassin of Trotsky) David Alfaro Siqueiros, painter María Izquierdo, union leader Vicente Lombardo Toledano, and composer Silvestre Revueltas. Their many talents and ideologies are brought under the national umbrella and placed at a safe historical distance.[11]

It is notable that some leftists have had to wait rather longer than others for interment in the Rotunda of Illustrious Persons. While the muralists Diego Rivera and David Alfaro Siqueiros—the former a rather heterodox communist, the latter a committed Stalinist—were interred in the years of their deaths, Ricardo Flores Magón, Vicente Lombardo Toledano, and Valentín Campa all had more circuitous routes to the Rotunda. Flores Magón, an anarchist famed for transnational agitating in the revolutionary era, died in a U.S. prison in 1922 in somewhat unclear circumstances. The return of Flores Magón's body was itself a contentious process: internationally, between the United States and Mexico, but also ideologically, as different factions of the Mexican labor movement attempted to claim credit and thus endow themselves with the revolutionary legitimacy that his legacy would bestow. He had been denounced by the dictator Porfirio

Díaz as a "bad Mexican," and his absorption into the pantheon tells us a good deal about the shift in national identity and narrative.[12] As World War II came to a close, he was interred in the Rotunda with public acknowledgment of his role in fomenting revolution. The timing of this was important for two reasons. First, the war had thrown Mexico and the United States into close cooperation, and it no doubt benefited the Ávila Camacho government to show that—contrary to appearances—a radical anti-imperialist anarchist "belonged" to its nationalist tradition. Second, enough time had passed that Flores Magón's own differences with the putative victors of the Mexican Revolution—as well as other leftist currents—could be papered over in a ceremony of healing, or perhaps of forgetting.

Lombardo Toledano and Campa present a pair of contrasting examples. Lombardo styled himself as a Marxist patriot and sought the ear of the government as a friendly interlocutor with organized labor.[13] This served him well in the 1930s, but he was increasingly sidelined in the 1940s. Flirting with oppositional politics, he set up the Partido Popular but as a "friendly critic"; even this was too much for the ruling PRI, which effectively stymied the party's establishment and growth. Lombardo's death came at an inopportune moment for the left, just a few weeks after the Tlatelolco massacre in 1968. However, unlike several leading figures both on the left and center of Mexican politics, he went out to bat for the government, denouncing the protesters as "provocateurs" and agents of foreign powers. His party's newspaper was similarly unsupportive of calls for democratic reform. For this he was rewarded—in death if not in life—with accession to the pantheon. Although it took until 1994 for his interment in the Rotunda to occur, he had been a loyal soldier for the regime; it was perhaps fitting that the burial took place under the eye of neoliberal president Carlos Salinas. As Daniela Spenser put it, "Lombardo took on the defence of the state, whose sovereignty he believed was challenged, covering up the tragedy that engulfed Mexico in the Plaza de las Tres Culturas in Tlatelolco on 2 October 1968."[14] By contrast, it is worth noting that the great communist writer and activist José Revueltas—who on the day of Lombardo's death was arrested and incarcerated at the infamous Lecumberri prison (itself now the rather chilling setting for Mexico's National Archive)—has been welcomed into neither the figurative pantheon nor the Rotunda, and lies in the peaceful setting of the French Cemetery a few kilometers away.

The case of Valentín Campa is almost the inverse to that of Lombardo Toledano. Campa was a prominent left-wing member of the Communist Party in the 1930s but was expelled in 1940 as the organization bitterly divided over both the attempted (and then successful) assassination of Trotsky, as well as the Nazi-Soviet Non-Aggression Pact. In the 1940s, Campa resisted the crackdown on the left and was a founder of the Mexican Worker-Peasant Party, then was jailed (one of thirteen sentences) following the 1959 railroad strikes. In contrast to Lombardo, Campa embraced the wave of protests in the late 1960s, and following his release from jail, scored a very respectable million-plus votes as a write-in candidate for a more-or-less united left. He remained a somewhat marginal figure, though, and while lionized by many, was far from a pantheon shoo-in, dying as he did in 1999 as Mexico was moving painfully but inexorably into neoliberal modernity.

It took the presidency of Andrés Manuel López Obrador to bring Campa back into the imagined community. In 2019, López Obrador solemnly oversaw the reinterment of Campa's remains among the Illustrious Persons of the Rotunda. However, this was not a moment of national unity but rather a restatement of contemporary divisions. For all that López Obrador has sought to portray himself as a left-wing break from the old parties, there are aspects to his rule that are paradigmatically *PRIista*. He no doubt saw the reinternment of a consistent, radical, and anti-PRI labor leader as a demonstration of left-wing legitimacy; his opponents chose to call his bluff and pretend that the burial was an attack on the Mexican state. Hence Campa has been made resident in the official physical pantheon, the Rotunda of Illustrious Persons, but thanks to the significantly altered rhetorical context, his position in the imagined roster of national heroes is yet to be confirmed.

The diversity of the pantheon has given it tremendous flexibility as a political tool. Its members range from firebrand revolutionary priests like Hidalgo and Morelos to lofty men of letters such as lawyer and murdered vice president Pino Suárez. While few women have been elevated into the group (Josefa Ortiz de Domínguez and Leona Vicario are notable exceptions), a number of Mexicans of Indigenous heritage are there, though whether they are representing a multiethnic nation or being used to hide its gross inequalities is another matter.[15] There is not space here to delve far into the state's attempts to appropriate, tame, and depoliticize Indigenous identities, but where Indigenous Mexicans are placed in the

Monument to the Revolution, Mexico City. (Photo by Ismael Villafranco, Wikimedia, Creative Commons Attribution 2.0)

pantheon it is firmly as "Mexicans"—no hint of ethnic separatism is brooked.[16] Mexican rulers have benefited greatly from having a large and silent supporting cast drawn from so many backgrounds. The result, as Alan Knight has suggested, is that "despite its hoary and ponderous image, tradition proved remarkably nimble."[17]

A final representation of revolutionary identity and memory—both physical, as a tomb, and metaphorical, as a symbol—is the Monument to the Revolution. Sited a little north of the Paseo de la Reforma in Mexico City and close to several other memorials—including those to Independence, Cuauhtémoc, Benito Juárez, and the women's struggle—it is one of the key embodiments of the imagined pantheon. Having sat unfinished for decades, the skeleton of a planned national legislative building was repurposed as a memorial to the revolution and, latterly, to its greatest leaders. As Thomas Benjamin put it, "Mexican history was refashioned, literally and physically, in iron, stone, and bronze." The first stone was laid in 1910 by the soon-to-be-overthrown President Díaz; the repurposing and transformation took place between 1933 and 1938, straddling the transition from *callismo* to *cardenismo*. Both the monument's form and the timing of its construction are seen by Benjamin as crucial to understanding its purpose: "to unify symbolically *la Revolución* and to heal the wounds of memory." Initially this monument was decoupled from the heroes and martyrs of the revolution. After all, each of them was a villain to many. "The collective memory of postrevolutionary Mexico was," Benjamin argued, "shaped by the unregulated multivocal expressions of competing revolutionary traditions."[18]

Thus, where supporters of Francisco I. Madero, Zapata, Felipe Carrillo Puerto, and Carranza had fought it out (often literally) to determine legitimacy—and ultimately supremacy—the postrevolutionary government wished to sidestep such conflict by honoring anonymous, ordinary citizens. Their fights for independence, for reform and the law, for peasants' rights, and for workers' rights were telegraphed in statue groups at each corner. However, this intended anonymity did not last long; the desire for martyrs and enforced enmeshing of their competing visions of the revolution won out. As the remains of Venustiano Carranza, Madero, Plutarco Elías Calles, Cárdenas, and Villa were placed beneath the monument between 1942 and 1976, their ideas and rallying cries were no longer visceral but rather marmoreal. At least that was the theory.

Notes

1. There is actually a third contender, that being September 13, when (in 1813) the Congress of Chilpancingo declared independence. This date has another patriotic connotation though: it is dedicated to the memory of the *Niños Heroes* (Boy Heroes), six young cadets who gave their lives rather than surrender Chapultepec Castle to the advancing U.S. Army in 1847, but that is another story.
2. See, *inter alia*, Timothy J. Henderson, *The Mexican Wars of Independence* (New York: Hill and Wang, 2010).
3. By far the most complete analysis of Villa's career, impact, and legacy is Friedrich Katz's monumental study *The Life and Times of Pancho Villa* (Stanford, CA: Stanford University Press, 1998).
4. See Edward Shawcross, *The Last Emperor of Mexico* (New York: Faber and Faber, 2023).
5. See Tanalís Padilla, *Rural Resistance in the Land of Zapata* (Durham, NC: Duke University Press, 2008).
6. See, *inter alia*, Neil Harvey, *The Chiapas Rebellion* (Durham, NC: Duke University Press, 1998).

7. See Claudio Lomnitz, *The Return of Comrade Ricardo Flores Magón* (Brooklyn, NY: Zone Books, 2014).
8. Benedict Anderson, *Imagined Communities* (London: Verso, 1983); Eric Hobsbawm and Terence Ranger, *The Invention of Tradition* (Cambridge: Cambridge University Press, 1983).
9. Alan Knight, "Popular Culture and the Revolutionary State in Mexico, 1910–1940," *Hispanic American Historical Review* 74, no. 3 (1994): 398.
10. Octavio Paz, *The Labyrinth of Solitude* (New York: Grove Press, 1985), 167.
11. For a wide-ranging and detailed discussion of the creation of a broad revolutionary identity, see Thomas Benjamin, *La Revolución: Mexico's Great Revolution as Memory, Myth and History* (Austin: University of Texas Press, 2000).
12. See Kelly Lytle Hernández, *Bad Mexicans: Race, Empire, and Revolution in the Borderlands* (New York: Norton, 2022).
13. See Daniela Spenser, *In Combat: The Life of Lombardo Toledano* (Leiden: Brill, 2019); for a critical view of Lombardo's role, see William A. Booth, "Hegemonic Nationalism, Subordinate Communism: The Mexican Left 1945–7," *Journal of Latin American Studies* 50, no. 1 (2018): 31–58.
14. Spenser, *In Combat*, 382.
15. Two prominent Afro-Mexicans, José María Morelos and Vicente Guerrero, are rarely referred to as such, reflecting a broader awkward history of Afro-Mexican identity in the imagined community.
16. Here the rather prickly position of Felipe Carrillo Puerto in relation to the pantheon is relevant. In the 1920s, he was widely mourned and praised, having been murdered during a failed coup in the winter of 1923–24. An advocate of "racial resuscitation" for the Mayan people, his brand of proto-decolonial socialism sits uneasily with the revolutionary narrative; he rests where he was shot, in a cemetary in Merida, Yucatán. See Peter Hulme, "Monuments and Promise: Maya Ruins and the Death of Felipe Carrillo Puerto," *Transmodernity* 9, no. 7 (2021): 143–71, and Ben Fallaw, "Felipe Carrillo Puerto of Revolutionary-Era Yucatán, Mexico: Popular Leader, Caesar, or Martyr?" in *Heroes and Hero Cults in Latin America*, ed. Samuel Brunk and Ben Fallaw (Austin: University of Texas Press, 2006), 128–48.
17. Knight, "Popular Culture and the Revolutionary State in Mexico," 398.
18. Benjamin, *La Revolución*, 117, 118, 123.

Performing Dessalines
STATE AND POPULAR APPROPRIATIONS OF HAITI'S
FOUNDING FATHER, JEAN-JACQUES DESSALINES

Erin Zavitz

Pow! Pow! The sound of gunshots ricochets through the central square near Haiti's Bureau d'Ethnologie (Bureau of Ethnology). People start running followed by a white mist. Tear gas. I quickly learn from the Haitians standing at the same corner that there are antigovernment protests occurring throughout Port-au-Prince. They offer me a packet of water to help with the stinging in my eyes. I explain that I am waiting for my moto-driver. More people are on the move. Pasteur calls my cell and asks, "Ki kote mwen ye?" (Where am I?) He is at the Bureau d'Ethnologie but cannot find me. I scan the crowd and see Pasteur with his bike at the corner. I rush over and hop on the back, securing my helmet strap as he accelerates. We ride up from downtown to the wealthy area of Pétion-ville. We pass the remains of more protests—I learn many of the men and women are out in support of a new movement, Kòdinasyon Desalin (Dessalines Coordination), or KÒD.[1]

KÒD is one of many Haitian political movements. According to anthropologist Chelsey L. Kivland, they are "a federation of urban activists named after the revolutionary general and Haiti's first head of state, Jean-Jacques Dessalines."[2] KÒD formed in early 2013 following the election of Michel Martelly to provide a progressive alternative to Martelly's government and continue the anti-imperialist movement that was begun by the Lavalas Family Party in the mid-1990s. Their acronym means rope (kòd) in Kreyòl, and the party's slogans create a play on words. KÒD will tie up the president, the UN forces, or imperialists.[3] The name could suggest more sinister actions such as hanging. It may also derive from the colonial-era conflation of the KiKongo term *kanga* and the French verb *amarrer*. David Geggus explains that both meant "bind or tie" but came to signify the use of supernatural forces to bewitch or render harmless.[4] Whether or not KÒD members are turning to Vodou to combat their enemies, the reference to tying up corrupt politicians alludes to the colonial usage of the verb. The name may illustrate how the urban, disenfranchised Haitians have adapted the language of slave resistance to new struggles. Unmistakably, it serves as a warning to politicians who understand the additional meanings of the name.

Weeks before KÒD's protest, President Martelly held a memorial service for Dessalines on the anniversary of his assassination, October 17.[5] Following a tradition begun over 150 years earlier with the first memorial service to Haiti's founder in 1845, Martelly employed the memory of Dessalines to demonstrate his connection with the Haitian majority. In all these performances, Haitians construct narratives of the revolution and offer competing interpretations of Haitian identity and social divisions. The original man Jean-Jacques Dessalines is lost to the myths that have emerged over the centuries after his death.[6] Dessalines was likely born into slavery and remained enslaved until liberating himself through the revolution. Yet, Dessalines became a property owner and even emperor. He is both a representative of the people and a former head of state. As the protests of KÒD and the memorial service of Martelly illustrate, Dessalines's memory retains the contradictions of his life and represents the legacies of slavery and the revolution in present-day Haiti. Haiti's founder is both an institutionalized hero employed by the state to unite Haitians and a popular hero used by the people to criticize the government and its failures.

Establishing Traditions: Dessalines and Celebrations of Independence Day

Haiti's revolution created the first postslavery and second postcolonial state in the Americas, and it encompassed the hemisphere's largest and first successful slave revolt. Defined by Haitian anthropologist Michel-Rolph Trouillot as "unthinkable," the revolution and the creation of an independent Black state challenged contemporary frames of reference (slavery, colonialism, European cultural superiority).[7] Building a Black state and nation in a world dominated by slavery and colonialism was a Sisyphean undertaking. Memories of the revolution were integral to Haiti's state and nation formation, in particular commemorations of Haiti's founder, Dessalines.

The declaration of independence on January 1, 1804, created—de facto—Haiti's first national holiday.[8] Independence Day celebrations combined print (newspapers) and performance to build a national community and reach the population of former enslaved people born on the island or in Africa and free-born people of color, as well as naturalized Europeans and visiting European and American officials, merchants, and government officials. In the aftermath of Dessalines's assassination (October 17, 1806), Haitian politicians and intellectuals expunged Haiti's founding father from official memory including Independence Day celebrations. Nevertheless, unofficial celebrations continued, and Dessalines remained a hero in popular memory until the 1840s.[9]

Beginning in 1847 with the "election" of Faustin Soulouque, official celebrations of Dessalines blossomed.[10] These included building monuments and new national holidays.[11] Although Soulouqe was ridiculed in the international press, he represented "a symbol of true independence" to formerly enslaved people who could now hold titles of their own. An important aspect of this political transformation and independence was the memory of Dessalines.[12] Soulouque revised the 1846 constitution and created a new holiday, January 2, Jean-Jacques Dessalines day.[13] Appearing first as a new law in December 1848 and then as part of a constitutional article, the day honored Dessalines for his service to the country.[14] For the next decade, Dessalines's holiday took its place next to Independence Day celebrations. Soulouque's resurrection of Haiti's first emperor and institutionalization of a holiday marked a milestone in the transformation of official memory. Even after the mixed-race leader Fabre Geffrard toppled Soulouque in 1859 and formed a new republican government, Dessalines had a constitutionally sanctioned national holiday.[15] Yet, with the fall of Geffrard, Dessalines Day disappeared. A more inclusive Heroes' Day began in the mid-twentieth century during François Duvalier's dictatorship, and October 17, the date of Dessalines's assassination, has evolved as an important commemoration, though it is only a legal holiday and not named in any constitutions.[16]

In the second half of the nineteenth century, as unity remained an elusive goal and threats to independence loomed on the horizon, the Haitian state and elite turned to the memory of Dessalines to reinvigorate the Haitian nation on its one hundredth birthday. Mounting state debt and political struggles, along with the increased national significance of 1904, provided a space that had not been available in annual celebrations for associations and individuals to work with the government in planning the event. Beyond fostering more public engagement, L'Association du Centenaire, founded to prepare for the nation's centennial, worked with Nord Alexis's government to return commemorations to the city of Gonaïves, where Dessalines had declared independence in 1804. And, foreshadowing the events of 1954, they reenacted January 1, 1804, including the reading and signing of the declaration. As Alexis explained in his speech that morning, "It is a great pleasure for me to come to the same place as the Founder to renew, on the Altar of the Homeland, our oath of Independence."[17] While the symbolic potential of 1904 would quickly dim, the centennial did offer one rebirth—the memory of Jean-Jacques Dessalines.

Dessalines's full entry into the national pantheon coincided with a historiographic shift at the turn of the century. Haitian authors began writing histories that placed Black Haitians at the center of their analysis, and they began to redefine specific aspects of peasant culture as positive.[18] The U.S. occupation of 1915–34 further spurred Haitian writers to embrace popular culture more thoroughly in the third wave of *indigénisme* in the 1920s and 1930s. Urban intellectuals launched nonviolent resistance through newspapers and cultural organizations. In their newspaper columns and discussions, a new generation of writers redefined Haitian identity. Similar to earlier waves of cultural nationalism of the 1830s and 1890s–1900s, these writers argued that the roots of Haitian identity lay in the culture of the Haitian folk, or the Black peasant majority. Unlike the earlier movements, this *indigénisme* did not dissipate. Instead, it initiated the adoption and at time cooption of folk culture, specifically Vodou practices and dance, by the Haitian elite. It also combined with *noirisme* (Black nationalism) to become an official national ideology that shaped the interpretation of Haiti's past. The removal of U.S. troops in 1934, the rise of a Black middle class, and the election of Dumarsais Estimé in 1946 facilitated the triumph of a new national vision.

Estimé came to power thanks to a politically active and demographically significant urban Black middle class who believed in the potential of Black political nationalism.[19] In particular, a group of radical Black nationalists, the *authentiques* (authentics), proclaimed themselves to be "the real inheritors of the legacy of Dessalines," and as Matthew Smith insists, they saw that it "was their responsibility to fulfill the historical promise of Toussaint and Dessalines." Fulfillment meant having "Black control of the state apparatus."[20] Key members of the *authentiques* included future dictator François Duvalier (Papa Doc), who employed the politics of memory and national myths to an extreme to justify his violent rule.

Commemorations of Independence Day reflected Haiti's political and cultural efflorescence in the mid-twentieth century. If 1904 symbolized a momentous achievement for the island nation, 1954 was even more significant, especially after fifteen years of U.S. occupation. President Paul Magloire, who had assumed power after the military intervened when Estimé tried to prolong his time in office by revising the constitution, ushered in a period of political expansion and economic growth. Haiti's franchise expanded to include all men over twenty-one and, after decades of campaigning, women.[21] Magloire promoted agricultural production, built new schools, and garnered U.S. support through his anticommunist campaigns. These actions ushered in a boom in tourism, particularly visitors from the United States.[22] In planning Haiti's sesquicentennial celebrations, Magloire, state officials, and intellectuals drew from 150 years of commemorative traditions for this notable anniversary and developed their own. While previous Independence Day celebrations had included international guests, 1954 illustrated a more concerted effort on the part of the state to "perform" Haiti for a foreign audience.[23]

Approaching an international audience took several forms. First was the publication of an oversized book with color photos. Entitled *Tricinquantenaire de l'Indépendance d'Haïti,* the book recounted Haiti's history and offered readers samples of Haitian literature alongside ads for the country's hotels and restaurants. The Office National de Tourisme and its New York counterpart, the Haitian Tourist Information Bureau, published the book through a Swiss press—Imprimerie Held S.A. (this publishing house would also print a book on Haitian military honors for the 150th anniversary). The bureau in New York actively worked through this publication and others to attract tourists to Haiti under Magloire's government. The president appointed Gérard de Catalogne to head the bureau. Catalogne, Chelsea Stieber states, was instrumental in combining interwar French fascism with Haitian ethnonationalism. Thus, his role at the bureau and in crafting an image for Haiti, including major state commemorations, is important for thinking about the evolution of Independence Day and the use of Haitian historical memory by Haitian officials. Catalogne would go on to work with François Duvalier, who capitalized on coopting historical myths and memories to bolster his dictatorship, not to fulfill Dessalines's "pathbreaking, radical, brilliant critiques of racism and systems of oppression."[24]

In terms of the book itself, one can imagine that this made a lovely coffee-table addition for the wealthy and adventurous tourist in the United States or Europe. The large color photos of Haitian cities, marketplaces, beaches, and mountains invited visitors to experience and explore the "sunny island where the historic charm of the Old World met the unparalleled picturesque of the Tropics."[25] The historic charm included the revolution, represented by photos of the Citadel (Henry Christophe's fortress constructed to protect the island from future French attacks) and paintings of revolutionary heroes. In addition, the book contained essays, short stories, and poems by contemporary Haitian intellectuals. In under 150 pages, the Tourist Bureau offered readers an introduction to Haiti, its culture, and landscapes to tempt them to come visit in person.

The book suggests one level of performance; for visitors who did attend Independence Day celebrations in Haiti, a more interactive experience awaited them. Similar to 1904, the festivities included a reading of the declaration. The strong anti-French language of the document shocked the French ambassador's wife, who broke down in tears according to the British ambassador or possibly even fainted.[26] The following day the Haitian Army reenacted the final battle of the revolution, Vertières. In band stands, Haitians and foreign dignitaries watched the battle.[27] In front of their eyes, the revolution was not just a memory but a living history. The passing of time condensed on the plains of Cap Haïtien. Festivities ended with a banquet in the ruins of Henry Christophe's palace, Sans Souci, during which Marian Anderson performed the Haitian national anthem "from the peristyle of the palace."[28] The four-day event was a lavish exhibit of Haiti's history and culture that paid homage to Dessalines and the country's founding.

Following these celebrations, Magloire faced increasing criticism as Hurricane Hazel destroyed crops, homes, and lives later in 1954. He had no more success than earlier presidents at changing Haiti's development path, and when the end of his term approached he also attempted to stay in office. The years 1956–57 were a period of violent political struggle that concluded with François Duvalier's assumption of power. Laurent Dubois aptly described the outcome: "Duvalier would offer his own response to Haiti's situation: a twisted synthesis of Estimé's populism and Magloire's conservatism, with a ferocious cult of personality at the center."[29]

A cornerstone of Duvalier's cult of personality was the cooption of Jean-Jacques Dessalines's commemorations. If previous heads of state had celebrated Dessalines, read founding documents, or staged reenactments, Duvalier surpassed them all by claiming to embody Dessalines and Haiti's other founders. To bolster his self-appointment as president for life in 1964, Duvalier and his officials published a state catechism that declared, "Dessalines, Toussaint, Christophe, Pétion, and Estimé are five distinct Chiefs of State who are substantiated in and form only one and the same President in the person of François Duvalier."[30] Duvalier did not just celebrate Dessalines; he was a reincarnation of the founder and other key Haitian leaders. To commemorate Haiti's revolutionary heroes was to celebrate Duvalier and any criticism of Duvalier was an attack on Haiti, its founding, and its history.

Haiti's newest national holiday, Heroes Day (January 2), facilitated this convergence of past and present. The holiday first appeared in the 1957 constitution, ratified months after Duvalier became president.[31] Duvalier and his new administration focused on the usual January 1 celebrations in 1958.[32] The following year, January 2 became its own holiday with a zealous speech by Duvalier in which he claimed to be renewing a tradition of addressing the Haitian people begun by Jean-Jacques Dessalines 156 years before.[33] Nevertheless, Dessalines's actions on January 2, 1804, included two proclamations, one that canceled all plantation leases and the second that standardized military uniforms.[34] Significant pronouncements, particularly the former, which moved to nationalize lands held by French colonists, suggest a different memory than January 1 and that unsurprisingly, Duvalier was manipulating history to serve his own ends.

The end of the Duvalier dictatorships marked a democratic opening for Haiti that never came to fruition. As political turmoil and disasters have marked Haitian history in the twenty-first century, Dessalines has remained a potent figure for all Haitians, despite Duvalier's corruption of his legacy.[35] Art historian Lindsay Twa proposes that representations of Dessalines, the only Haitian hero to be incorporated into the Vodou pantheon, shift with each individual or, I would add, group, similar to the *lwa* (Vodou spirit) mounting a Voduisant. Twa contends that "Dessalines's spirit and legacy has only grown more powerful as representations continuously reconstitute, rework and repair this mercurial hero."[36] Dessalines remains a figure of radical critique, and his memory offers an alternative vision for Haiti.

Returning to the 2013 protests, KÒD members and others who had joined declared "yo pral kay Pétion." They are going to Pétion's house, meaning Pétionville, the wealthy city/suburb up the hill from the heat and stench of Port-au-Prince, founded by mixed-race president Jean-Pierre Boyer in honor of Pétion, Haiti's first president and revolutionary hero but also a conspirator in Dessalines's assassination. The protesters continued, "Dessalines yo vle pale." The command could be translated as "Dessalines wants to talk." Yet, the Kreyòl *yo* leaves open several interpretations. *Yo* is both the third-person plural "they" or plural article. Thus, perhaps the rallying call was "The Dessalines want to talk," meaning that all the protesters became Dessalines that day.

The invocations of Haiti's revolutionary heroes on the streets of Port-au-Prince condense the two hundred–plus years that have passed since the declaration of Haitian independence. The revolutionary past merges with present political tensions to continue the revolution begun over two hundred years ago. Dessalines and Pétion are still alive; they take on or perhaps possess new bodies and come to symbolize new struggles and divisions. The wealthy, educated, French-speaking Haitians of any hue signify Pétion, as do their air-conditioned SUVs, generators, and gated houses. The undereducated, underemployed, politically disenfranchised, Kreyòl-speaking urban masses are Dessalines, and they are marching on.

Notes

1. Erin Zavitz, "Revolutionary Memories: Celebrating and Commemorating the Haitian Revolution" (PhD diss., University of Florida, 2015), 359.
2. Chelsey L. Kivland, "'The People' Exposed: Spatio-Racial-Affective Alterity in Haitian Popular Protest," *Latin American and Caribbean Ethnic Studies* 15, no. 3 (2020): 219.
3. Kim Ives, "The Dessalines Coordination Launches Itself as a New Party," *Haïti Liberté* 7, no. 31 (February 2014), http://haiti-liberte.com/archives/volume7-31/The%20Dessalines%20Coordination.asp.
4. David Geggus, "Haitian Vodou in the Eighteenth Century: Language, Culture, Resistance," *Jahrbuch für Geschichte Lateinamerikas* 28, no. 1 (1991): 28–29.
5. Robenson Geffrard, "Pour Dessalines, Martelly veut tourner le dos à la confrontation," *Le Nouvelliste* (Port-au-Prince), October 18, 2013, https://www.lenouvelliste.com/article/122811/pour-dessalines-martelly-veut-tourner-le-dos-a-la-confrontation.

6. For more on Dessalines, see Julia Gaffield's forthcoming publication *I Have Avenged America: Jean-Jacques Dessalines and Haiti's Fight for Freedom* (New Haven, CT: Yale University Press, 2025).
7. Michel-Rolph Trouillot, *Silencing the Past: Power and the Production of History* (Boston: Beacon Press, 1995), 82.
8. For a more detailed discussion of Haitian Independence Day, see Erin Zavitz, "Revolutionary Commemorations: Jean-Jacques Dessalines and Haitian Independence Day, 1804–1904," in *Haitian Declaration of Independence: Creation, Context, and Legacy*, ed. Julia Gaffield (Charlottesville: University of Virginia Press, 2016), 219–37, and Zavitz, "Revolutionary Memories."
9. Thomas Madiou, *Histoire d'Haïti* (1847–48; reprint Port-au-Prince: Henri Deschamps, 1988–91), 3:406; Beaubrun Ardouin, *Études sur l'histoire d'Haïti* (Paris: Dézobry et E. Magdeleine, 1853–60), 6:74n1.
10. In nineteenth-century Haitian politics, presidents were often selected by a process called "politique de doublure." Translated as "the politics of the understudy," it was a system devised by lighter-skinned elites to select Black puppet presidents who would support their agenda. See Laurent Dubois, *Haiti: The Aftershocks* (New York: Metropolitan Books, 2012), 131, 145, for more discussion.
11. *Le Moniteur* (Port-au-Prince), May 8, June 12, 1847; Carlo A. Célius, "Neoclassicism and the Haitian Revolution," in *The World of the Haitian Revolution*, ed. David Patrick Geggus and Norman Fiering (Bloomington: Indiana University Press, 2009), 381.
12. Murdo MacLeod, "The Soulouque Regime in Haiti, 1847–1859: A Revaluation," *Journal of Caribbean Studies* 10, no. 3 (1970): 36. For a longer study of Soulouque's rule, see Emmanuel Lachaud, "The Emancipated Empire: Faustin I Soulouque and the Origins of the Second Haitian Empire, 1847–1859" (PhD diss., Yale University, 2021).
13. Louis Joseph Janvier, *Les Constitutions d'Haïti, 1801–1885* (Paris: C. Marpon et E. Flammarion, 1886), 261.
14. "Le peuple s'enivre avec calme à ses réjouissances ordinaires, a l'occasion de l'anniversaire de notre indépendance qui cette année, a été suivi de la fête instituée en l'honneur de l'illustre auteur de cette Indépendance. La veille de ces fêtes, un grande nombre de prisonniers politiques ont été rendus à la liberté." "Secrétaire Général à Ardouin," January 6, 1849, Maximilien Eugene Collection, New York Public Library.
15. Janvier, *Les Constitutions*, 272; *L'Opinion Nationale* (Port-au-Prince), January 5, 1861.
16. No twentieth-century Haitian constitution lists Jean Jacques Dessalines Day (October 17) as a holiday. The 1957 constitution does name

Heroes' Day, January 2. Constitution de la République d'Haïti, 1957, article 183, Digital Library of the Caribbean, https://ufdc.ufl.edu/aa00000620/00001. The constitutions do state that legal holidays are established by law, and Jean Jacques Dessalines Day is listed as a legal holiday in 1986 communications with the French Embassy. "Calendrier des Fêtes Légales," série B 524/PO/B/226, Centre des Archives Diplomatiques de Nantes, Nantes, France.

17. "C'est une bien grande satisfaction pour moi de venir à la même place que le Fondateur, faire renouveler sur l'Autel de la Patrie notre serment d'Indépendance." *Le Moniteur,* January 2, 1904.
18. For example, Hannibal Price's *De la Réhabilitation de la Race noire par la République d'Haïti* (Port-au-Prince: Imprimerie J. Verrollot, 1900) refuted foreign authors' racist portrayals of Haiti and in the process secularized Vodou. By so doing, he worked to legitimate discussions of Vodou in elite circles as a motivating force for the enslaved in the revolution.
19. For a detailed discussion of the factors and "revolution" of 1946, see Matthew Smith, *Red and Black in Haiti: Radicalism, Conflict, and Political Change, 1934–1957* (Chapel Hill: University of North Carolina Press, 2009), 71–101.
20. Smith, *Red and Black,* 108; Matthew Smith, "Vive 1804! The Haitian Revolution and the Revolutionary Generation of 1946," *Caribbean Quarterly* 50, no. 4 (2004): 25, 35.
21. Chelsea Stieber, *Haiti's Paper War: Post-Independence Writing, Civil War, and the Making of the Republic 1804–1954* (New York: New York University Press, 2020), 255; Smith, *Red and Black,* 151. For a thorough discussion of women's political activity in the twentieth century, see Grace Sanders Johnson, *White Gloves, Black Nation: Women, Citizenship, and Political Wayfaring in Haiti* (Chapel Hill: University of North Carolina Press, 2023).
22. Dubois, *Haiti,* 318–19; Stieber, *Haiti's Paper War,* 255.
23. For much of the nineteenth century, intellectuals and heads of state realized that foreigners viewed performances of nationhood, be they national holidays, history, or literary works, as symbols of Black potential or failure. See Marlene Daut, *Tropics of Haiti: Race and the Literary History of the Haitian Revolution, 1789–1865* (Liverpool: Liverpool University Press, 2015); Karen Salt, *The Unfinished Revolution: Haiti, Black Sovereignty and Power in the 19th-Century Atlantic World* (Liverpool: Liverpool University Press, 2019); and Stieber, *Haiti's Paper War.*
24. Building on the work of Lyonel Trouillot and Marlene Daut, Stieber has contended that Dessalines initiated a "radical critique" of Enlightenment universalism which avowed Black humanity. Stieber, *Haiti's Paper War,* 6–10, 246, 254, 255n2.

25. *Tricinquantenaire de l'Indépendance d'Haïti* (Lausanne, Switzerland: Imprimerie Held, 1954), title page.
26. J. Mill Irving to Anthony Eden, January 8, 1954, FO 371/103493/AT1961/4, National Archives of the United Kingdom, Kew; David Geggus, "Haiti's Declaration of Independence," in Gaffield, ed., *Haitian Declaration of Independence*, 32.
27. Irving to Eden, January 8, 1954, FO 371/103493/AT1961/4; "Haiti Proud Anniversary," *Time Magazine*, January 11, 1954, https://content.time.com/time/subscriber/article/0,33009,819332,00.html; "Haiti Marks 150th Anniversary of Freedom Won from France," *New York Times*, January 2, 1954.
28. Irving to Eden, January 8, 1954, FO 371/103493/AT1961/4.
29. Dubois, *Haiti*, 320.
30. Quoted in Dubois, *Haiti*, 343.
31. The 1957 election took place on September 22, and the National Assembly ratified the constitution on December 19. Constitution de la République d'Haïti, 1957, Digital Library of the Caribbean, https://ufdc.ufl.edu/aa00000620/00001.
32. "La Proclamation de Chef d'État Le 1er Janiver 1958," *Le Nouvelliste* (Port-au-Prince), January 1, 1958, Digital Library of the Caribbean, https://ufdc.ufl.edu/uf00000081/10591.
33. "Le Message du Président Duvalier, le 2 Janvier 1959, à l'occasion du Jour des Aieux," *Le Nouvelliste*, January 3, 1959, Digital Library of the Caribbean, https://ufdc.ufl.edu/uf00000081/10906. Here the *Nouvelliste* editor has named the holiday Ancestors' Day while the 1957 constitution uses Heroes' Day. The holiday, which remains in the Haitian constitution, is today known as Ancestors' Day, a less overtly nationalistic title. See Constitution de la République d'Haïti, 1987, Digital Library of the Caribbean, https://ufdc.ufl.edu/aa00000627/00001.
34. Jean-Jacques Dessalines, "Arrêté," January 2, 1804, MFQ 1/184, National Archives of the United Kingdom, https://haitidoi.com/2015/12/08/dessalines-reader-2-january-1804/; Jean-Jacques Dessalines, "Arrêté Relatif au Costume," January 2, 1804, MFQ 1/184, National Archives of the United Kingdom, https://haitidoi.com/2015/12/08/dessalines-reader-2-january-1804-2/; Madiou, *Histoire d'Haïti*, 3:153; Ardouin, *Études sur l'histoire d'Haïti*, 6:45–46.
35. Most recently Dessalines has been invoked by gang leaders, in reference to the assassination of Jovenel Moïse, and in protests similar to those led by KÒD in 2013; see Worlgenson Noël, "Jean-Charles Moïse: Pitit Dessalines restera dans les rues pour poursuivre la lutte contre le système," *Le Nouvelliste*, November 14, 2019; Peter Beaumont, "Sick of Corruption, Haiti Looks Back to Its Revolutionary Hero for Hope," *The Guardian* (London),

December 7, 2019; DeNeen L. Brown, "The Haitian Leader Assassinated after an Anti-Slavery Revolution Two Centuries Ago," *Washington Post*, July 9, 2021, https://www.washingtonpost.com/history/2021/07/09/haiti-jean-jacques-dessalines-assassination-moise/; and Jon Lee Anderson, "Haiti Held Hostage," *New Yorker*, July 17, 2023, https://www.newyorker.com/magazine/2023/07/24/haiti-held-hostage.

36. Lindsay A. Twa, "Jean-Jacques Dessalines: Demon, Demigod, and Everything in Between," Romantic Circles, 2011, https://romantic-circles.org/index.php/praxis/circulations/twa, paragraphs 24, 27.

Scenes from Hong Kong

REVOLUTION OF OUR TIME, HISTORIES IN REAL TIME

Noah Shusterman

I wrote this piece in December 2019. More specifically, I wrote most of it on a plane from Hong Kong back to the United States for winter break—exhausted by the upheavals I'd just witnessed, but also by a tenure review that had begun in April and was still dragging, dragging, dragging on. I was ready for a reset.

A lot that I wasn't expecting would come next, starting with that being our last trip to the United States—or anywhere—for more than two years. Life in Hong Kong was about to change because of the pandemic and the political crackdown, two factors that fed into each other. Nor did I know that my days as a runner would soon end, courtesy of an aging body that I'd been pushing too hard for too long. I had known that I'd have to give up running at some point. Hong Kongers also knew that there would be some sort of crackdown from Beijing. Both just came sooner than anyone expected.

The Hong Kong I live in now is a tamer place. Although the protests were largely leaderless, the people who commanded the most respect from the protesters—politicians, writers, artists—are almost all now either in exile or in prison. The graffiti has been painted over. In this essay, there are photos below of the Tai Po Lennon Tunnel and the Goddess of Democracy statue, both gone. My university's administration removed the statue around one year after I wrote this; the tunnel is now just what it was before the protests started, a utilitarian underground passageway.

There are no markers on campus commemorating the protests, nor should there be—but as has happened in many places in Hong Kong, the sidewalk bricks photographed below have been replaced by concrete, a wound, a scar that hasn't healed.

I'm grateful that the editors of *Age of Revolutions* pushed me to write this, and grateful that they chose to include it in this volume. I have not, however, followed their advice in presenting this piece. They asked me to change it from present tense to past. A fair enough request, as it describes a Hong Kong that no longer exists, but making those changes felt wrong. It's shorter now and I've added a few notes, but otherwise this is the text I wrote back when these events were still fresh on my mind. I've made a career writing secondary texts, histories of past events. This one I lived through and witnessed and, though I meant this as a kind of analysis at the time—an iconology of protest art, even if I did not yet know the term—this was a primary text and I prefer to leave it as such.[1]

THE PROTESTS in Hong Kong began in June and spread quickly. So did the response from the police. Since then, politics have been everywhere: on the news, in daily conversations, in the constant updating of which train lines are running. Politics have been all over the walls of Hong Kong too, including the relatively quiet areas of the New Territories where I live. "Relatively" is the key term here—the population density here in the Shing Mun River Valley is well beyond anything folks from the United States are used to. There are people everywhere, and tons of commercial activity. At night, the paths along the waterfront bristle with energy. Yet it's not the central business district that Hong Kong Island or parts of Kowloon are. It's not central for much of anything. And it wasn't much for politics until this past summer. Word that there were posters in a nearby pedestrian tunnel last June was a sign that something really was changing—really? there? Now there's a cycle taking place in that pedestrian tunnel, like everywhere else around here: a round of graffiti or postering, then a round of cleanup, then the whole thing starts again.

Things did come to a head in November when—among other things—my campus became the site of a standoff between students and protesters on one side and the Hong Kong police on the other. The students barricaded the campus for several days. Police fired tear gas into the campus while students threw Molotov cocktails at the police. The quiet, out-of-the-way university where I worked was suddenly the center of attention of the international media. There were photos in the *New York Times* of buildings I'd known for years. Politics didn't come here, until it did. And when it did, it took over the walls and much of the ground as well.

I didn't do anything special to get these photos. I took them while living a life that was, as much as possible during the upheavals, my normal

Graffiti on the side of a building on the Chinese University of Hong Kong (CUHK) campus during the standoff. By the time I saw it, rebellion had already arrived. (All photos in this essay by the author)

everyday life. I teach in the history department at the Chinese University of Hong Kong—CUHK, or just CU—in the Shatin District of the New Territories. We live just a few kilometers from campus, so it was easy to get there during the standoff, when public transportation was shut down and cars could not go through. I took two trips to campus then. My hope was to help somehow, but, like the rest of the CU faculty, I failed on that count. A number of the photos here are from those two trips, though I avoided taking photos that would include the protesters themselves. As for the rest of the photos, most are of places that many other residents of the New Territories also go. I'm a runner so I see more of them than other people do, but I don't see anything different. I go through the tunnels and underpasses of the city that before were of little interest other than for getting from one side of a highway to the other. Since the summer, they've been full of spray-painted slogans and glued-on posters. (I've never seen people doing the spray painting. I have seen people gluing on the posters—including students still in their uniforms.)

A few slogans have dominated since the start, especially "Restore Hong Kong, Revolution of Our Times" and "5 Demands, Not One Less." The other most common slogan has evolved. At first it was "Hong Kongers, Add Oil!" (This phrase, "Add Oil"—加油, or *ga1 yau4*—is one

Graffiti on a wall on the CUHK campus during the standoff. The characters on either side of the helmeted head with a gas mask say "Restore HK, Revolution of our times." The characters on the helmet say "Resist."

of the Cantonese sayings that most nonlocal people here know. "Step on the gas" would be a more accurate translation, but the literal translation, "Add Oil," is too entrenched to change). As the protests have evolved, "Add Oil!" has given way to "resist," and then "revenge," in both the call-and-response chants and the spray-painted slogans.

As for the slogan "Restore Hong Kong"—this idea of "restoration" might turn off readers at *Age of Revolutions*. What state is being "restored" if not the pre-1997 British colonial one?[2] There is a strong nostalgia among Hong Kongers for colonial Hong Kong, both among local Han Chinese and among the large number of people here—mostly white, largely British—who identify as expats. I wish folks here were more critical about the history of British imperialism as a whole, but the contrast between colonial Hong Kong, on the one hand, and the China of the Great Leap Forward and the Cultural Revolution on the other, makes Colonial Hong Kong look good by comparison.

If the protesters are naive about British imperialism and contemporary U.S. politics, they also have an almost instinctual understanding of Beijing's goals and the means it will use to achieve them. Beyond that—and this is the focus of the remaining photos—is the deep sense of history in much of the protest art. Since July the protesters have been declaring that reclaiming Hong Kong is 時代革命—the revolution of our times. But the protesters pay attention to past moments as well—past revolutions, past struggles for freedom and against oppression, old ideas about law and justice. Much of the art and graffiti tries to put Hong Kong into a distinctly Western tradition of revolt, a hodgepodge where Latin phrases and Patrick Henry quotes can mingle with echoes of Mai '68. But more than anything, the protesters who spray-paint and poster the walls draw attention to the history that they themselves are creating as they go, telling the story of their own movement as it unfolds, and by doing that, placing their own actions into the history they also evoke.

A banner at CUHK making the case against the Mass Transit Railway Corporation. Train cars run through the banner, and the top line of each section is a date from 2019.

Often, the need to tell the history of the movement comes with dates and events. In this photo, a section of a banner that hung by the University Mass Transit Railway (MTR) station lists the times when protesters feel the MTR betrayed the people. (The dates here are in Chinese characters, which is unusual). Looking at two of the specifics: the first on the left (beneath the train) is July 21, when the police stayed away from Yuen Long Station while a mob of men in white shirts beat up the people in the trains as the trains stayed in the station. The third is from August 31, when the police themselves rushed into the trains and beat people there. Protesters since then have been calling on the MTR Corporation to release the footage from the internal cameras there—CCTV—which the corporation has not yet done. These two dates—usually referred to as 7.21 and 8.31—can be seen all over Hong Kong. It's hard to emphasize how central these dates are in the minds and the vocabulary of protesters here. One of the chants this past autumn was "7-2-1, didn't see anyone; 8-3-1, beat someone to death," referring to the police inactions of July 21 and the police violence of August 31.[3]

A poster from Tai Po's Lennon Tunnel representing two young Hong Kongers who had died in recent months

The protest movement also commemorates its martyrs. There are photos and drawings of a Chow Tsz-lok, a twenty-two-year-old student who fell to his death from a parking garage during fights between the protesters and the police in November, and Chan Yin-lam, a fifteen-year-old high school student whose body was found at sea in September. Her mother has asked people to stop speculating on her death, but protesters continue to put her name and drawings of her face on the walls of Hong Kong. Physically—and I realize that talking about Chan Yin-lam's appearance and ignoring that of Chow Tsz-lok is problematic—she seems perfect for the part, her wide eyes looking like a living version of the Japanese animation that inspires some of the best Lennon Wall artists.

The Lennon Walls are themselves a way for Hong Kongers to put themselves into a Western tradition of resistance to oppression; they tie the people's resistance to Beijing to Eastern Europeans' resistance to Moscow

Art from the Tai Po Lennon Tunnel. This combines two common features of the Lennon Walls in Hong Kong: the extensive use of Post-It notes and the influence of Japanese animation.

The main entrance to the Tai Po Lennon Tunnel. The characters above the entrance say "Tai Po Lennon Tunnel."

during the 1980s, even if the Hong Kong Lennon Walls have since surpassed their Eastern European predecessors.

Of the many Lennon Walls near where I live, only one was famous throughout Hong Kong, and that was the Lennon Tunnel of Tai Po, around five miles away. When the Tai Po Lennon Tunnel was at its peak, it was impossible to put even a quarter of it into one photograph; it stretched out hundreds of meters, around turns, down different branches leading out to different bus stops, malls, and housing estates. People came from Hong Kong Island to see it, which is like getting people who live in Manhattan to come out to Queens. The art mixed preprinted posters with home-drawn art, along with the thousands of Post-It notes.

It's not all slogans and posters; there has been a lot of destruction. Protesters have torn up brick sidewalks during the last several months. Some protesters have thrown bricks at police and at counterprotesters, and killed one man in doing so.[4] Most of the bricks are reused to make barricades or to place on the ground in case of a rush by the riot police, whose heavy gear and protections make it hard to move fast when the ground is uneven. It's a practical measure—not a matter of messaging or

SCENES FROM HONG KONG   187

A poster in the Tai Po Lennon Tunnel. I don't know the etiquette regarding posting over earlier postings; at this point in the fall, space on the walls was at a premium.

an intentional statement about its place in any sort of revolutionary tradition. But whenever I see these sidewalks, I think of the events of May 1968 in Paris.

For people who know that history, it's one of many such parallels—the student protests, the fights for control of a university campus, tearing bricks from the ground to build barricades. Sometimes, though, the protesters make the parallel explicit. One piece of graffiti at the athletic field near the bridge where students and police fought read, *"je me révolte, donc nous sommes"*—"I rebel, therefore we are."[5]

References to the French Revolution are rarer, as one might expect, but they are around. Before the poster at the top of this post started appearing, there was an earlier remake of *La Liberté guidant le peuple* with a female protester holding the flag and leading the crowd (but without any wardrobe malfunctions). That was more fitting, both in terms of recreating Eugène Delacroix's painting and in recognizing the enormous role that women play in the protests. This is the one that has spread though.

The American revolutionary tradition, broadly speaking, is more present. There are often U.S. flags at protests. There are calls for freedom and democracy that cite the United States' tradition, with little investigation

A road at CUHK during the standoff, the bricks from the sidewalks ready to be repurposed.

into the role of slavery in the founding generation. Hence a prominent "Give me liberty or give me death—Patrick Henry" not far from the CUHK library (I didn't get a photo). Even when they are not explicit references, to me they fit in with the kinds of slogans I'd see next to a Gadsden Flag or among a group of Revolutionary War reenactors. There are also many paintings and drawings of Guy Fawkes masks, which have arrived in popular culture via the movie *V for Vendetta*. (The circled-V from that movie is also a frequent sight, as seen in the bottom of the second photo in this piece.)

For an American like me, it's also hard not to see the CUHK Goddess of Democracy as a kind of local Statue of Liberty, even though it's not (and explicitly so). It's based on a larger such statue that the protesters of Tiananmen Square built in 1989. The Goddess of Democracy has stood strong through the months of protests. As far as I've seen, the "Five Demands—Not One Less" poster has been there the whole time. Other symbols of the protests—the gas masks, the construction helmet—have come and gone.

While the protesters show an understanding of Beijing's politics and a quirky but broad understanding of many events of European history, their understanding of contemporary U.S. politics is often quite weak. Passage of the Hong Kong Human Rights and Democracy Act was a goal of the protesters here, which they achieved in November. Still, there is a

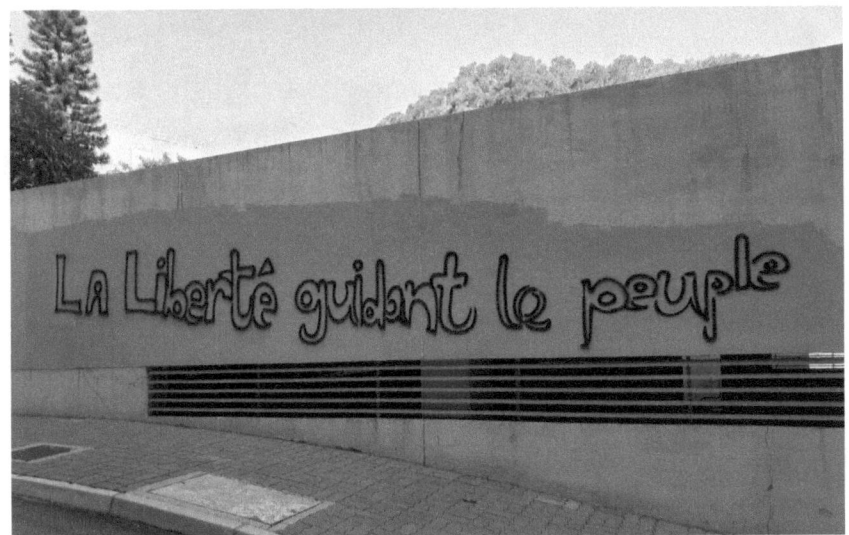

"La Liberté guidant le peuple" spray-painted on a wall at CUHK across from the entrance to the building that houses the history department

"You can't make a free people kneel" spray-painted on the road at CUHK during the standoff

CUHK's Goddess of Democracy. A yellow hard hat was placed on her head, and the poster hanging from her neck reads, "Five demands, not one less" in Chinese

naiveté here about which U.S. politicians could—or should—help Hong Kong. Part of this comes from the actions of prominent Republicans. Some seem to really enjoy calling mainland China "Communist," even as it's unclear what that word means these days. Supporters of Beijing seem no better informed; Trump was hesitant to sign the Hong Kong Human Rights and Democracy Act and called President Xi his "friend," but pro-Beijing protesters still burned him in effigy.

The biggest shock came when I was on campus a few weeks after the standoff. Most of the campus had been cleaned up by then, but the area of the greatest fighting was still as-is, with piles of food and water bottles stacked, along with umbrellas and medical tape and other supplies. One of the banners there was folded up, so I wanted to know what was on it. Not the face I was expecting to see there. The quote is from an editorial McConnell wrote in the *Wall Street Journal:* "Sooner or later, the rest of the world will have to do what the protesters are doing—confront Beijing."

There have even been posters and spray-painted slogans appearing in Latin on the CUHK campus, showing off their erudition. This is not

This painting of CUHK's Goddess of Democracy, given a yellow hard hat, appeared near Siu Lek Yuen.

a completely uncritical praise of the Western tradition. I dislike seeing them so I avoid photographing them, but Hong Kong is full of comparisons of Beijing and the Chinese Communist Party to the Nazis. Walls that have "Chinazi" written on them are a frequent sight. There are also a lot of spray-painted swastikas. I get the idea—they're trying to compare Xi with Hitler, today's Beijing with the Berlin of the 1930s and World War II. I still hate it. As far as I am concerned, I'd rather not see swastikas, period. It's worth noting that there are very few direct references to European communism—neither to the Bolsheviks nor to Karl Marx himself. Or if they *are* there, I miss them.

I'll repeat what I wrote earlier: my view of the protests is skewed. There is a lot that I miss in the posters and the graffiti: references to events that I've never heard of; phrases I can't read and don't take the time to look up. There's also an enormous amount of wordplay. Like any academic, I'm hyperaware of even the most distant reference to the events I study.

A banner showing a quote from Mitch McConnell against the stars of the American flag lay after the standoff at CUHK near the bridge that was the site of most of the fighting.

"Si Vis Pacem, Para Bellum" (Latin for "If you want peace, prepare for war") appeared next to the history department's building at CUHK.

Nor—in case I have not made this clear enough thus far—do I endorse everything the protesters do. But I recognize the overall outline of the events. The Hong Kong protesters are on the frontlines of the global fight against authoritarianism. They are not on the only such frontline, so I don't know if what's happening in Hong Kong right now qualifies as the Revolution of Our Times, as the protesters claim. Nor do I have any idea what the future has in store.

Notes

1. My thanks to Jacob Henry Leveton for explaining this idea of an iconology of protest art to me.
2. After this essay was published, several scholars of China reached out to me and corrected me on this issue. The Chinese phrase here for restore (光復) refers to Sun Yat-Sen's Nationalist Revolution at the start of the twentieth century.
3. There were rumors early on that the police had killed someone on August 31 and covered it up, but no details ever surfaced to support those rumors, nor were there any people reported missing during that period who could have been there.
4. Looking back today, this sentence is far too nonchalant about a man's death. His name was Luo Changqing; he was seventy years old and worked as a cleaner for the government. This essay was not about the protests' violence per se—at the time, there were many articles that did talk about violence, and I did not want to just be one more. Still, "and killed one man" was dismissive in a way that pains me when I reread it.
5. The original version of this essay included a photo of that graffiti, which the editors removed because the painted words would not be clear enough in a black-and-white version of the photo. I mention this here because, as of this writing, of all of the graffiti and art included or mentioned here, this is the only piece that has not yet been removed or painted over. None of the other graffiti on campus lasted until the summer of 2020, but "*je me révolte, donc nous sommes*" remains there six years later, faded but present.

The Bastille and the Roundabout

POPULAR PROTEST AND THE REVOLUTIONARY PAST OF THE GILETS JAUNES

Andrew W. M. Smith

"Everyone is looking for their own revolution," editorialist Abel Mestre wrote in *Le Monde* when surveying the profusion of historical references in the *gilets jaunes* protests of winter 2018–19.[1] The diffuse nature of these protests evaded traditional interpretations of a social movement; tribunes deliberately avoided the legacies of particular (potentially divisive) movements and instead shifted the frame of reference to historical revolutions.[2] Calls to storm the Bastille were certainly not absent, nor references to the Paris Commune, nor even to 1848. For newly mobilized protesters from a wide sweep of society, these references to historic events were less exclusive than complex political debates and understandably more energizing than critiques of specific taxation measures. As a group of anthropologists observed after speaking with *gilets jaunes* protesters in Rennes: "The term 'revolution' is more of a unifying symbol than a word describing a well-defined political process."[3] Yet, as historian Ludivine Bantigny has noted, these "presences in the present" can be distorted in their reuse for political purposes, flattening and pacifying historical conflicts.[4] There was among the *gilets jaunes* no serious attempt to seize the mechanisms of state nor means of production, no serious attempt to impose a rival political system. Yet, the scope and vibrancy of these protests looked and felt revolutionary, especially as the language and images of past revolutions were deployed in earnest. Using the language of the French Revolution represented in part an attempt to inscribe the protests in the *roman national* (or national story), lending them greater significance in the well-worn tale of the country's political evolution. By first setting out the events of the protests, then analyzing the historical referents applied therein, this essay considers the memory culture that retooled revolutionary heritage to help order and explain a diffuse movement, both by actors involved in the mobilizations and by those seeking to analyze it from without.

The Revolution of the Roundabouts

Combining an openly neoliberal policy stance with a patriotic restatement of French values, Emmanuel Macron's meteoric rise to the presidency in 2017 sought to cast him as politically neither right nor left. For others, this was a new form of "extreme centrism" in which Macron positioned himself as the only bulwark against what he described as "chaos."[5] As such, his victory was defined in opposition to extremism (particularly his runoff against Marine Le Pen on the extreme right) and had a notable lack of express voter attachment to his program. He won just 18 percent of registered voters in the first round of the election.[6] Likewise, despite publishing a campaign book entitled *Revolution*, his emphasis on *laissez-faire* economic liberalization jarred with opponents for whom negative suspicions were confirmed by his early abolition of the wealth tax on those with assets over 1.3 million euros.[7] Resistance to this vision of Macronism found social and political voice in the *gilets jaunes* movement, which emerged in November 2018 and was at its peak until January 2019. The symbol of the protest wave was the high-visibility yellow vest, effective by dint of its ubiquity and a symbol of government regulation (it is a legal requirement to carry one in motor vehicles, and drivers can be stopped by authorities to check if one is present in the vehicle). This first phase of the movement saw large numbers of people across France participating in diverse actions such as the occupation of roundabouts and the commandeering of motorway tollbooths. This was a context in which "cultural insecurity" could be marshalled as an antielitist force, reflected in the preponderance of *gilets jaunes* activity in the "*diagonal du vide* . . . the least populated rural and semi-urban regions characterised as having an ageing population and weakening economic growth rates."[8] Sophie Wahnich, in turn, described the sociological makeup of the protests as akin to the sans-culottes yet notably more feminine.[9]

Visibility spread outside regular media channels, often through virtual forums. An online petition calling for reductions in the price of fuel, for example, was launched by a small business owner, Priscilla Ludosky, in May 2018 and received millions of signatories. This fed popular engagement and momentum, and in October, Narbonnais service technician Ghislain Coutard recorded a short video on Facebook encouraging people to place their yellow vests on their vehicle dashboards as a way to show their annoyance at the rising cost of living. Listing checks, taxes, costs, and contradictions affecting the ordinary motorist, so too did the Breton hypnotherapist Jacline Mouraud, who became a Facebook sensation in a video rebuke to the presidency that went viral. These cognate online protests fueled a growing trend of complaints about how government measures (such as increasing fuel taxes to offset carbon emissions) seemed to be exacerbating pervasive, daily frustrations about prices and regulation.[10] According to Jérôme Fourquet of polling organisation IFOP: "The price of fuel now is as politically and sociologically sensitive as the price of wheat was in the days of the *ancien régime*."[11] The first widespread days of action in November 2018 were organized by national and local groups over Facebook, and this is where some of the other key figures of the movement emerged, such as Eric Drouet, a thirty-three-year-old truck driver who proposed blocking traffic by encouraging protesters to drive slowly around roundabouts; Jérôme Rodrigues, a trainee plumber who frequently supported Drouet's critiques of the cost of living online; Maxime Nicolle, a video-blogger and delivery driver with the pseudonym "Fly Rider"; and Ingrid Levavasseur, a low-paid nurse who became a frequent media fixture.[12] These prominent spokespeople represented the novelty of the movement, with most lacking any sustained engagement with party politics (and thus allowing a wider than normal range of engagement across the political spectrum).

On November 17, 2018, 280,000 people protested across France, wearing yellow vests and gathering at roundabouts or tollbooths to disrupt traffic.[13] From there, each weekend marked a new "act" in the ongoing drama of the protest movement. This first phase of the movement from November 2018 to January 2019 involved the most intensive and popular mobilizations, and an opinion poll showed 21 percent of French people actively considered themselves to be *gilets jaunes*.[14] Other polls from the period showed the movement had 70 percent approval ratings, indicating both a high rate of participation and a much wider halo of popular support.[15] Amid rising tensions caused by the expansion of the protests, the government sought to strike up a dialogue. Yet, as in the early days of the French Revolution, these popular mobilizations "do not seem to have needed organizational structures to develop their political demands," and the decentralized movement made finding interlocutors challenging.[16] Eventually, on November 26, a "delegation" of eight "official communicators" was constituted to negotiate with the government. These attempts by Prime Minister Edouard Philippe to meet with protesters descended into farce—of eight invited leaders, only two attended and one left instantly, citing threats and pressure from other protesters. The status of these official communicators was immediately challenged within the movement and the body quickly dissolved (just as Jacobin fears of the corruptibility of representative assemblies took hold in 1793).[17] According to Pierre Rosanvallon, this demonstrated a contemporary impression that democratic representatives could be bypassed, and that "representation can be immediate and individualized. It is the internet age; all intermediaries are guilty."[18]

From the end of November, the state response was increasingly characterized by coercion and repression, as the convergence of protests in Paris led to violence and disorder. The mayor of Paris lamented 3–4 million euros of damages, and police alleged that protests were being taken over by *casseurs* (wreckers or, more accurately, thugs). There was strong evidence of excessive force used by police against protesters too, and memories remained fresh of the political scandal in July 2018 when President Macron's aide Alexandre Benalla was discovered to have donned police gear and engaged willingly in violence against Mayday protesters.[19] As Sophie Wahnich highlighted, the violence "at the height of the December mobilizations resembled the capture of the Tuileries, which did not take place at the start of the French Revolution, but came after calm attempts to demand justice had failed."[20] On December 8, the police union Alliance diagnosed an "insurrectionist situation," and in the ensuing protest some 1,300 arrests were reported, with over 900 held in police custody.[21] Samuel Hayat saw in the Paris demonstrations distorted echoes of the 1848 Revolution: those protests had involved the reclamation of neighborhoods in the *quartiers populaires* (working-class neighborhoods) of Paris, relying on networks of community solidarity, yet in the Paris acts of the *gilets jaunes*, working-class people targeted the centers of power in the heart of the city.[22] The violent intensification of protests changed media narratives but was also accompanied by the broadening of Lycée occupations by students, challenging (as ever) the "hierarchy and conservativism" of the state.[23] Across France, scenes of police dealing roughly with teenagers played badly, such as in Mantes-la-Jolie, where police lined up school students on their knees with hands above their heads, creating a pose that was redeployed by *gilets jaunes* in protests across France. Another flashpoint surrounded the protester Jérôme Rodrigues, who lost an eye because of police violence. As protests intensified, the movement splintered in the face of violence and destruction of property, with many moderate voices seeing a deviation from the original protest.

In his address to the nation on December 10, President Macron attempted to appease popular anger. The reduction of taxes, assurance of minimum levels of payment for retirees, and a spate of social measures worth up to 10 billion euros were all important, but perhaps the most symbolic response was the huge listening project that started with a seven-hour townhall meeting hosted by Macron. This placed the president as a direct intermediary to the people, recalling the *ancien régime* practice of the king holding his parliament.[24] In early 2019, the encampments set up on occupied roundabouts began to be destroyed, and this diminished the number of participants and presaged internal shifts within the wider protest movement. This period also saw a "convergence of struggles," as *gilets jaunes* groups began to develop more "formal associations" with political groups (such as those opposing pension reforms on the left).[25] The presidential address meant to mark the end of Macron's Grand Debate was unexpectedly postponed by the fire in Notre-Dame Cathedral in Paris.[26] The imposed "mourning period" that followed this heritage catastrophe brought the first of many interruptions to the momentum of the *gilets jaunes*. While sporadic action continued, the movement began to lose its centrality within France's social conflict as 2019 moved on and the advent of the COVID-19 pandemic signaled its end, notwithstanding a minor resurgence in 2021 (when popular anger was directed against the policy of a vaccination-dependent health pass, with one Annency protester declaring themselves "the *gilets jaunes* of Covid").[27] This stuttering end to the protests somewhat belied the momentum it had gathered in the winter of 2018, when France appeared in the grip of a major political crisis.

Characterized both by its spontaneity and ultimately its ephemerality, the movement constructed no real institutional infrastructure that would sustain its presence.[28] These protests drew unfamiliar actors into social debates and political engagement, and the social media structures that had popularized the cause and mobilized protests offered no ready system for governance or representation. As Donald Reid noted, the "violence in Paris may have been what won concessions from Macron, but it was the political culture of the roundabouts that fascinated historians of the revolutions of 1789 and 1848 and the Paris Commune of 1871."[29] To understand how revolutionary memory culture evolved during the *gilets jaunes* protests, we can track two key themes: first, references to the moral economy of Macronism and the ways in which protests were a rightful response to injustice, and second, how concepts of the people were deployed both by protesters and commentators.

Moral Economies of Macronism

Samuel Hayat turned to the concept of "moral economy" as an explanatory model for the claims of the *gilets jaunes*.[30] E. P. Thompson originally coined this concept as a response to George Rudé's call to better understand the rationality of claims made by the so-called mob during the French Revolution. Thompson unpacked how beyond France, the eighteenth-century social experience of economic injustice could breach personally held yet collectively shared values of fairness, provoking popular mobilization as "shock passes into fury."[31] Frustrations around motoring were thus parceled into the larger concern of *pouvoir d'achat* (purchasing power) as the leitmotif of the *gilets jaunes* protests.[32] Perhaps the clearest articulation of any coherent *gilets jaunes* policy platform was the list of forty-two demands produced from an online consultation in which thirty thousand people took part, subsequently published as "people's directives."[33] This language of economic justice reflected the movement's popular foundations, settling around the injustice of the costs of green energy transition and climate policies landing on those struggling to make ends meet. As one protest placard read, "Macron worries about the end of the world, while we worry about the end of the month."[34] The prominence of motoring issues mobilized protesters from beyond the city centers, whose reliance on car travel meant their purchasing power was dented by duties on fuel. Attempts by the government to characterize *gilets jaunes* as resistant to necessary change or irresponsible in terms of the environment chafed among protesters.[35] In rejecting this frame, protesters drew attention to social imbalances and economic injustices, reinforcing images of Macron as favoring the well-off. Returning to Fourquet's comparison of wheat prices in the *ancien régime* and gas prices in contemporary France, we can see where suspected breaches of the moral economy mobilized broad social coalitions against an elite decried as out-of-touch and exploitative.[36]

The unifying force of a personal dislike of President Macron rallied protesters around the term "President of the rich" (graduating from accusations of being the "Candidate of the rich," which Marine Le Pen hammered during the election campaign).[37] This parcels in a class-based discourse of wealth as much as it does cultural remoteness, eliding forerunners like former President Nicolas Sarkozy (often caricatured as a "bling-bling" president) alongside references to King Louis-Philippe's caricatured bourgeois decadence during the July Monarchy.[38] So too the recurrent depictions of Macron as King Louis XVI on protest placards demonstrated how his self-depiction as a Jupiterian president and continued sidestepping of intermediary bodies rankled.[39] Danielle Tartakowsky quoted protesters chanting "Macron to the Bastille" as a sign of the Revolution's continued usefulness for protesters, helping mobilize moral claims of the past in service of contemporary critiques of power.[40] The editor of *Médiapart*, Edwy Plenel, attributed at least some of these direct comparisons to the poignant similarities audiences saw on cinema screens in September 2018, when Pierre Schoeller's film *Un peuple et son roi* lavishly depicted "the progressive divorce between Louis XVI and the French people."[41] Needless to say, when the assumptive heir of the Bourbon throne, the self-styled Louis de Bourbon, endorsed the *gilets jaunes*, things were in a very strange place indeed (conjuring farcical echoes of a reverse 1830).[42]

Clearly, such demands for economic justice are not novel nor specific to one period of time, and it is within this wider context that symbols of the revolutionary past have found traction. Ludivine Bantigny pointed to a banner flown by protesters in Nîmes on December 22, 2018, that included article 35 of the Declaration of the Rights of Man and Citizen. She noted that "the past is a living present," affirming the contemporary complaints of protesters in the context of a wider revolutionary heritage.[43] Here, memory culture both helped to explain complex sociopolitical developments and affirm the language used to protest them while offering a wider rallying cry. Enduring concepts like moral economy spoke across chronological gaps, helping smooth the ragged edges of revolutionary references.

Popular Democracy and Postcards of the Past

Drawing on the historiography of the French Revolution, we can see that the concept of "the people" is plural, disputed, and politically exigent. We might break the term down into at least three constituent groups: "the crowd, the [people defined as the political] sovereign, and popular groups [or associations]."[44] This plurality helps navigate discussions of the *gilets jaunes*, and the accumulated scholarship around the French Revolution provides a guide. Protesters themselves drew continuities using the concept of the people, grounding their demands in a memory culture that affirmed their popular sovereignty. Michelle Zancarini-Fournel described a relevant slogan written on a yellow vest that declared, "1789, 1968, 2018, the people."[45]

The protesters' generalized demands for a *referendum d'initative citoyen* (Citizen's initiative referendum, or RIC), which would grant the general population a means to trigger national decision-making processes, were ill-fated but representative of a desire for greater popular sovereignty within the structures of the Fifth Republic. This echoed the revolutionary practice of compiling *cahiers de doléances* (lists of grievances written up for submission to the Estates General).[46] Indeed, the pursuit of the RIC was justified by reference to the Declaration of the Rights of Man and Citizen, specifically article 6, which states, "The law is the expression of the general will. All the citizens have the right of contributing personally or through their representatives to its formation."[47] For Edwy Plenel, "This same Declaration sets out the right that the *gilets jaunes* are reviving today, that of changing the rules and the hand they've been dealt in this political game."[48] Calls for direct democracy were explicitly voiced in the language of moral economy, the tenor of which could involve both the memory culture of the Revolution and the everyday language of working people (contrasted against the precise and crafted language of political elites, represented *par excellence* by President Macron). This clamor for direct democracy was in part an attempt to avoid the "political recuperation" of the movement (by being absorbed into a party structure or subsumed by bourgeois political elites), "which you would find with the sans-culottes in 1792–1794, the citizen-fighters of February 1848, the Communards of 1870–1871 and the anarcho-syndicalists of the Belle Époque."[49] Facebook gave a platform to people who felt marginalized when expressing themselves through writing or public speaking. By disregarding traditional conventions of written communication, Facebook provided greater flexibility in how users could interact, from self-recorded videos that could be quickly reshared to comments on discussion threads in local, national, and international groups then promoted into users' newsfeeds. This is exemplified by the popularity of "camera-facing" videos made by *gilet jaunes* protesters, such as the opinion pieces from people like Jacline Mouraud and Ghislain Coutard, or the witness videos highlighting instances of police brutality.[50] Online spaces provided a means to converse and a contrast with official media sources, facilitating a sense of direct connection and privileging popular languages of direct democracy.

We do not have to look far into the *gilets jaunes* protests to find the physical enactment of the rituals of popular democracy. During protests, tollbooths were widely occupied and opened for free passage. One couple even tied the knot at an occupied toll plaza in the Hautes-Pyrénées. Decked out in high-vis finery, the protesters declared their revolutionary love in symbolic nuptials presided over by the local magistrate.[51] While the burning of customs gates into Paris in 1789 fueled the festival atmosphere leading up to the storming of the Bastille, the freedom of the roads and the occupation of the roundabout represent an opportunity for social encounters and the development of further action.[52] There are contemporary and revolutionary roots to the methods of the *gilets jaunes* protest, especially those involving the occupation of space: from the occupation of public squares during the *Nuit Debout* movement (a 2016 social movement that targeted labor reforms) to the expansion of ZADs (*zones à défendre*) in relation to the resistance movement against airport construction at Notre-Dame-des-Landes. So too for *gilets jaunes* the presence on roundabouts became a form of social space in which protest burgeoned, ideas were exchanged, and the participatory nature of the action could be understood. Here we can see the invention of democratic public spaces, as described by Alain Cotterreau in the Revolution.[53] In particular, the creation of "barracks" on roundabouts across France meant that there was a democratic hub to these diffuse protests, sites of "collective solidarity built from bric a brac with the skills of anyone."[54] Placards on the roundabouts implored passersby to "turn off your TV and join us" in an appeal to reject the passive consumption of news and participate in a democratic process of discussion in the protest space.

As noted by Donald Reid, the *gilets jaunes* were drawn from "the popular classes (le populaire), a term that refers to 'the people' (le peuple) but without the hegemonic political and homogeneous social qualities that 'the people' can convey."[55] Protesters shaped connections in these spaces of popular democracy, bridging political differences with reference to shared calls for economic and social justice. This diversity of background also meant they brought different experiences to the protests. Some commentators noted the profusion of Phrygian bonnets at protests as well as the number of protesters who preferred to sing the *Marseillaise* over the *Internationale*, while others saw the profusion of flags and anthems a more likely legacy of France's World Cup win that year, which had seen national merchandise fly off the shelves in celebration.[56] The connection to football is a useful one, demonstrating the ways in which negative depictions of crowd behavior by authorities could inform police attitudes. Donald Reid pointed to President Macron's "use of the archaic 'laboring classes' to speak of the *gilets jaunes*," which recalled "a term for the threat to civilization posed by the lower classes in the July Monarchy" as well as attempting to conjure up a host of other "deplorable" characteristics in the present.[57] The concept of the mob is one that has dogged histories of the Revolution, especially when seeking explanations of violent excesses. As more violent elements clashed with police in Paris, imagery of masked protesters against backgrounds of flames were splashed across front pages, eroding public support.[58]

The opening of the trial against people accused of damaging the Arc de Triomphe during the Paris acts of the *gilets jaunes* represented an emotive and symbolic process, therefore. At the time, in December 2018, national and international newspapers focused on the destruction of national symbols to convey the significance and upheaval of the protests, shifting public sympathies from the popular classes to the nation as shorthand for the sovereign people. One lawyer condemned the accused protesters by declaring that even the Communards had not attacked the Arc de Triomphe.[59] Eyes were drawn to what was called "a vandalised statue of Marianne, a symbol of the French Republic, inside the Arc de Triomphe."[60] The shattered face of the statue was a striking leader for many newspapers, though this was not an image of Marianne as a symbol of the republic (an unlikely subject for tribute when the statue was created during the July Monarchy) but rather a plaster cast for the main frieze designed by François Rude depicting *Le Départ des volontaires de 1792* (which itself remained largely undamaged—the figure is that of Victory floating symbolically above the volunteers levied to defend the young republic against the armies of the First Coalition).[61] Amid the "total hysteria" of the wider protests described by *Le Figaro,* there was some acknowledgment that defendants in the trial of those who had entered the Arc de Triomphe were not the "main culprits," and some were charged with relatively minor crimes: "In the ransacked souvenir shop, Valentin N. 'automatically' picked up four postcards. 'Two of the Arc de Triomphe and two of the Eiffel tower' noted the judge. It is for this theft that he is being tried."[62] This symbolic trial, of a young man without previous criminal conviction accused of stealing postcards of the past amid historic unrest, offered a compelling marker of the state's failure to engage with the protests. The substitution in the media of a shattered statue's face as symbolic victim, rather than the mutilated protesters—such as the aforementioned Jérome Rodrigues—highlighted a changing media narrative that made the political claims and the personhood of the protesters abstract.[63] By way of example, the damaging of a statue of Maréchal Juin in Place d'Italie led Geneviève Darrieussecq, secretary of state to the minister for the armed forces to symbolically appeal for popular unity in the face of "casseurs de mémoire" (memory wreckers).[64] The past was no longer being used to unify protesters on the roundabouts in an act of popular democracy but instead weaponized against them to represent the symbols of a sovereign nation coming under attack.

In the developing media narrative about the Paris acts of the *gilets jaunes,* protesters were no longer considered to be making individual claims as part of a collective but rather viewed as an undifferentiated mob, presenting a danger to wider symbols of the nation. Violence became overrepresented in media imagery, and images of fire or damages provided compelling content that outweighed emphases on creativity in signs or costumes, or the conviviality of protests on the roundabouts.[65] Yet it also showed how revolutionary memory culture provided the means by which competing claims of who represented "the people" could be fought out in the media, echoing the historiography of the Revolution itself (and particularly conservative dismissals of its violence). This symbolic prosecution of the supposed mob amid the wider concerns of those who felt forgotten by the state made the story of the twenty-five-year-old Breton Valentin somewhat instructive: the broader structural issues of inequality and alienation, the violence and destruction of that protest, and a hearty disdain for the central state all combined to see a young man fined for stealing postcards of the past.[66]

THE GILETS JAUNES protests took place in a memory culture suffused with revolutionary heritage. Its principal issues were conceived in reference to contemporary political phenomena, though they would not be wholly alien to past revolutionaries. Calls for radical reconfigurations of popular sovereignty and for greater economic justice resonated despite their respective historical contexts. The reappearance of *cahiers de doléance*, the donning of Phrygian bonnets, and the citation of the Declaration of the Rights of Man and Citizen all confirmed that revolutionary memory culture had a role. By contrast, the movement was also characterized by complaints about the cost of driving, which spread rapidly across social media through videoclips and livestreaming. Yet despite the chronological gulf between revolutionary references and the vagaries of Facebook livestreams, consistent themes of fairness and socioeconomic justice helped bridge the centuries. Many of the revolutionary references deployed by protesters and by commentators were hazy, yet as Danielle Tartakowsky noted, 1789 as a "foundation of our history, resurfaces when we don't know how else to describe something."[67] This useful past was both rallying cry and riposte. Refracted through the lens of revolutionary memory culture, these protests drew similar appeals on behalf of "the people," framed variously as a democratic force to be drawn into the struggle, an abstract political ideal, and a mob to be feared. The *gilets jaunes* movement generated its own politically useful history (which may well be captured by more radical political movements in the future), even as it reached for languages of the Revolution. The past does not belong to historians, just as politics does not belong to politicians. Instead, in the popular reclamation of politics and history on the roundabouts and streets of France, we are reminded, as Ludivine Bantigny states, that in our modern world "there remain Bastilles still to storm."[68]

Notes

1. Abel Mestre, "'Gilets jaunes': Chacun cherche sa révolution," *Le Monde* (Paris), December 9, 2018.
2. Ludivine Bantigny and Samuel Hayat, "Les Gilets jaunes une histoire de classe?" *Mouvements* 4, no. 100 (2019): 13.
3. Barbara Doulin-Dimopoulos, Elsa Koerner, and Isabelle Siffert, "Le baraquement comme espace de résistance du mouvement des gilets

jaunes," *Condition humaine / Conditions politiques* 2 (2021), https://revues.mshparisnord.fr/chcp/index.php?id=524.
4. Ludivine Bantigny, "Un passé ravivé: La Commune dans les engagements du présent," *Revue d'histoire du XIXe siècle* 63 (2021): 97–111, 100 (quotation).
5. Pierre Serna, *L'Extrême centre ou le poison français* (Ceyzérieu, France: Champ Vallon, 2019), 243.
6. Edwy Plenel, *La Victoire des vaincus* (Paris: La Découverte, 2019), chap. 1.
7. Charles Devellennes, *The Gilets Jaunes and the New Social Contract* (Bristol, U.K.: Bristol University Press, 2021), 3.
8. Frédéric Royall, "The *Gilets Jaunes* Protests: Mobilisation without Third-Party Support," *Modern and Contemporary France* 28, no. 1 (2020): 99–118. This has been referred to by Christophe Guilluy as the "nation's urban peripheries"; see Guilluy, *Twilight of the Elites: Prosperity, the Periphery, and the Future of France* (New Haven, CT: Yale University Press, 2019), 84–88.
9. Sophie Wahnich, "Sans-culottes et gilets jaunes," in *Le fond de l'air est jaune: Comprendre une révolte in-édite*, ed. Joseph Confavreux (Paris: Seuil, 2019).
10. Pierre Boyer et al., "Les déterminants de la mobilisation des Gilets jaunes," *Revue économique* 71, no. 1 (2020): 109–38.
11. Quoted in William Drozdiak, *The Last President of Europe* (New York: Public Affairs, 2020), 27.
12. Boyer et al., "Les déterminants de la mobilisation des Gilets jaunes," 109–38.
13. M. Della Sudda and E. Reungoat, "Understanding the French Yellow Vests Movement through the Lens of Mixed Methods: A French Touch in Social Movement Studies?" *French Politics* 20 (2022): 303–17, https://doi.org/10.1057/s41253-022-00188-8.
14. Marc Lazar, "Gilets jaunes: L'entrée dans la 'peuplecratie,'" AOC Media, May 7, 2019, https://aoc.media/opinion/2019/05/07/gilets-jaunes-lentree-peuplecratie/.
15. Patrick Chamorel, "Macron Versus the Yellow Vests," *Journal of Democracy* 30, no. 4 (October 2019): 52.
16. Micah Alpaugh et al., "Peuple et révolution française," *Annales historiques de la Révolution française* 402, no. 4 (2020): 131–58.
17. Ruth Scurr, *Fatal Purity: Robespierre and the French Revolution* (New York: Holt, 2006), 264.
18. Quoted in Donald Reid, "History at the Roundabout: The Pasts and Presents of the Gilets Jaunes," *Histories of the Present* 12, no. 2 (2022): 189.
19. Plenel, *La Victoire des vaincus*, chap. 1.
20. Wahnich, "Sans-culottes et gilets jaunes."

21. Ludivine Bantigny, "Un événement," in Confavreux, ed., *Le fond de l'air est jaune*.
22. Olivier Fillieule, Samuel Hayat, and Sylvie Monchatre, "Trois regards sur le mouvement des 'Gilets jaunes,'" *La nouvelle revue du travail*, November 1, 2020, http://journals.openedition.org/nrt/7377.
23. E. Chabal, *A Divided Republic* (Cambridge: Cambridge University Press, 2015), 209.
24. Serna, *L'Extrême centre*, 236–37.
25. Sudda and Reungoat, "Understanding the French Yellow Vests Movement," 303–17.
26. Ewan Barcelo, "Perspectives sur les Gilets jaunes et l'incendie de Notre-Dame de Paris," *Au regard des sciences sociales*, December 15, 2022, http://journals.openedition.org/insituarss/2067.
27. William Audureau, "'Les gens n'ont pas besoin de mesures sanitaires qui les déshumanisent': L'ode à la joie des antirestrictions à Annecy," *Le Monde*, March 21, 2022, https://www.lemonde.fr/societe/article/2021/03/22/a-annecy-l-ode-a-la-joie-des-antirestrictions_6074056_3224.html.
28. Chamorel, "Macron Versus the Yellow Vests," 60.
29. Reid, "History at the Roundabout," 197.
30. Samuel Hayat, "L'économie morale et le pouvoir," in Confavreux, ed., *Le fond de l'air est jaune*.
31. E. P. Thompson, "The Moral Economy of the English Crowd in the Eighteenth Century," *Past and Present*, no. 50 (1971): 76–136.
32. "Naissance d'un mouvement citoyen," *Midi Libre*, November 6, 2018, https://www.midilibre.fr/2018/11/06/naissance-dun-mouvement-citoyen,4770628.php.
33. Thibaut Lehut, "DOCUMENT—Les gilets jaunes publient une liste de revendications," *FranceBleu*, November 29, 2018, https://www.francebleu.fr/infos/societe/document-la-liste-des-revendications-des-gilets-jaunes-1543486527.
34. Drozdiak, *The Last President of Europe*, 28.
35. Reid, "History at the Roundabout," 189–90.
36. Quoted in Drozdiak, *The Last President of Europe*, 27.
37. See, for example, "Les intox du grand débat de la présidentielle," *Libération*, May 21, 2017, https://www.liberation.fr/politiques/2017/03/21/les-intox-du-grand-debat-de-la-presidentielle_1557189.
38. Victoria Dailey, "A Pear, a Bear, and Some Hair: Caricature and Freedom of the Press," *LA Review of Books*, August 21, 2017, https://lareviewofbooks.org/article/a-pear-a-bear-and-some-hair-caricature-and-freedom-of-the-press.
39. Wahnich, "Sans-culottes et gilets jaunes."

40. Mathieu Dejean, "Quand une historienne spécialiste des mouvements sociaux analyse les 'Gilets jaunes,'" *Les Inrockuptibles*, November 29, 2018, https://www.lesinrocks.com/actu/quand-une-historienne-specialiste-des-mouvements-sociaux-analyse-les-gilets-jaunes-183886-29-11-2018.
41. Plenel, *La Victoire des vaincus*, chap. 1.
42. "Gilets jaunes: Louis de Bourbon, héritier au trône de France, soutient 'le peuple de France,'" *Ouest France*, December 10, 2018, https://www.ouest-france.fr/societe/gilets-jaunes/gilets-jaunes-louis-de-bourbon-heritier-au-trone-de-france-soutient-le-peuple-de-france-6120556.
43. Bantigny, "Un événement."
44. Alpaugh et al., "Peuple et révolution française," 131–58.
45. Michelle Zancarini-Fournel, "On est en train de faire l'Histoire," in Confavreux, ed., *Le fond de l'air est jaune*.
46. Zancarini-Fournel, "On est en train de faire l'Histoire."
47. Devellennes, *The Gilets Jaunes*, 26.
48. Plenel, *La Victoire des vaincus*, chap. 2.
49. Gérard Noiriel, *Les gilets jaunes à la lumière de l'histoire* (Paris: Editions de l'Aube, 2019), chap. 3.
50. Olivier Ertzscheid, "De l'algorithme des pauvres gens à l'Internet des familles modestes," in Confavreux, ed., *Le fond de l'air est jaune*.
51. "Ces deux Gilets jaunes se sont dit 'oui' au péage de Séméac," *La Dépeche*, December 10, 2018, https://www.ladepeche.fr/article/2018/12/09/2921375-ils-se-sont-dit-oui-au-peage-de-semeac.html.
52. Noelle Plack, "Drinking and Rebelling: Wine, Taxes and Popular Agency in Revolutionary Paris, 1789–1791," *French Historical Studies* 39, no. 3 (2016): 599–622.
53. Alain Cottereau, "La désincorporation des métiers et leur transformation en 'publics intermédiaires': Lyon et Elbeuf, 1790–1815," in *La France, malade du corporatisme? XVIIIe–XXe siècles*, ed. S. Kaplan and P. Minard (Paris: Belin, 2004), 97–147.
54. Doulin-Dimopoulos, Koerner, and Siffert, "Le baraquement comme espace de résistance."
55. Reid, "History at the Roundabout," 186–87.
56. Wahnich, "Sans-culottes et gilets jaunes."
57. Reid, "History at the Roundabout," 189.
58. Jérémie Moualek, "L'image disqualifiante de la 'violence populaire' en démocratie," *Socio* 16 (2022): 139–58.
59. "'Gilets jaunes': Le procès du saccage de l'Arc de triomphe, lourd de symbole, s'ouvre lundi," *Europe1*, March 22, 2021, https://www.europe1.fr/societe/gilets-jaunes-ouverture-du-proces-du-saccage-de-larc-de-triomphe-4033052.

60. "The Aftermath of the Gilets Jaunes Riots in Paris—in Pictures," *The Guardian* (London), December 2, 2018, https://www.theguardian.com/world/gallery/2018/dec/02/the-aftermath-of-the-gilets-jaunes-riots-in-paris-in-pictures.
61. Aymeric Parthonnaud, "'Gilets jaunes': La statue saccagée de l'Arc de Triomphe n'est pas une Marianne," *RTL*, December 3, 2018, https://www.rtl.fr/culture/arts-spectacles/gilets-jaunes-la-statue-saccagee-de-l-arc-de-triomphe-n-est-pas-une-marianne-7795790252.
62. "Procès du saccage de l'Arc de Triomphe: 'C'était l'hystérie totale,' racontent les prévenus," *Le Figaro* (Paris), March 22, 2021, https://www.lefigaro.fr/faits-divers/proces-du-saccage-de-l-arc-de-triomphe-c-etait-l-hysterie-totale-racontent-les-prevenus-20210322.
63. Moualek, "L'image disqualifiante de la 'violence populaire' en démocratie," 139–58; Bantigny, "Un événement."
64. Geneviève Darrieussecq, "Stèle du maréchal Juin dégradée: Unissons-nous face aux casseurs de mémoire!" *Le Figaro*, November 22, 2019, https://www.lefigaro.fr/vox/societe/stele-du-marechal-juin-degradee-unissons-nous-face-aux-casseurs-de-memoire-20191122.
65. Moualek, "L'image disqualifiante de la 'violence populaire' en démocratie," 139–58.
66. "Au procès du saccage de l'Arc de triomphe par des 'gilets jaunes,' des peines modestes et une relaxe," *Le Monde*, March 21, 2021, https://www.lemonde.fr/societe/article/2021/03/26/au-proces-du-saccage-de-l-arc-de-triomphe-des-peines-pedagogiques-et-une-relaxe_6074530_3224.html.
67. Dejean, "Quand une historienne spécialiste des mouvements sociaux."
68. Bantigny, "Un événement."

Red, White, and Blood

AN ESSAY ON WHITE TERROR AND GREAT FEAR, 1789-2021

Beatrice de Graaf

"White terror" or "reactionary terror" has always been the twin brother of "revolutionary" or "red terror." Modern history since the French Revolution has witnessed an effervescent parade of rebellions, insurrections, insurgencies, and proper coups—but they almost always came in pairs: revolutionary terror (against sitting feudal, authoritarian regimes) and white terror, counterrevolutionary violence, directed against the alleged or original revolutionary, socialist (after 1917) activists and dissidents.

Empirically, the first references to terrorism, terrorists, and terror in our "modern" sense of the word can be found in French and other European journals in the years after 1795. Before the French Revolution, "terror" (*terreur*) had been part of the political vocabulary as well, but back then (and this interpretation continued in public texts throughout the nineteenth and twentieth centuries), it denoted the righteous, salutary, and majestic "terror of God"—that capacity of gods and princes to instil fear in their enemies.[1]

Since Maxmilien Robespierre's Reign of Terror, however, the concept morphed into a secularized version, the "terror of the people," the "tyranny of the multitude": in short, into a "term of abuse that could be used to discredit political adversaries." In Dutch discourse, for example, references to terrorism pointed to the French Revolutionary or Bonapartist system of governance without law; it could indicate "fanaticism," "Jacobinism," or despotism—with the Dutch brand christened "Batavian terror." Moreover, through the Revolutionary and Napoleonic Wars, the semantic field of terror/terrorism became connected to chaos, disorder, and anarchy as well. The agents of this reign of terror could, however, be located in two places: within the government, engaging in terror and abuses of power, or among the "radicals" aiming at revolutionizing society and overthrowing government.[2]

As Rudolf Walther in his seminal piece "Terror, Terrorismus," for Reinhart Koselleck's monumental series on "conceptual history," explained, modern-day terrorism assumed an ambivalent, dual character: negative and positive, future-oriented and backward-reaching, aimed to overthrow the state or launched to push back to an earlier state in history. Since the French Revolution terror could manifest itself as a "terrorism of the revolution," but it could equally be seen as a *terminus technici* for the "terrorism of the reactions," or a "terrorism of the revisions." For example, in the case of the reactionary paramilitary organizations in the interwar period in Germany in the 1920s, right-wing shock troops of advancing national socialism roamed the streets and carried out acts of terror and premeditated attacks against political targets. In one of its last formal acts on August 9, 1932, the Weimar Republic issued a "Verordnung gegen politischen Terror," a decree prohibiting acts of politically motivated (lethal) violence, that specifically addressed both types of terrorism: left-wing and right-wing terrorism, revolutionary and reactionary violence.[3]

As we know from social psychology, the way people perceive and structure their mental representations of sensitive concepts, such as race and gender but also terror and terrorism, will be aligned with their surrounding social and cultural systems. These systems in turn have been produced and reiterated by historical events and context. The social and political stereotypes we unwittingly think and argue with do not come out of thin air but are encoded in our culture through specific trajectories of appropriation and instrumentalization of these categories by the dominant classes. The way terror and terrorism have been handled by the dominant institutions (mostly those of the state), therefore, can be considered formative in how present-day stereotypes on terrorism are structured.[4]

In overviewing the complex and dual conceptualizations of terror and terrorism throughout history, it may just be the case that applying this dichotomy of terror to the wave of insurrections and revolts occurring in our day and age helps us to put its dynamics in a broader historical context and unpack stereotypes that we unwittingly reproduce. This essay is an attempt to unmask in particular the stereotype of the "terrorism of the reactions" that has proven so lethal and detrimental in the course of the development of our modern-day open societies.

The Great Fear

With the "Red Scare" having ingrained itself in American collective and national memory, it is easy to forget that for Europeans, "white terror" as a politics of vengeance was always the natural partner to occurrences of "red revolutions." What connects the two faces of terror is historically evident from the perspective of European history. It is *la Grande Peur,* the great fear, that is encoded in the way we perceive terror and terrorism, as the accompanying dynamic of autosuggestion, or the near-subconsicious adoption of an idea derived from one's own conscious. In his famous and still highly relevant account of the French Revolution, the monograph *La grande peur de 1789* (1932), French historian Georges Lefebvre introduced the notion of the general panic, the "great fear" that urged peasants and local communities nationwide to launch an assault on the feudal system in 1789.[5]

Fueled by *fausses nouvelles* (fake news) and rumors, they believed that a foreign force would burn their crops, robbers were on their way to burn their houses, and aristocrats were hatching a "famine plot" to starve the population and force them back into obedience and acquiescence. In anticipation of this plot, and propelled by this fear, peasants and townspeople but also artisans and members of the bourgeoisie attacked the estates of the feudal nobility and tried to find and destroy documents recording feudal privileges. This panic-inspired revolt then triggered the National Assembly in Paris to do away with the feudal regime, thereby kickstarting the proper French Revolution that same year. The ensuing waves of insurrection, the overthrow of the monarchy, the upending of the estates system, and the abolishment of feudal privileges and expropriations came to be known as a "regime of terror": a terror anchored forever in history by Robespierre's mechanization of the noose, the guillotine.

Yet, with their executions and arrests the revolutionary committees immediately prompted a counterrevolutionary wave of white terror to wash over the country in 1795. This wave was not directed from above. It included mob lynchings, uncoordinated attacks, and protests staged by victims' relatives and other people opposing the Jacobins. However, in southern France, the counterrevolutionary violence was organized and carried out by underground associations of royalists, who had been preparing to hunt down Jacobins participating in the Reign of Terror. The epitaph "white" derived from the fact that they were said to adorn their caps with white cockades, the color of the Bourbon monarchy.

In 1814 and 1815, after Napoleon was defeated, waves of white terror erupted again and engraved themselves not just in French collective memory but also in that of the allied powers that were to watch over France's stabilization and de-bonapartization with their Allied Army of Occupation. During the summer of 1815, the Allied Commission received numerous reports on ultra-royalists in southern France launching a literal manhunt for "Bonapartist brigands," Jacobins, and revolutionaries: in short, for anyone whom they took to be an enemy of the Bourbon Restoration.[6]

Although the Allies, with their occupation force and administration, kept a close eye on the dynamics of revolutionary or reactionary unrest in northern and western France and in Paris, anarchy and a struggle for power did hold sway for a few months in the south, where no Allied troops were deployed. The Duke of Angoulême (the eldest son of the Count of Artois, also known as "Monsieur"), who ruled in those parts, tried with all his might to counteract the directives and attempts at control coming from Paris, where his uncle King Louis XVIII tried to direct the country toward a politics of reconciliation. As a consequence, a new wave of White Terror swept over the Midi, the Vendée, Brittany, and Maine. Royalist groups went around pillaging, kidnapping, and terrorizing the population. They had a large following especially around Marseilles and Toulouse, where the conscription quotas had been very high and economic life lay in ruins because of the continental blockade.[7] In these areas, royalist gangs not only killed dozens of Napoleonic soldiers but were able to create a veritable people's revolt. In addition to the murder of Guillaume Brune in Avignon on August 2, General Jean-Pierre Ramel also fell at the hands of the White Terror on August 15. Armed gangs in the department of Gard in the Languedoc region vented their anger against alleged "nests" of Bonapartist supporters. Protestant towns were heavily afflicted; dozens of Protestant Christians lost their lives, were persecuted, ended up in prison, or simply chose to flee. Between July and October 1815 in Nîmes alone—the capital of the department—2,500 people were forced to leave their homes, including 400 employers, 1,500 employees, and 600 day laborers and farmers. They left, taking half a million francs as capital with them. In the end, hundreds of civilians were lynched, 70,000 alleged prorevolutionary and pro-Bonapartist officials purged, and thousands put to trial.[8]

For Lefebvre, the pivot to understanding such outbursts of violence were the concepts of social fear and autosuggestion—something that worked for both types of violence. Obviously, there were deeper causes and transitions that had ripened the climate for rebellion, but the trigger for the insurrections were the self-generated beliefs allowing historical actors to feel that their worst fears were already coming true before they in fact were. As Lefebvre noted, "Now when an assembly, an army or an entire population sits waiting for the arrival of some enemy, it would be very unusual if this enemy were not actually sighted at some time or other."[9]

Terrorism of the Reaction

As an unprecedented and tectonic rupture in the political, economic, cultural, and even historical fabric of society, the French Revolution came to be the blueprint of every social panic since 1789. The Paris Commune and the Red Terror of 1917 only further carved out this primordial trope in history.[10]

The Russian Revolution and the Cold War translated the Red Scare into a veritable literary and cultural industry, with radio plays and movies invoking all kinds of looming conspiracies—apocalyptical days of reckoning included. The Cold War deepened and hardened Lefebvre's notion of the *grande peur* in the heart of all-centrist, conservative parties in the liberal democracies of the West. Lefebvre was spot on with his focus on "history of below" and the notion of autosuggestion as the motor for revolutions (as opposed to the idea of central coordination from above), but he could have highlighted its effect on the proponents of the "terrorism of the reaction" with far more emphasis.

Because that is where the autosuggestion and primordial fears for revolution have been mostly at home: with the perpetrators of this "terrorism of the reaction and of the revisions" and their conspiracy-driven politics of vengeance. Since 1795 onward, via the second wave of white terror in 1815 and the Russian white terror in 1917–23, the trope of counterrevolutionary violence against so-called traitors, enemies of the public, revolutionaries, communists, or fifth columns proliferated throughout history. In the 1960s until the 1980s in Italy, the fear of a left-wing takeover or a revolutionary upswing was felt so urgently that elements within the secret service conspired to stage acts of terrorism that were presented as being perpetrated by left-wing terrorists. According to this "strategy of tension," attacks were committed with the intention to create unrest and prompt a societal call for law and order—amounting to the thesis of the *stragi dello state,* "massacres operated by state institutes."[11]

When terror morphed into "terrorism" as a discourse and dispositive since the late nineteenth century, the dichotomy was there from its inception. We could even argue that, following the theory of political scientist David Rapoport on the "four waves" of terrorism in modern history (anarchism, anticolonial terrorism, left-wing terrorism, and "holy" terrorisms), each wave of terrorism saw an accompanying shadow wave of parasitic, reactionary, and counterrevolutionary terrorism trying to push back against, undo, and delegitimize the changes and transformations wrought by emancipatory movements. Sometimes this wave was propelled by paramilitary or anticolonial organizations, such as in the 1920s in Germany or in the 1960s in France. Sometimes the reaction was initiated by secret services, such as when the tsarist secret police, the Ochrana, set up numerous conspiracies against alleged anarchist networks in Germany.[12]

The question is whether this "terrorism of the reaction" was a similar bottom up or societal reaction as the grassroots revolutionary terrorist groups of the various waves of terrorism, or whether it is always, to a greater or lesser extent, a ploy or ruse in the hands of the government. Take for example the frenzy of ultraroyalist bloodletting in the Midi, the abovementioned second wave of "white terror" in 1814–15. Under the pretext of rooting out revolutionary and bonapartist networks, underground associations and vindictive royalists conspired, returned from exile, organized raids in the department of the Gard, and killed thousands of their enemies. Terrified Protestants (who were singled out on many occasions) wrote in despair to the allied minister of police in Paris, complaining about a *seconde Barthelemy,* referring to the St. Bartholomew Day's massacre carried out by royalist forces and Catholic mobs against French Calvinists in 1572. But the security forces and government in Paris sat still and waited for the counterrevolutionary terror to wash over. That suited them better in their quest for consolidating their power. In this instance, the white terror was not a direct ploy in the hands of the government. Yet, French royalist and allied forces chose to let the terror play out, in order to keep their immature and instable reign intact.

Again, a similarly ambivalent background of anticolonial terror presented itself in the 1960s: were French secret services or other authorities complicit in their knowledge of existing anticolonial terror networks in the homeland? As in 1815, the autosuggestion of the antifeudal revolution translated into the fear of colonial uprisings and insurgencies in the twentieth century, with the paramilitary and rogue army officers as terrorists enacting their white terror attacks in France in the 1960s. The mechanisms of creating a social scare and a moral panic were not that different from that of the right-wing terrorist organization Ordine Nuovo in Italy implied in the attacks of 1972 and 1974 in Peteano and Brescia, or that of the similarly right-wing terrorist group Nuclei Armati Rivoluzionari on the train station of Bologna in 1980.

Similarly, alleged communist takeovers and expropriations were always high on the agenda of anticommunist witch hunters within government institutions, who in countries as dispersed as Spain, Italy, West Germany, the United States, and Chile resorted to counter-coups and political killings in the 1970s and 1980s, sometimes killed out by front organizations of the state, in other instances committed by "deviating" forces or rogue groups that affiliate themselves with the powers of law and order.

Today's White (Supremacist) Terror

Even more pertinent for today, in the United States and elsewhere, the trope of reactionary white terror is also translated into the especially deep-seated fear for supposedly antiwhite and allegedly socialist agendas. This fear demonstrably also sits deep in the bosom of the institutions that maintain and enforce security, be it the police, security, or military organizations.[13]

Here, in the case of the U.S. Capitol riots, the epitaph "white" mutated from indicating a political, cultural, or social denominator for a specific type of reactionary protest and violence into its most racial outgrowth: "white terror" came to be equated with "anti-Black" terror. This form of terror came to the fore on January 6, 2021, when a mob of hardcore Donald Trump supporters, militiamen, white supremacists, anti-maskers, and diehard QAnon adepts launched a coup to stop Congress from certifying President-elect Joe Biden's election victory. At the same time it was a counter-coup against the democratic process itself. Arguably, with the participation of domestic terrorist groups, it could be considered a form of "terrorism of the reaction," since the assault was projected and announced as being directed against an anticipated, alleged left-wing, socialist elite takeover of the country. It was moreover a form of anti-Black terror as well, with race and fear of diversity permeating this wave of "great rage." Confederate flags were swayed. Tie-wrap cuffs were wielded. Gallows and nooses were erected around the Capitol, recalling the lynchings of Black people (and perhaps even unwittingly reminiscent of the guillotine as the method of choice in the hands of the Committee of Public Safety of 1793–94).[14]

Stereotypes never fall out of thin air. Deep, globally felt reverberations such as the Atlantic and French Revolutions have left behind traces and scars in the fabric of our collective memory and our social systems. Traces of great fears, of conspiracy theories, of terrorist and counterterrorist shadows lurking behind seemingly "normal" law-and-order dispositions have been encoded in iterative moments of revolution, revolt, and counterrevolution. These traces and stereotypes are now so deeply engraved that stereotypes of a "revolutionary coup," or the threat of a "Great Replacement," can be invoked to mobilize riots by means of autosuggestion and "great fears" in a way completely unattached to reality. A conspiracy theory such as QAnon, disseminated by the *fausses nouvelles* machine that is social media today, serves to light the fuse of the powder keg.[15]

The autosuggestion of Lefebvre regarding the mobs and masses turning wild against an enemy that they themselves propped up, and inspired by an apocalyptic panic that they themselves through their media outlets generated, was always more appropriate for "the terrorism of the reaction." With its reactionary, backward-looking direction, it was and is worlds apart from the thrust of the original farmers' and citizens' revolts that were driven by emancipatory ideals against an unjust system. As a stereotype, it needs to be identified, exposed, and deconstructed into the parts that it is made of: fear, class- and/or racially inspired hatred, and the desire to remain dominant.

Note

1. Ronald Schechter, *A Genealogy of Terror in Eighteenth-Century France* (Chicago: University of Chicago Press, 2018), 204–5.
2. Beatrice de Graaf, "Why Do We Need to Historicize Terrorism, and How Should We Do It?" in *Conceptualizing Extreme Beliefs and Behaviors: Definitions and Relationships between Phenomena*, ed. Rik Peels and John Horgan (Oxford: Oxford University Press, 2025), 35–36.

3. Rudolf Walther, "Terror, Terrorismus," in *Geschichtliche Grundbegriffe: Historisches Lexikon zur politisch-sozialen Sprache in Deutschland*, vol. 6, ed. Otto Brunner, Werner Conze, and Reinhart Koselleck (Stuttgart: Klett-Cotta, 1990), 418–21.
4. Ryan F. Lei, Emily Foster-Hanson, and Jin X. Goh, "A Sociohistorical Model of Intersectional Social Category Prototypes," *Nature Reviews Psychology* 2 (2023): 297–308.
5. Georges Lefebvre, *The Great Fear of 1789: Rural Panic in Revolutionary France*, trans. Joan White (Princeton, NJ: Princeton University Press, 1973).
6. Beatrice de Graaf, *Fighting Terror after Napoleon: How Europe Became Secure after 1815* (Cambridge: Cambridge University Press, 2020), 217–28.
7. Daniel Philip Resnick, *The White Terror and the Political Reaction after Waterloo* (Durham, NC: Duke University Press, 1966), 5–6; Rafe Blaufarb, *Bonapartists in the Borderlands: French Exiles and Refugees on the Gulf Coast, 1815–1835* (Tuscaloosa: University of Alabama Press, 2005), 3.
8. Resnick, *The White Terror and the Political Reaction after Waterloo*, 55–56; De dGraaf, *Fighting Terror after Napoleon*, 223.
9. Lefebvre, *The Great Fear of 1789*, 50.
10. Walther, "Terror, Terrorismus," 394–96.
11. Tobias Hof, "The 'Moro Affair'—Left-Wing Terrorism and Conspiracy in Italy in the Late 1970s," *Historical Social Research* 38 (2013): 235.
12. Beatrice de Graaf and C. Zwierlein, "Historicizing Security: Entering the Conspiracy Dispositive," *Historical Social Research* 38, no. 1 (2013): 46–64.
13. Teun Van Dongen et al., "Right-Wing Extremism in the Military," International Centre for Counter-Terrorism-The Hague, ICCT Research Paper, 2022.
14. Miles T. Armaly, David T. Buckley, and Adam M. Enders, "Christian Nationalism and Political Violence: Victimhood, Racial Identity, Conspiracy, and Support for the Capitol Attacks," *Political Behavior* 44, no. 2 (2022): 937–60.
15. Andrew H. Kydd, "Decline, Radicalization and the Attack on the US Capitol," *Violence: An International Journal* 2, no. 1 (2021): 3–23.

Afterword

Lynn Hunt

Since this deliberately provocative collection sweeps across three centuries and a dizzying array of countries, the first question must be whether "Age of Revolutions" is still a useful concept. Is there a definite epoch if revolutions can be traced back to the 1600s and forward to the present? Those who wrote about the Age of Revolutions in the past often took the American Revolution and especially the French Revolution of 1789 as their starting points, but the authors of these essays consider events around the globe from Japan and Hong Kong to West Africa, Mexico, and Haiti. To me, nonetheless, the temporal and spatial range of the essays proves that "Age of Revolutions" remains relevant, if only because it can incite this diversity of reflections and analysis. This is true even when, or perhaps especially when, the authors chafe at the confines set out by earlier proponents of the term. The writing of history often proceeds by contesting what previous historians have done, but in all fairness, it has to be admitted that the predecessors most often cited here—Robert R. Palmer and Eric Hobsbawm—differed about chronology and about the meaning of what happened in the Age of Revolutions. In short, the phrase has never been a settled concept or a clearly demarcated era but it has proved fruitful even so.

Despite many justifiable complaints about the Eurocentric focus of much previous scholarship on the Age of Revolutions, the events originally in question, in particular the French Revolution of 1789, still exercise great gravitational pull. Republicanism appears repeatedly in these essays because France set up the first republican form of government in a major global power. The Dutch republic did not have the same influence because it was based on a loose federation of provinces of comparatively small size that could compete economically but not militarily. Although the American example inspired the French, no one at the time thought that a country of 2.5 million people, one-fifth of whom were enslaved, provided a global model. In contrast, metropolitan France had 26 to 28 million people in 1789. The French Revolution served as an exemplar in part because the French abolished both monarchy and noble status in making way for a republic, and in part because they imposed republics on other countries during the wars of the 1790s. The models of linked social and political revolutions and of exporting revolution resonated across the globe for many generations. The use of the Goddess of Liberty (or Democracy) in Chinese protests in 1989 and again in Hong Kong in 2019–20 shows that the French example still echoes; the Statue of Liberty in New York Harbor (1886) was given by France, designed by a Frenchman, and based on female representations of the French republic that go back to 1792.

If we start with the Protestant debates of the late 1600s, as this volume does, then it becomes clear that republicanism (much less democracy) was never a straightforward choice, and that it could be caught up in religious disputes since religion was believed by most Europeans at the time to be essential to legitimizing public authority. The French Revolution had the impact that it did because the French deputies broke with this traditional religious justification, which held that kings ruled because the Judeo-Christian God ordained it so. The deputies proposed the sovereignty of the nation and the guarantee of rights as the new basis of governmental legitimacy. That move prompted other questions that bedevil us still, as essays in this volume demonstrate: Is the nation the same as the people? Is a republic necessarily democratic? Who speaks for the people? Can the people's voice be represented best through elections of representatives or through popular mobilization, whether in clubs, paramilitary groups, or protest movements? The issues brought up in the late 1600s did not disappear: Were republics dangerous because they could not provide a firm foundation for social order, or were they an inevitable step toward what seemed to be political modernity in which more and more people gained access to political participation?

Lurking inside these abstract political dilemmas is the question of violence (and nonviolence). The authors of the essays in this volume compel us to recognize that popular sovereignty could be expressed in countless, endlessly creative ways: rioting in Martinique over fears of a ship carrying the plague with its cargo, North American Cherokees refusing to engage with their would-be European American subjugators, the numerous and recurrent revolts of the enslaved across the Atlantic world, a mutiny by convicts against their captors in the South China Sea, reading forbidden books in Iran, putting banners where everyone can see them in Hong Kong, and wearing yellow vests while stopping traffic in French roundabouts. Agency, inventiveness, forceful demands to be heard, and violent attacks on established authority were not concocted or perfected by the American or French Revolutions of the late eighteenth century. Wherever they were in the world, and long before and after 1776 or 1789, people who felt beleaguered, oppressed, or threatened with annihilation found ways to work with what they had at their disposal, which sometimes meant evoking memories of past forms of resistance, such as references in Peru to Túpac Amaru, the leader of an Indigenous revolt against the Spanish in 1572, but just as often it meant finding something new, such as Post-It notes or yellow vests. The authors of these essays rightfully insist that we learn this truth about the creativity of popular forms of resistance, long occluded by narratives written to glorify founding fathers, boost national identity, or explain the supposed successes of colonial and postcolonial domination. Even faced with overwhelming force against them, people did not simply cower; they fashioned unexpected ways of pushing back, undermining, or running off to set up their own new communities.

Resistance could be found everywhere and at every time, but though it is a necessary condition of revolution, it is not a sufficient one, as protesters have learned repeatedly over the centuries. Here again the American and French Revolutions have exerted their influence and not only because they invoked fresh principles of human rights and national sovereignty. In the American and French cases, revolutionaries, most often of the property-owning classes, managed to displace their former rulers and devise new sources of power: novel institutions such as the presidency and congress in the United States and the national assembly and administrative uniformity in France. The overthrow of rulers by internal military forces, such as occurred in Siam in 1688, may have been described by contemporaries as "revolutions," but they meant revolution in the pre-1776 or pre-1789 sense, a coming full circle rather than this kind of leap forward to recast the future. Such "revolutions" could be momentous, as the one in Siam in 1688 surely was because it inaugurated a century of internal instability even while dashing all French hopes of gaining a colonial toehold there. But they are not revolutionary in the same way because they only changed the hands holding the levers of power and did not alter the levers themselves.

As many of the essays in this collection attest, however, we can no longer explain revolutions such as the American and French ones by reference to exclusively internal factors such as the colonists' desire for independence from Britain or the contradictions of the "feudal" regime in France. The causes of those revolutions were not just Atlantic but also global, and their effects were also global. In the competition for dominance within Europe, the Atlantic countries (Spain and Portugal first, then the Dutch provinces, Britain, and France) discovered that overseas trade and in particular the slave trade could gain them an advantage against each other and other European powers. The vertiginous expansion of the slave trade in the second half of the eighteenth century produced the conditions for the third of the great revolutions of this Age of Revolutions, the Haitian Revolution of the enslaved against their masters. More than 200,000 African men and women were forced on to French ships and taken to Saint-Domingue (Haiti after 1804) just between 1781 and 1790. Because of increasing resistance to the trade in West Africa, the subject of an essay in this volume, the enslaved population in Saint-Domingue came from many different locations and spoke many different languages. The memory of the resistance back home may have inspired them, and in any case, as recent arrivals, many vividly remembered life before capture and enslavement.

Global factors shaped all three revolutions. The British North American colonists would not have gained independence without the direct military assistance of France and the indirect financial assistance of the Dutch. The French helped the colonists in order to contest British dominance after the Seven Years' War, and the French king's inability to finance the debt from the American war created the opening for 1789. The news of revolution in metropolitan France then ignited a failed uprising by free Blacks in Saint-Domingue in 1790 and helped set off the great revolt of the enslaved in 1791. The insurrection of the enslaved in Saint-Domingue counts as a revolution in the sense I am using it here because it showed that enslaved men and women could overthrow their masters and run the country on their own terms, using a mixture of models imported from elsewhere and developed on their own. Despite the determined efforts of leaders in the United States and France, the Haitian example spread through rumors, songs, and stories told and retold across the Caribbean and North and South America, and played a significant role in prompting the abolition of slavery in Mexico and Spanish South America. The

AFTERWORD

French revolutionaries abolished slavery in 1794 in a desperate attempt to keep control of Saint-Domingue. Napoleon reinstituted it as part of his effort to gain an advantage against Britain. The United States began its march westward by purchasing the Louisiana Territory from Napoleon, who had managed to capture Toussaint L'Ouverture, original leader of the Haitian Revolution, and yet failed to reconquer Saint-Domingue, which declared its independence as Haiti in 1804.

Given the indisputable importance of global competition, some would argue that the Age of Revolutions is defined not by republicanism or democracy but rather by shifts in international power alignments, such as the westward expansion of the United States, the transfer of French colonial interest from the Caribbean toward Algeria, and the shift of British imperialism away from the lost North American colonies toward India. Enabling these realignments was the development of fiscal and military techniques for expanding state powers. The Haitian Revolution's turn toward authoritarianism would seem to further weaken the argument for the importance of republicanism and democratic aspirations. Moreover, the American and French Revolutions invoked new democratic principles for largely fortuitous reasons; neither was part of the original programs. The thirteen British North American colonies wanted better treatment from Britain and then independence. The French revolutionaries of 1789 aspired to constitutional monarchy with a national debt that could be managed more equitably. The leaders in the British North American colonies came to republicanism for lack of any other option and resisted demands for democratic participation, not to mention the abolition of slavery. Very few of the French leaders could even imagine setting up a republic in 1789 and only did so under the impact of war and the treachery of the king and his court. Since the French ended up with Napoleon I as emperor at virtually the same moment that Jean-Jacques Dessalines declared himself emperor in Haiti, the authoritarian turn can hardly be summoned as a reason to discredit the Haitian Revolution.

Still, the contingent appearance of republicanism and democratic aspirations did not make them any the less important for the future after 1776 and 1789. True, national or popular sovereignty and broader democratic participation proved to be powerful ways of demanding more from citizens, from more taxes to justification of conscription into bigger and bigger armies. But they also opened the way to new demands for participation and the guarantee of rights, not just in the United States, France, and Haiti but across the globe. The example of the Haitian Revolution reinforces two points made by the essays here: that information shapes the form that revolution will take and most of all that the collective memories of revolution and resistance continue to animate demands for freedom and equality. The essays also demonstrate the mutability of those collective memories. The Rotunda of Illustrious Persons in Mexico's most important cemetery welcomes bodies previously overlooked as the political winds shift, and as regimes change in Haiti the memory of Dessalines is repeatedly repurposed.

The examples of the twin emperors, Napoleon and Dessalines, serve as reminders that republicanism and aspirations for freedom and democracy sometimes produce authoritarianism. The final essay in this collection brings in two other dynamics that need to be included in any consideration of the Age of Revolutions: terror and counterrevolution. Do revolutions necessarily devolve into terror because they rely on violence to get underway and because the "nation" and "the people" are too volatile and indefinable to settle as foundations for legitimacy? Or do revolutions produce violence and counterrevolution simply because they attack the traditional forms of legitimacy? Does the violence of the reaction undermine the legitimacy of revolution or confirm it? Endlessly varied and contradictory answers have been offered to these questions, which only goes to prove once again that the "Age of Revolutions" has not lost its charge.

CONTRIBUTORS

BRYAN A. BANKS is Associate Professor of History at Columbus State University. His research focuses on religious and intellectual histories of revolution and refugee studies. He is the author of *Write to Return: Huguenot Refugees on the Frontiers of the French Enlightenment* and is the coeditor of *Freedom and Faith: The French Revolution and Religion in Global Perspective*.

WILLIAM A. BOOTH is a historian of twentieth-century Latin America with a particular interest in Mexico and U.S.–Latin American relations. His research largely focuses on socialism and communism in the Americas, on radical transnational networks, and on the historiography of the Cold War. He has taught at Warwick, Oxford, London School of Economics, Johns Hopkins, and the UCL Institute of the Americas.

KATLYN MARIE CARTER is Associate Professor of History at the University of Notre Dame. A political and intellectual historian of the eighteenth-century Atlantic world specializing in the American and French Revolutions, she is the author of *Democracy in Darkness: Secrecy and Transparency in the Age of Revolutions*.

DENISE Z. DAVIDSON is Professor of History at Georgia State University. She is the author of *France after Revolution: Urban Life, Gender, and the New Social Order* and *Surviving Revolution: Bourgeois Lives and Letters,* and coauthor, with Anne Verjus, of *Le roman conjugal: Chroniques de la vie familiale à l'époque de la Révolution et de l'Empire*.

LAURENT DUBOIS is the John L. Nau III Bicentennial Professor in the History and Principles of Democracy at the University of Virginia. A specialist on the history and culture of the Atlantic world who studies the Caribbean (particularly Haiti), North America, and France, he is the author of seven books, including *A Colony of Citizens: Revolution and Slave Emancipation in the French Caribbean, 1787–1804,* which won the Frederick Douglass Prize, among other book prizes.

DAN EDELSTEIN is the William H. Bonsall Professor of French at Stanford University. He is a specialist of eighteenth-century France with research interests in literature, history, political thought, and digital humanities. He is the author or editor of eleven books, including most recently *The Revolution to Come: A History of an Idea from Thucydides to Lenin*.

CINDY ERMUS is the Charles and Linda Wilson Professor in the History of Medicine, and Director of the Humanities in Medicine program at the University of Nebraska–Lincoln. She specializes in the history of medicine and the environment, especially epidemics and other disasters, in eighteenth-century France and the Atlantic world. She is the author of *The Great Plague Scare of 1720: Disaster and Diplomacy in the Eighteenth-Century Atlantic World* and *Urban Disasters*.

BRONWEN EVERILL is the former Director of the Centre of African Studies at the University of Cambridge. She now teaches in the Princeton Writing Program and is a Research Affiliate of the Laboratory for the Economics of Africa's Past at Stellenbosch University as well as a Fellow of the Royal Historical Society. Her most recent books are *Africonomics: A History of Western Ignorance* and *Not Made by Slaves: Ethical Capitalism in the Age of Abolition*. Her research on Africa in the Age of Revolutions is forthcoming with Princeton University Press.

GIDEON FUJIWARA is Associate Professor of History and Asian Studies Coordinator at the University of Lethbridge. His research looks at early modern to modern Japan, focusing on intellectual networks, *kokugaku* (Japan studies), community, nation and nationalism, and information access. He is the author of *From Country to Nation: Ethnographic Studies,* Kokugaku, *and Spirits in Nineteenth-Century Japan*.

KATE FULLAGAR is Professor of History at the Institute for Humanities and Social Sciences, Australian Catholic University, and Vice President of the Australian Historical Association. She specializes in the history of the eighteenth-century world, particularly the British Empire and the many Indigenous societies it encountered. She is the author of *Bennelong and Phillip: A History Unravelled; The Warrior, the Voyager, and the Artist: Three Lives in an Age of Empire;* and *The Savage Visit;* editor of *The Atlantic World in the Antipodes: Effects and Transformations since the Eighteenth Century;* and co-editor with Michael A. McDonnell of *Facing Empire: Indigenous Experiences in a Revolutionary Age*.

BEATRICE DE GRAAF is Distinguished Professor of International Relations and History at Utrecht University. She studies the emergence of and threats to security arrangements from the nineteenth century until the present. She is the author of several works, including *Fighting Terror after Napoleon: How Europe Became Secure after 1815*.

LYNN HUNT is Distinguished Research Professor at the University of California at Los Angeles. She is the author most recently of *The Revolutionary Self*, *History: Why It Matters*, and, with Jack Censer, *The French Revolution and Napoleon*.

MIGUEL LA SERNA is Bowman and Gordon Gray Term Professor and Chair of the Department of History at the University of North Carolina at Chapel Hill. He is interested in the relationship among culture, memory, and political violence in modern Latin America. He is the author of several books, most recently *With Masses and Arms: Peru's Tupac Amaru Revolutionary Movement*.

CHRISTY PICHICHERO is Associate Professor of History, French, and African and African American Studies at George Mason University. A specialist in race, gender, slavery, and the African diaspora, she is the author of *The Military Enlightenment: War and Culture in the French Empire from Louis XIV to Napoleon*. Her articles on critical race theory, Afro-feminist microhistories, French exceptionalism, and critical digital humanities have appeared in *PMLA*, *Historical Reflections/Réflexions historiques*, *Contemporary French and Francophone Studies*, *French Historical Studies*, and other venues.

NOAH SHUSTERMAN is Associate Professor of History at the Chinese University of Hong Kong. His recent research focuses on the history of militias and armed citizens in the eighteenth-century Atlantic world. His books include *Armed Citizens: The Road from Ancient Rome to the Second Amendment* and *The French Revolution: Faith, Politics, and Desire*.

ANDREW W. M. SMITH is Senior Lecturer in Liberal Arts at Queen Mary University of London. He is a historian of modern France interested particularly in ideologies and strategies of resistance, and how identities are shaped by interactions with the state. He is the author of *Terror and Terroir: The Winegrowers of the Languedoc and Modern France* and *Make Cheese Not War: Transnational Resistance and the Larzac in Modern France*.

NAGHMEH SOHRABI is the Charles (Corky) Goodman Professor of Middle East History and the Director for Research at the Crown Center for Middle East Studies at Brandeis University. She is the author of *Taken for Wonder: Nineteenth Century Travel Accounts from Iran to Europe* and numerous articles on Iranian history, politics, and culture.

JUNKO THÉRÈSE TAKEDA is Professor of History at Syracuse University. Her research and teaching interests include the histories of early modern globalization, revolutions, migration, displacement, and disease. She has authored two books, *Between Crown and Commerce: Marseille and the Early Modern Mediterranean* and *Iran and a French Empire of Trade, 1700–1808: The Other Persian Letters*.

ERIN ZAVITZ is the Upper School Humanities Department Leader and a Humanities Teacher at Bosque School. Her writing has appeared in *The Cambridge History of the Age of Atlantic Revolutions* (edited by Wim Klooster) and in *Atlantic Studies*.

INDEX

Abd al-Qadr Kane, 111
academic publishing, ix
Adams, John, 21–25, 29–30, 32, 38
Age of Revolutions (website), ix–x, 2, 3
Aide toi, le ciel t'aidera, 47
Ainu, 121
Aizu, 126, 129
Alexis, Nord, 170
Algerian Revolution, 138–39
Amaru, Túpac (1572), 5; execution of, 146–52
Amaru, Túpac II (José Gabriel Condorcanqui, 1742–1781), 5, 57, 147–52
American Revolution, 1, 3, 19–28, 37, 41, 80, 108, 117, 219; memory of, 187
anarchism, 15, 23, 33, 160–62, 201, 210–15
Ancestors' Day, 177
Anderson, Marian, 172
Andes, 147–48
Ani-Yunwiya, 85–88
anticolonialism, 4, 52–61, 92, 146–52, 215
antiracism, 5, 149–51, 152
Arc de Triomphe, 203–4
Argenson, Marquis d', 25
Arnaud-Tizon, Amélie, 43
Arnaud-Tizon, Catherine, 43
Asante, 114
Association du Centenaire, 170
Atlantic history, 5, 54, 101–8
Atlantic revolutions, 1, 93, 103
Attakullakulla (Tsalagi), 81–84
Aurelius, Marcus, 20
authoritarianism, 27, 45, 158–60, 193, 210, 223–24
autosuggestion, 212–17
Aymara, 57

Ayutthaya Kingdom, 11, 91–98. *See also* Thailand

Baker, Keith Michael, 25, 95
Barbet, Jacques, 47
Bastidas, Micaela, 147
Bastille, 194–205
Battle of Sandy Creek, 86
Bayle, Pierre, 3, 15–18
Behrangi, Samad, 139
Beijing, 179–91
Bénard, Charles, 70–75
Biedermeier culture, 42
Bight of Benin, 114
Bilbao, Spain, 72
Black Lives Matter, 109
Black Panther Party (U.S.), 149
Bois Caïman, 60
Bolsheviks, 191
Bonaparte, Napoleon. *See* Napoleon
Bordeaux, France, 73
Bordes, Jean-Baptiste, 69–72
Boshin civil war, 126, 128, 130
Boukman, Dutty, 60
Bourbon Restoration, 47, 213
Boyer, Jean-Pierre, 174
Brazil, 58, 60, 112
Britain, 19, 21, 46, 81–83, 108, 115, 121, 222–24
British penal system, 56–58
broadsides (*kawaraban*), 122, 130
brocade pictures (*nishiki-e*), 122

Calvinism, 12, 15–16
Camisard Wars, 12
Campa, Valentín, 161, 163
Carnival, 47
Catalogne, Gérard de, 171

229

230   INDEX

Caveirac, Jean Novi de, 12–13
Chan Yin-lam, 185
Chávez, Hugo, 150
Cherokees, 5, 80–89, 220
Chickamauga, 85, 88
China, 58–61, 92, 121, 182, 190
Chinese University of Hong Kong, 181
Chōshū, 126–27, 130, 133
Chota, 81, 86
Chow Tsz-lok, 185
Citadel (Henry Christophe's fortress), 172
Condorcet, Marquis de, 21, 27
Confederate flags, 217
Conseil supérieur (Martinique), 75–76
conspiracy, 214, 217
Controverse, 13, 17
convicts, 52
Coutard, Ghislain, 196, 202
COVID-19, 198
Cuba, 53, 56, 112, 138
Curaçao, 57–58

Dahomey, 114
Declaration of Independence, 19, 22, 169
Declaration of the Rights of Man and Citizen, 19, 200–205
decolonial, 5, 52, 148, 150–52
Dessalines, Jean-Jacques, 101, 156, 160, 167–74, 223–24
Dinwiddie, Robert, 81, 87
D'Orléans, Pierre-Joseph, 11
Dostoevsky, Fyodor, 28
Dragging Canoe (Tsiyu Gansini), 81, 84–86
Du Rieux, Pierre Henri Miraillet, 75
Duvalier, François, 169–73

Edo, 122, 130
education, 43, 45–46, 125
"Eight-Point Plan" (*Senchū hassaku*), 125, 127
enslaved peoples, 5, 53–60, 74, 102–8, 113, 116–17, 168–69, 219–22

epidemics, 69, 92
États de Languedoc, Les (vessel), 69–72
Eurocentrism, 4–5, 52, 55, 219
exile, 15, 43, 48, 93, 137–38, 147, 179, 215
"Expel the Barbarians" movement, 123, 126

Fake News/Fausses Nouvelles, 212
Fanon, Frantz, 52–53
Fante, 114
fatherhood, 42
Fatta, 111–12
Fawkes, Guy, 188
Feuquières, François de Pas de Mazencourt, 70–76
Flores Magón, Ricardo, 160–62
Fort Duquesne, 82
Franklin, Benjamin, 19, 21
freedom of conscience, 11, 14–15, 18
French Revolution of 1789, 1–6, 19–20, 24, 36–37, 42, 47, 54–60, 93, 96–97, 103–5, 187, 194–201, 210–17, 219–23
fūsetsudome, 121–23, 127, 129–30
Futa Toro (Fuuta Toro), 54, 111–17
Fuuta Jalon, 54

Gaoulé, 75–76
Geffrard, Fabre, 169
gender, 6, 41–48, 106, 121, 211
Geneva, 12
Georgia, 84–85
Glen, James, 81–82
Glissant, Édouard, 53
Global North, 52–55
Global South, 59, 138
globe, Le, 47
Glorious Revolution, 21–23, 92
Goddess of Democracy, 179, 188, 190–91, 220
graffiti, 6, 179–91
"great fear," 210–18
"Great Replacement," 217
Grito de Dolores, 156–58
Guadeloupe, 74–75

Guajiros, 56–57
Guevara, Ernesto "Che," 142, 152
Guizot, François, 47

Haiti, 27, 58, 60–61, 101–10, 167–78, 222–24
Haitian Revolution, 1, 5–6, 54, 58, 60, 101–10, 167–78, 222–24
Haitian Tourist Information Bureau, 171
Hakodate, 123
Hamaguri Gate Incident, 126–28, 131
Hamilton, Alexander, 23, 34
Henderson, Richard, 83–87
Henry, Patrick, 183
heresy, 12
Heroes Day, 173
Herouville, Louis-Balthazar de Ricouart, 74
Hidalgo y Costilla, Miguel, 156–58, 163
Hirao Rosen, 122–23, 126, 128–30
Hirosaki, 122–24, 126, 128–30
Hobsbawm, Eric, 113–14, 219
Hong Kong, 6, 58–59, 179–93, 219–21
Huguenots, 12–17. *See also* Calvinism
Hyogo port, 123–25

iconology, 180
Independence Day, 156–57, 168–72
Indigenous peoples, 5, 56–57, 61, 80–89, 102–3, 147–51, 160–63, 221
Indonesia, 58
Industrial Revolution, 1, 7, 41
Iran, 137–45, 221
Iranian Revolution, 5, 137–45
Ireland, 58
Islam, 26, 98, 111, 115, 138–39, 142–44
I'tisam al-Din, Mirza, 55
Iturbide, Agustín de, 157–58

Jackson, Andrew, 101
Jacobinism, 197, 210, 213
Jamaica, 54, 117
James, C. L. R., 54, 103, 105, 108, 113

Jefferson, Thomas, 19, 101
Jesuits, 11–12, 26, 93–94
jihad, 54, 111
Jordan, Camille, 42
Jurieu, Pierre, 12–18

Katari, Tomás, 57
Khomeini, Ayatollah Ruhollah, 137
Kido Takayoshi, 127
Kivland, Chelsey, 167
Kòdinasyon Desalin (Dessalines Coordination; KÒD), 167
kokugaku (Japan studies), 122, 123
Komiyama Tōbei, 126
Kongo, 105
Konoe family, 126, 128
Konoe Tadafusa, 127–29
Konoe Tadahiro, 128–30
Koselleck, Reinhart, 211
Kyoto, 123, 126, 130
Kyushu, 127

Lafayette, Marquis de, 19
Languedoc, 69–73, 213
Lascars, 55
Lavalas Family Party, 167
Lee, Richard Henry, 22
Lefebvre, Georges, 212–17
Lenin, Vladimir, 138–39, 142
Lennon Tunnel of Tai Po (Hong Kong), 179, 184–87
Lennon Walls, 185–86
Le Pen, Marine, 195, 200
letters of health, 72
Levant, 73, 96
Liberté guidant le peuple, La, 187, 189
Lombardo Toledano, Vicente, 161–63
Louis Alexandre de Bourbon, 74
Louis XIV, 12–14, 21, 91, 93, 95
Louis XVI, 32, 43, 97, 200, 213
Lyttelton, William, 82, 87

Macron, Emmanuel, 195, 197–203
Madison, James, 23–24, 35–36

Magloire, Paul, 171–72
Maimbourg, Louis, 12
Malabar, 55
Maladie de Siam, 72
Malaysia, 58
Malê Revolt, 60
mambo, 60
Marseille, France, 69–73, 213
Marseille Plague of 1720, 4, 69–76
Martelly, Michel, 167–68
Martinique, 69–76, 220
Marx, Karl, 27, 54, 139, 143, 191
Mass Transit Railway (MTR, Hong Kong), 183–84
Matsudaira Katamori, 126, 129
Maurepas, Comte de, 75
May 1968, 140, 187, 201
Mazzei, Philip, 35
McConnell, Mitch, 192
Meiji, Emperor, 121, 128
Meiji nikki or *Meiji Diary*, 122–27, 129–30
Meiji Restoration, 4, 121–31
Meiji sesquicentennial, 121
Mercier, Louis-Sébastien, 26–27
military-fiscalism, 112
monarchies, 12, 14, 18, 27, 28, 80, 92, 95, 137, 143, 200, 203, 212, 220, 223
Morelos, José María, 157–58, 163
Moria, Guinea, 111, 117
Morris, Gouverneur, 34
motherhood, 42
Mouraud, Jacline, 196, 202
MRTA (Movimiento Revolucionario Túpac Amaru, Peru), 148–49
Mujahedin-e Khalq Organization, 139

Nana Asma'u, 116
Nantes, France, 73–74
Napoleon, 27, 42–45, 96–97, 101, 213, 223–24
Napoleon III, 158
Narai the Great (king), 91–100
National Convention, 26–27, 32, 43

national polity (*kokutai*), 125
Native Americans. *See* Indigenous peoples
Nazis, 191
necropolitics, 52, 60
New France, 71
New York Times, 180
Nicole, Pierre, 14
Nipissing, 81
Nishidate Heima, 126
Nova Scotia, Canada, 71

Obama, Michelle, 109
octroi, 74, 79
Oratorian School, Lyon, 42
Ortiz de Domínguez, Josefa, 158, 163
Ostenaco (Ustanaqua), 81, 86–89
Ostrovsky, Nicolai, 138
Ōu Etsu Domainal Alliance, 129
oungan, 60
Oyo, 114

Paine, Thomas, 23, 33–34
Palestinian struggle, 138
Palmer, R. R., 19, 33, 108, 113, 219
pandemic (COVID-19), 179, 198
Panteón de Dolores, 160–61
Paris, 43, 46, 76, 97, 197, 199, 202–4, 212, 215
Paris Commune of 1871, 194, 214
patriarchy, 4
Penang, 59
Périer, Casimir, 42
Perry, Matthew C., 120
Persia, 4, 91–99, 138–40
Peru, 57, 146–52, 221
Pétion, Alexandre, 167, 173–74
Pétionville, 167, 174
Phaulkon, Constantine, 91–94
pirates, 59, 71
plague, 4, 69–79
Plato, 23
police, 52, 151–52, 160, 180, 184–87, 193, 197–98, 203, 215–16

Polybius, 20, 28
Pontiac's War, 82–83
Port-au-Prince, 167, 174
Potosí, Dámaso, 57
Price, Richard, 26
Provence, 69–76
Provence, Plague of, 69–76
Pulau Obi, 59

QAnon, 216–17
Qazvin, 137, 141
Qom, 139
quarantine, 70–72
Quechua, 57, 147

race, 6, 52–61, 107, 112, 211, 217
racial capitalism, 52
racism, 4, 50, 149–50, 170. See also antiracism
rape, 52, 106
Rapoport, David, 215
"Red Scare," 210, 212
referendums, 32, 201
religion, 3, 12, 52, 60, 94, 106, 115, 220
rentier, 44, 46
reparations, 4, 53, 56
republicanism, 11–17, 32, 80, 96, 219–20, 223–24
Republic of Letters, 16
Revocation of the Edict of Nantes, 12–14, 17
Revolt of the Tailors, 58
Revolutions of 1848, 194, 197, 199, 201
Robespierre, Maximilien, 36–37, 210, 212
Roquelaure, Duc de, 72
Rouen, France, 43–47
Rousseau, Jean-Jacques, 1, 24, 26, 34, 96
Roux, Vital, 44
Russian Revolution, 214

Safavids, 92, 95
Saigō Takamori, 126
Saint Domingue. *See* Haiti

Saint Lucia, 71
Saint-Pierre, abbé de, 25
Sakamoto Ryōma, 125, 127
Sala, Milagro, 150
Samizdat, 139–40
Sans Souci, 172
São João Bautista (slave ship), 101
Satsuma, 126–30
Satsuma-Chōshū (Sat-Chō) Alliance, 127
Scotland, 58
seconde Barthelemy, 215
secularism, 3, 11, 16, 60, 143, 176, 210
self-emancipation, 58
Sendai, 129
Sète, France, 69–78
settler colonialism, 56, 121
Seven Years' War, 1, 55, 82, 222
Shah, Nader, 92, 96–97
Shakur, Tupac (rapper), 149–50
Shawnee, 85
Shays's Rebellion, 23
Shimoda, 123
Shining Path (Sendero Luminoso, Peru), 148–49
Siam, 3–4, 11, 72, 91–100, 221. See also Thailand
Simpson, Audra, 86
Singapore, 59
skepticism, 15, 24
slavery, 52–64, 101–10, 113–18, 168, 188, 222–23. *See also* enslaved peoples
Sokoto Caliphate, 54, 111–12, 116–17
Sons of Liberty, 118
South Carolina, 81–82, 84, 87
sovereignty, 4, 5, 32–37, 53, 56–57, 61, 80–84, 103, 149, 162, 201, 205, 220–23
Soviet Union, 139–40
Spain, 216, 222
Sri Lanka, 58
Statue of Liberty, 188, 220
Stuart, John, 84–85
Suchet, Louis Gabriel, 44, 46
Switzerland, 13, 43
Sycamore Shoals, 83, 85

Tacky's Revolt, 54
Taller Túpac Amaru (California artists' collective), 151
Tang China, 121
Tasmanians, 56
Tehran, Iran, 138–44
terror/*terreur*, 6, 43, 48, 210–17, 224
terrorism, 210–17
Thailand, 11, 59. *See also* Siam
Thucydides, 20, 23
Tiananmen Square, 188
Tokugawa shogunate, 122, 124, 125, 128–30
Tokugawa Yoshinobu, 123–25, 128
Tokyo, 130
Tomotley, 81, 86
Tosa, 125, 127, 130
Treaty of Amity (1854), 123
Treaty of Dewitt's Corner (1777), 84, 88
Treaty of Finckenstein (1807), 97
Treaty of Long Island (1777), 84
Treaty of Paris (1763), 96
Treaty of Tellico Blockhouse (1794), 86
Trouillot, Michel-Rolph, 54, 103, 168
Trump, Donald, 190, 216
Tsugaru clan, 126, 128
Tsugaru Tsuguakira, 128–29
Tubman, Harriet, 101
Tula, 57
Tupamaros, 149–50
Turgot, Anne Robert Jacques, 23, 25–27

Uthman dan Fodio, 111, 116

Velasco Alvarado, Juan, 148
Venezuela, 27, 56, 150, 154
Vertières, 172
V for Vendetta, 188
Victorian England, 42
Vietnam War, 139
Vilcabamba (Inca kingdom), 147–51
Virginia, 22, 81–88, 101
Vitet, Amélie (née Arnnaud-Tizon), 47
Vitet, Louis, 43
Vitet, Ludovic, 47
Vitet, Pierre, 41–42, 48
vodou, 60, 168, 170, 173, 176
Voltaire, 21, 24, 26

Wall Street Journal, 190
Wars of Religion, 3, 12
Washington, George, 82
Webster, Noah, 34
"white books," 141–42
white supremacism, 52, 113, 216. *See also* racism
"white terror," 6, 210–17
Williams, Eric, 103, 108
Williamsburg, 81
Winthrop, John, 22
Wood, Gordon, 24, 37
Wynter, Sylvia, 52

Yamanouchi Yōdō (Tosa lord), 125

The Revolutionary Age

Barbary Entanglements: Realizing American Independence on the World Stage
John M. Chamberlin

The Course of Human Events: The Declaration of Independence and the Historical Origins of the United States
Steven Sarson

Napoleon in America: Bonaparte and the Rhetoric of US Empire
Mark F. Ehlers

Before Manifest Destiny: The Contested Expansion of the Early United States
Nicholas G. DiPucchio

Revolutionary Diplomacy: Spanish Connections and the Birth of the United States
Thomas E. Chávez

Declarations of Independence: Indigenous Resilience, Colonial Rivalries, and the Cost of Revolution
Christopher R. Pearl

Dishonored Americans: The Political Death of Loyalists in Revolutionary America
Timothy Compeau

The American Liberty Pole: Popular Politics and the Struggle for Democracy in the Early Republic
Shira Lurie

European Friends of the American Revolution
Andrew J. O'Shaughnessy, John A. Ragosta, and Marie-Jeanne Rossignol, editors

The Tory's Wife: A Woman and Her Family in Revolutionary America
Cynthia A. Kierner

Writing Early America: From Empire to Revolution
Trevor Burnard

Spain and the American Revolution: New Approaches and Perspectives
Gabriel Paquette and Gonzalo M. Quintero Saravia, editors

The American Revolution and the Habsburg Monarchy
Jonathan Singerton

Navigating Neutrality: Early American Governance in the Turbulent Atlantic
Sandra Moats

Ireland and America: Empire, Revolution, and Sovereignty
Patrick Griffin and Francis D. Cogliano, editors

www.ingramcontent.com/pod-product-compliance
Lightning Source LLC
Chambersburg PA
CBHW032057230426
43662CB00035B/589